the ethical consumer

Guide

to everyday shopping

GW00691920

First published in Great Britain 1993
by ECRA Publishing Ltd
16 Nicholas Street, Manchester M1 4EJ

An Ethical Consumer Books Original

ECRA Publishing Ltd is a non profit-making ICOM co-operative.
It is the publishing arm of the Ethical Consumer Research
Association (ECRA), which exists to research and publish
information on companies behind brand names, and to promote
the ethical use of consumer power.

Typesetting at Caxton's Final film, Manchester. Tel 061 236 8288
Printed on recycled paper by: RAP Ltd. 201 Spotland Rd,
Rochdale OL12 7AF. Tel 0706 44981.
All material © ECRA Publishing Ltd. Non profit-making and
voluntary groups may use any of the material appearing in this
book, providing that all such material is credited. No part of this
publication may be reproduced by commercial organisations
without written permission from ECRA Publishing Ltd.

Preface & Acknowledgements

The Ethical Consumer Guide to Everyday Shopping is one of a series of three books which aim to provide people with information which allows them to integrate some of their ethical beliefs with their economic decisions. The Series comprises:

The Ethical Consumer Guide to Everyday Shopping (Food, Drink and Household Products)

The Ethical Consumer Guide to Major Purchases (Transport, Electrical Goods, Sport and Leisure Products)

The Ethical Consumer Guide to Money (Banks, Building Societies, Insurance, Pensions and Investments)

In the introduction to this book we argue that a culture which encourages consumers to choose products without questioning the possible effects of each decision on other humans, animals and the environment, cannot expect to have an economic system which does not systematically damage the environment and human and animal rights. We also argue that the presence of consumer choice in the market gives purchasers enough potential economic power to massively influence the future direction of the economic system in regard to these kind of issues.

The rest of the book presents detailed information about the main ethical issues arising in 30 broad product areas. The information is presented in a way which emphasises the possibilities for immediate practical action to address a range of pressing global ethical concerns.

The contents of this book have been compiled and edited collectively by Jane Turner, Rob Harrison, Bruce Bingham and Ruth Binns.

Also providing valuable contributions at various stages during the four year production of this book have been Paul Harrison, Chayley Collis, Catriona Smith, Katie Foster, Peter Clift, Anna Thomas, Bridget Norman, Wendelmoet Rotmans, Gerk-Jan Kuipers, Florian Kohler, Caroline Watson, Liz Stout, Sara Osman, Joseph Ryan and Jenny Harris.

Thanks to P.J. Polyp, David Holland and Sarah Guthrie for the cartoons, and to Angela Smith for the cover design.

Thanks also to the readers of the Ethical Consumer magazine who have sent us copies of their correspondence with companies. Also thanks to the companies who have taken the trouble to contact us to discuss their ratings. Finally, thanks to the more than one hundred investors in ECRA Publishing Ltd, whose financial support has made this project possible.

Contents

In our common everyday needs the great industries of the world take their rise. We - the mass of common men and women in all countries - also compose the world's market. To sell to us is the ultimate aim of the world's business. Hence it is ourselves as consumers who stand in a central relation to all the economies of the world, like the king in his kingdom. As producers we go unto a particular factory, farm or mine, but as consumers we are set by nature thus to give leadership, aim and purpose to the whole economic world. That we are not kings, but serfs in the mass, is due to our failure to think and act together as consumers and so to realise our true position and power.

(Percy Redfern: The Consumer's Place in Society, 1920)

Chapter 1

How to Use this Book

This Book This book aims to provide information about ethical issues in a way which allows people with different beliefs to consider their own ethical priorities before choosing what to buy. It contains 30 product reports, each report containing three sections:

(i) A **table** which rates companies against fourteen ethical issues;

(ii) A **text-based discussion** of the broader issues relating to each product;

(iii) A **Best Buys** section which provides a summary of the information in (i) and (ii).

The Tables The tables are designed to show whether a company which owns a particular brand has been criticised for its activities in a particular area. Therefore, when we have discovered evidence that a company has been criticised for activities that damage the environment, a square or half-square will appear against the brand name in the environment column. This 'negative information' allows people to avoid giving their money to companies involved in activities which they wish to discourage. People will sometimes choose to consider information from only one or two columns if they do not feel the others are important to them.

In order that readers may check to see why a mark has appeared in a particular column, every mark on every table is explained under the appropriate company's name in the Companies Section.

The Text Along with each table is a text-based discussion of the broader product-related issues. These sections provide information about any cruelty-free or environmentally-friendly or fair-trade products which are available. This 'positive information' allows people to identify and buy from companies which they feel are particularly progressive. These sections also discuss health-related issues where appropriate and any general issues which relate to the particular product under discussion.

Best Buys provide an overview or summary of the information on the tables and in the text. Since these sections give equal value to all the columns on the tables, they will only be useful to people who are broadly sympathetic with all the issues covered.

Best Buys

All the negative information appearing on the tables comes from previously published sources. These sources will often include publications by campaign groups such as Friends of the Earth, Survival International and the British Union for the Abolition of Vivisection as well as more mainstream magazines, newspapers and business directories.

We try to use a five year rule which excludes from the ratings criticisms relating to events that occurred before May 1987.

Where Does the Information Come From?

In this section companies are listed in alphabetical order and specific criticisms are prefaced by letters indicating the issue to which they relate (such as ENV for environment and AT for animal testing).

For people who wish to discover even more detail about each criticism, a reference number will indicate the specific source (listed in Appendix 1) from which the evidence was drawn. Where a company has received too many criticisms to list individually, critical publications simply appear as numbers in brackets e.g. (See also refs: 1234, 1324).

Therefore we can see for example that the company Kodak receives a mark in the Irresponsible Marketing column of the Toothpaste table because:

Companies Section

> **IM:** In 1989, its drug company Sterling Winthrop, was criticised for its marketing of the painkiller, dipyrone, for minor applications in the Philippines and Indonesia and many other Third World countries...[279]

This information comes from the publication numbered 279, ie. Dipyrone - a drug no one needs (Health Action International-Europe/ BUKO-Pharma-Kampagne 1989).

Any other companies referred to in the text of the Companies Section will be subsidiaries of the company under discussion unless otherwise stated. Quite a lot of abbreviations occur in this chapter which are explained in Appendix 3.

Key to the Tables The categories used to rate companies on the tables reflect a broad range of human rights, environmental and animal rights concerns. They have been chosen either because the issues have surfaced previously as specific consumer campaigns or because ethical investment organisations have identified interest in avoiding these areas. More details about the system we use, including information on the way we rate supermarkets, appear in Appendix 2 (Technical Information about Ratings).

The meaning of the shaded squares is generally as follows:

■ Independent commentators have raised questions about the involvement or malpractice of this company group within the last five years

◢ Independent commentators have raised questions about a lesser degree of involvement or malpractice within the last five years

For more specific definitions please see each issue below. The grey shaded lines running from top to bottom are to make the tables easy to read. Blank squares mean that no evidence of involvement has been found.

▦ Lighter squares will show the record of a related organisation. An explanation will appear in the Companies Section.

South Africa

SA: A square or half-square in this column shows any involvement in South Africa, including companies which operate licensing, distribution or franchise agreements for their products there. At the time of writing it appears that an end to the ANC's call for economic sanctions may be quite close. This may put readers in the position of not having to consider the information in this column.

Oppressive Regimes

OR: A square or half-square in this column shows that a company has operations in a regime which has been criticised in the Amnesty International Report 1991 for:

(i) Torture and

(ii) Extra-judicial executions or disappearances and

(iii) Prisoners of conscience

and in 'World Military and Social Expenditures 1991' for

(iv) 'Frequent official violence against the public'.

The 39 regimes which fall into these categories and more details about the rating system in this column appear in Appendix 2.

A company group will not receive marks in this column if all its products sourced from these regimes are marketed as fair trade.

Trade Union Relations

TU: A square or half-square in this column indicates that there have been problems of trade union recognition or commentators have criticised particularly heavy-handed responses to industrial action.

Wages and Conditions

W&C: A square or half-square in this column shows that there has been criticism of wage levels that may not be enough to live on - or of dangerous working conditions.

Land Rights

LR: A square or half-square in this column provides information about criticisms of specific instances where indigenous peoples have been removed from their land or seriously disrupted in order to facilitate corporate operations. Information in this column is most likely to come from the campaign group Survival International.

Key to the Tables

Environment

ENV: A square or half-square in this column will show that a company has been criticised for activities which pollute or damage the environment or for lobbying against environmental improvements. This is the most widely drawn category so it will be particularly useful to look up specific criticisms in the Companies Section. Companies will not receive marks in this column simply for producing products (such as cars) which have been criticised for their impact on the environment.

Irresponsible Marketing

IM: A square or half-square in this column identifies companies marketing dangerous products or marketing products in a way that has been criticised as being detrimental to physical health. Commonly appearing in this column are tobacco companies, pharmaceutical companies, pesticide manufacturers and companies marketing baby-milks in the Third World.

Nuclear Power

NP: A square or half-square in this column shows evidence of corporate involvement in mining of uranium, production or distribution of technology, or research into nuclear energy.

Armaments

ARMS: Any company involved in the manufacture or supply of weapons and/or other combat equipment will be identified by a square or half-square in this column.

Animal Testing

AT: A square or half-square in this column will identify companies with a licence to vivisect or which are involved in vivisection or are subscribers to BIBRA. (See the Abbreviations in Appendix 3). Because the marks in this column will not necessarily identify whether a company is testing its consumer products on animals or whether it is testing its pharmaceuticals on animals, it may be worth checking the specific references in the Companies Section if this distinction is important for a decision.

Factory Farming

FF: This column shows evidence of intensive farming techniques which have been criticised by animal welfare campaigners and/or the supply of products or services which contribute to inhumane husbandry. A half square will show that a company operates in an area of animal husbandry where inhumane farming techniques are widespread, and where no evidence has been found that the product range is marketed as free-range or humanely reared.

Other Animal Rights

OAR: A square or half-square in this column, designed especially for vegetarians, shows evidence of involvement in the production of meat, leather or fur. It also identifies companies providing essential supplies to the meat industry.

Political Donations

PD: This column shows evidence of direct or indirect donations to any political party or individual politician anywhere in the world. An abbreviation in this column will provide some information about the destination of each donation and specific information will appear in the Companies Section and the Abbreviations appendix.

Boycott Call

BC: A square will indicate that a boycott of the company is currently being called somewhere in the world. More information about the reasons for the boycott and the group calling it will appear in the Companies Section.

An address for more information about each boycott appears in Appendix 4.

Products and Companies The hugely successful 'Green Consumer Guide' (Elkington & Hailes 1988) provided information about product-oriented issues but did not ask questions about the companies which provided the products. Ethical Consumer Guides, whilst considering relevant product-related questions, also address company-oriented issues and there are four main reasons for this.

(i) A combined product and company based approach allows each consumer to maximise the economic effects of each purchase. If it is 'good' for the environment to choose recycled paper it may be even better for the environment to choose recycled paper from the company with the best environmental record. Similarly, whilst it may be good to avoid products that have been tested on animals, it may be better to buy from a company with a policy of no animal testing. This approach discourages companies from cynically niche-marketing a range of 'green' products whilst maintaining a 'business as usual' policy for the rest of their operations.

(ii) A company-based approach can allow consumers to influence a wider range of corporate activities. If a company has damaging iron-ore mining operations on tribal lands in the Amazon, campaigners cannot really boycott the iron-ore but they may be able to boycott the washing-up liquid of a subsidiary of the same company.

(iii) Ethical issues, by their very nature, cannot be separated from ideas about responsibility. It is nonsensical for a company to claim to be ethical or responsible for a small part of its operations whilst ignoring its responsibility for the rest.

(iv) A company-based approach allows people to understand the power and influence of the world's major industrial conglomerates, and therefore makes them better placed to campaign against activities with which they may disagree.

Ethical purchasing works most effectively if consumers can communicate the reasons for their decisions to the companies concerned. If a company is losing sales and is at the same time receiving letters saying for example 'I have decided that I will no longer be buying your company's products until you announce an end to your policy on animal testing', it will at least be able to connect the loss of sales to this particular activity.

In the same way, a company receiving letters informing them that customers are particularly attracted to their products because they are, for example, organic will be able to use this information to further develop its policies in this area. Therefore, addresses for all the companies in this book appear in the Companies Section. Obviously it is not practical to write to every company in the book and most people will restrict their letter writing to those companies whose activities concern or please them the most. ECRA, the publisher of this book, produces two standard-form postcards for sending to companies to inform them about changes in buying patterns. More details about how to get hold of these appear in Appendix 5.

Writing to Companies

It is commonly recognised that almost every ethical principle will be faced with the question of compromise at some stage. In terms of buying ethically, most people get round this by establishing a list of their own personal priorities. These will comprise perhaps one or two principles that they will always try to abide by, such as not buying from companies in Oppressive Regimes or from companies which test their products on animals, and then a list of secondary issues which they will observe where possible. As we argue later, the other option, of giving up because it's all too complicated, simply serves to perpetuate a very destructive economic system. Lastly, it should be noted that just because this guide does not include information about the price and quality of these products does not mean that these issues are not important. It is simply that they are covered in some detail in other publications (such as the Consumers' Association's Which? magazine). Ethical purchasing is, after all, about considering ethical issues as well as, not instead of, price and quality at the point of purchase. Not to do so would simply be foolish.

The Art of Compromise

The Limits of this Information The sheer volume and complexity of information in this book means that it is useful to be aware of three main limiting factors:

(i) **The Rating System**

Because the method of screening companies that we use requires the existence of published information, the absence of a square or half-square in a particular column does not necessarily mean that a company has no activities in that area. It simple means that we have <u>discovered no evidence</u> that it has. Obviously we try to ensure that the research materials that we use help us to avoid this problem wherever possible.

(ii) **Subcontracting**

Although some companies control the entire production, manufacture, packaging and distribution of all their products, many do not. Some will subcontract part or all of these processes to other companies or even licence another company to produce the entire product. Because of 'commercial confidentiality' these kind of arrangements are not a matter of public record and so it is impossible to guarantee that every company rated on every table is the final manufacturer of a particular product. Unless otherwise stated, the company group we have rated is the one which owns or controls a particular brand name. We use a special method to rate supermarket own brands which is explained in Appendix 2.

(iii) **Limited Resources**

The Ethical Consumer Research Association (ECRA), which produced this book, is a voluntary organisation with limited resources. Whilst the ratings for most of the companies in this book have been checked for accuracy to April 1993, we can only guarantee that every company's rating was accurate at May 1992. And because companies are always buying and selling brand-names or subsidiary companies or taking each other over, it will be worth keeping an eye on the press to spot the obvious changes. Another option would be to subscribe to the Ethical Consumer magazine (see Appendix 5) whose 'updates' section is specifically designed to perform this task.

All the product reports in this book have appeared before in various issues of this magazine, and though the tables and Best Buys have been systematically updated, the text accompanying

10

each report has not been re-researched (but any obvious amendments have been made). Therefore the original date of publication for each report appears at the end of the text.
It should also be noted that although almost every item of information has been published at least twice before, the ratings have not been systematically checked with the companies prior to publication.
More details about the rating system and research methods appear in Appendix 2.

Although many of these limitations are actually quite severe, waiting for the availability of perfect information was, in our opinion, an even more undesirable path to follow since the very pressing nature of the global issues around us require an urgent response. However, at the same time, ECRA campaigns for changes in the law which would help facilitate ethical purchasing and 'freedom of information' is an important aspect of this campaigning.

Freedom of Information

ECRA believes that, as a minimum requirement, all companies trading in the UK should be obliged to publish information in their annual reports about environmental, employment and animal welfare policies and practice (including any court decisions taken against them). This would harm no one and acknowledge the potential value to society of weighing issues other than price and quality at the point of purchase.
At the same time governments should seriously consider the effects of the doctrine of commercial confidentiality on ethical purchasing. For example, the secrecy surrounding the ultimate suppliers of supermarket own-brands is particularly problematic for people wishing to consider ethical issues. Also ECRA believes that due consideration should be given to the possibilities of mandatory product labelling as the ultimate medium for providing purchasers with information on wider ethical issues.

Chapter 2

Why Buy Ethically?

An Introduction to Ethical Purchasing Theory

I DONT UNDERSTAND ALL THIS
BOYCOTT NONSENSE, THE FELLER
HASNT PLAYED FOR ENGLAND IN YEARS

Part One:

The Story So Far

Ethical buying is about considering ethical issues, as well as price and quality, at the point of purchase. We have already explained that it can be either product-oriented (asking questions about the impact of a product) or company-oriented (asking questions about the impact of a company). Ideally it should be a mixture of both.

All that ethical purchasing requires to operate are two elements: choice and information. It is generally accepted to have manifested itself in three main forms; boycotts, positive buying and the fully-screened approach.

Boycotts Although boycotts have appeared throughout history in cultures as diverse as those in China and Ireland,[1892] there is little doubt that both their frequency and success-rates have increased over the last ten years. For example, boycotts called by animal rights groups in the 1980s have persuaded three of the world's four biggest cosmetic companies to announce the abandonment of animal-testing. (For more information see the Cosmetics Report.) At the same time, anti-apartheid campaigners have used international boycotts to successfully stop banks lending to South Africa, and environmental pressure groups have used consumer boycotts to considerable effect on issues as diverse as CFCs, whaling and peat extraction.[1893]

Recent concrete examples of this kind of success have very largely put paid to a pervasive cynicism about consumer boycotts which was apparent in the UK in the 1970s. In many ways this cynicism was always misplaced because asking the question 'do boycotts work?' is a bit like asking the question 'do market mechanisms work?' As any ten-year-old child will be able to explain, if a lot of people don't buy the products of a company, it is faced either with changing its approach or going out of business.

Recent surveys have also provided evidence of a very widespread understanding of both boycotts and the issues they can address. In 1991 for example, a survey of UK consumers which had taken into account such variables as age, social class and geographical location, revealed that 80% of people would consider environmental issues when choosing products or services, 55% would consider animal welfare issues and up to 42% would consider other ethical issues such as irresponsible marketing, political donations and operations in oppressive regimes.[1894]

Positive Buying

The growth of positive buying has followed a similar pattern to that of boycotts. Although the idea that a business could and should be able to pursue ethical as well as financial goals is at least as old as the co-operative movement and some Quaker companies in the eighteenth century, the idea that these kind of companies could sell their products by emphasising their ethical features is a more recent phenomenon. And over the last ten years, consumers choosing to positively select ethical produce from the shelves of their local shops has brought about a mushrooming of small companies which specialise in such things as 'environmentally-friendly' or 'cruelty-free' or 'fair-trade' products. Some of these companies, such as the Body Shop with its campaigning slogan 'Against Animal Testing', are now no longer particularly small.

The Fully-Screened Approach

The trouble with boycotts was that you could never be sure whether the company you were switching to was not up to the same thing, only more discreetly. Equally, with positive buying there could always be a nagging doubt that there might be some even more ethical product around missing out on your support. Similar questions led ethical investment campaigners in the 1970s to develop methods to screen all the companies in a specific sector against specific ethical issues. This approach was later transferred to consumer products in publications like 'Rating America's Corporate Conscience'[1394], the Ethical Consumer Magazine, and 'Shopping for a Better World'.[1446,1447] However there was always more to these type of publications than making consumer boycotts and positive buying more effective. Within them was embodied the idea that once it was accepted that consumers had the power to influence <u>any</u> company's policy, it made sense for consumers to use every purchase to influence every company's policy on which they expressed an opinion. This idea can be described as the logic of ethical purchasing.

Why Buy Ethically?

Voting with your Money

Another way of explaining the logic of ethical purchasing is by looking at the idea that each purchase represents a vote.

Like the UK parliamentary vote, the purchase is a clumsy tool which can only deliver a simple yes/no message rather than indicate a like or dislike of particular policies. There is no way for example to buy something from a company in a way which says 'I like your product but I'm not so keen on your policies in Indonesia'. Therefore each purchase will be one which the company can only understand as a general vote of approval. And since all products or companies must have some environmental or human impact, a vote that only considers price and quality cannot but say that the impact of manufacture on the outside world is unimportant. This has the net effect of actually maximising environmental destruction and minimising human and animal wellbeing, since the company that cuts the most corners on such 'externalities' should logically be able to offer the most competitive price and quality.

Moreover, a purchase which doesn't consider ethical issues is not an 'abstention' but a vote for the worst environmental and ethical conditions of manufacture. The only way to abstain, is to buy nothing at all.

Voting by purchasing has also been used to develop notions of consumer power and consequent ideas of consumer responsibility.

Collective Purchasing

The words 'ethical consumer' or 'green consumer' can sometimes be misleading by implying that this way of looking at purchasing is only open to individuals. In reality, it has now long since been accepted that ethical purchasing can be particularly effective if it is collectively organised. Ethical purchasing is currently being practised around the world by clubs, societies, trade unions, campaign groups, health authorities, businesses and local and national governments. For some of these a special language has developed and, for example, ethically-screened purchasing by local authorities is known as 'contract compliance' and by governments as 'sanctions'. Perhaps surprisingly, a rapid growth area over the last few years has been large companies screening their suppliers in order to be able to substantiate green marketing claims.

In the USA, public policy on employment discrimination against women and minorities is enhanced by the requirement that government departments screen their suppliers against these issues, and only purchase from companies meeting set standards. In the UK however, not only are public authorities not required to screen supplier companies but they are actually prohibited by law from doing so. The growth of contract compliance by Labour local authorities in the early 1980s led the Conservative government to severely contain it by clauses in the Local Government Act 1988. ECRA believes that this Act as it relates to screened purchasing should be abolished and that all public authorities should consider the possibility of promoting their goals by the mandatory adoption of targets for supplier companies. This would be particularly beneficial at the moment in the field of environmental performance.

It should be noted that 'purchasing' can apply to any products or services, from insurance and investments to machine tools and toothpaste. The potential significance of collective ethical purchasing is not a reason to ignore or belittle the importance of individual shoppers considering ethical issues for the kind of products covered in this book. The logic of ethical purchasing described above, explains that the system will only work properly if the ethical dimensions of <u>every</u> purchase are considered.

What is Ethical?

The word 'ethical' is used in this book in its broadest possible sense and includes political, religious and moral ideas about how people should behave towards each other, the environment and animals. An essential feature of ethically-screened purchasing, from its early development within the ethical investment movement, is that it does not define what is ethical and what is not. It assumes, in other words, that people will naturally have conflicting beliefs. So whilst this book provides information for a broadly left-of-centre audience, purchasers in the USA have used boycotts to pursue right-of-centre values such as discouraging trade with communist states. However, this should not give the impression that ethical values as they relate to the purchasing and production of goods can mean anything, nor does it mean that different ethical approaches do not tend to reach common conclusions. These conclusions congregate around ideas of 'corporate responsibility', or in other words the idea that companies should behave responsibly towards their customers, employees, the environment and other parties affected by their activities.

This highly complex subject is further confused by the fact that companies may be targeted for ethical issues that do not relate directly to the way in which goods are produced. Boycotts, for example, have also been used to address issues such as anti-abortion campaigning.

A Reaction to Disempowerment It is now fairly widely accepted that consumer boycott campaigns will almost always emerge where 'normal political processes' don't appear to be working. The green consumer revolution of the late 1980s can therefore be seen as a response to the complete failure of national governments to be seen to be taking environmental issues seriously. Similarly, the spur to a series of successful boycotts by anti-vivisection groups can be seen to be rooted in an impatience with politicians who continued to ignore animal issues. And the peoples' sanctions or boycotts of companies investing in South Africa can be seen as rooted in a frustration with the lukewarm approach to economic pressure from some Western nations.

Part Two:

The Nature of Ethical Purchasing

The observations in Part One allow us to begin to compile a list of some of the key features, both explicit and implicit, of ethical purchasing.

(i) Use of the competitive mechanism

It creates both positive and negative incentives for companies to pursue ethical as well as financial goals. The fully-screened approach is clearly designed to maximise the use of the carrot and stick mechanisms of competitive capitalism to encourage the pursuit of ethical goals.

(ii) Democratisation and empowerment

The idea of using each purchase as a vote is both democratic and devolves decision-making power about ethics away from companies and towards individuals or groups. The advantage of this kind of vote is that, unlike general elections where people can express their opinions once every five years, purchasers could be voting on an almost daily basis. Interaction on this kind of scale opens up interesting opportunities for a highly subtle influence on the world's producers. The disadvantage of this kind of voting system is that it is not equal. The richest people have proportionally more voting power.

(iii) Multicultural

The refusal to define a fixed system of ethics within ethical purchasing theory can in itself be described as favouring multiculturalism.

(iv) Non-Violent

Ethically-screened purchasing gives competing systems of ethics the opportunity to resolve disputes through non-violence. Competing systems can use economic rather than physical power to regulate activities with which they disagree. In an apparently increasingly turbulent world, the importance of this aspect of ethical purchasing cannot be over-emphasised. This has been discussed in more detail in other publications.[1892,1896]

(v) Critical of unregulated capitalism

Ethical purchasing has been described as 'implicitly socialist in its analysis'.[1895] And in the discussion of purchasing as a vote in Part One we saw how the purchase decision made on price and quality alone of necessity was seen to encourage companies to externalise environmental and human costs more effectively. This analysis is identical to the socialist critique of capitalism in that it argues that there is a flaw in the market mechanism which will systematically threaten a whole range of interests.

(vi) Immediacy of action

Because ethical purchasing is about trying to use existing market mechanisms to pursue ethical goals, people can begin to take immediate practical action today. This of course is the purpose of providing the information in this book. Although there are no doubt many legislative measures which could enhance and improve the opportunities to purchase ethically, none of them are necessary for the mechanisms to start working.

(vii) Internationalist

If we look at the kind of issues which ethical purchasing has addressed so far, there is a tendency for them to be global in nature. The South African boycott, the Nestlé boycott and whaling and deforestation campaigns have all had an international dimension. Lobbying national governments in the usual way was simply not an option for these campaigns because, even if governments had been sympathetic, they did not have the power to legislate outside their own national boundaries.

(viii) A regulatory mechanism for industry

In theory, a campaigning organisation in the 1980s aiming to remove CFCs from aerosols could be said to have had the option of either lobbying the government to pass legislation banning or regulating their sale, or to persuade purchasers not to buy these products. The net effect, of making the production of CFC-propelled aerosols impossible, would have been the same. In the UK the purchasing method was used.

Although we have now identified some features of ethical purchasing which make it an attractive campaigning option for pressure groups or other political organisations, there is still some way to go before we can describe it as capable of going to the heart of the global crisis around us. The key to understanding how this can happen lies in analysing how regulation by ethical purchasing relates to regulation by government.

Part Three:

The Potential of Ethical Purchasing

A Crisis of Ideologies

With traditional socialist governments in retreat all over the world, the idea that socialism is in crisis is pretty widely accepted. However the notion that this somehow represents a triumph for capitalism is neither logical nor borne out by the evidence around us.

Governments appear powerless in the face of massive economic forces outside their control and people feel powerless because their governments don't seem to listen. Hunger and malnutrition live side by side with opulence and excess, and the global ecosystem itself is on the verge of collapse because, in the midst of an economic recession, we cannot 'afford' to clean it up. Although the list of absurdities is arguably much longer, these few examples on their own would seem to indicate neither success nor triumph but an ideology hard-pressed to explain, let alone control, what is going on around it. These kind of observations are causing economists all over the world to argue that 'ethics' somehow need to be re-integrated into economics.

The Success of State Regulation

Up until the 1950s, society chose to impose ethics upon economics through the mechanisms of state regulation. For example, maximum working hours and child labour laws clearly setting ethical boundaries first appeared in the UK in the nineteenth century.

The mechanism of democratically elected governments setting guidelines within which competitive capitalism operated, was seen to be sufficient at the time.

The Erosion of Government Regulation

However, after 1950, huge technical advances in transport and communications meant that industrial production did not necessarily have to take place within state boundaries. This 'internationalisation of production' effectively presented every single manufacturer with the option of circumventing the ethical boundaries of state regulation by relocating overseas. And it only took one unscrupulous manufacturer to relocate to a country without tiresome health and safety or environmental controls, before the others had to follow or go out of business.[615] Without sealing borders to all imports and exports, governments effectively became powerless to stop the least ethical companies from setting the agenda for everybody else.

Therefore it was no accident that ethical purchasing campaigns and boycotts began to emerge in the 1970s as a way of trying to control some of these events. Nor is the current fashion for de-regulation among right-of-centre economists any co-incidence, since the option of state regulation of industry effectively ceased to exist some time ago. 'Rolling back the state' and the unwillingness to even properly enforce existing controls, can therefore be seen as little more than disguises for the attempt to attract international investment. Governments then appear powerless in the face of massive economic forces because they are powerless. In the 1990s global production has escaped entirely from ethics.

Why Buy Ethically?

What are the Options? Assuming that letting the whole thing run out of control until the global ecosystem collapses is not on the agenda, there appear to be two solutions. The first is to re-introduce ethical boundaries through regulation by international institutions such as the UN. The second is to recognise that the engine which is driving the monster ever onward is purchasers choosing what to buy on price and quality alone.

International regulation by institutions has had modest success with the Montreal Protocol on CFCs and some tentative ideas on Codes of Conduct from the UN. However, the barriers to progress are considerable and require a much greater convergence of opinion and will than has been evidenced so far.

The widespread adoption of ethically-screened purchasing is no easy answer either because the practice of buying on price and quality alone is very deeply embedded in Western culture. To some extent this can be seen as having been reinforced by a faith in governments' ability to regulate in the pre 1950 period.

Answering the Critics Since the idea of ethical purchasing could be described as a strange sort of fusion between left-wing and liberal ideals on the one hand and the efficient competitive mechanisms of a market economy on the other, a lot of established political beliefs can appear to be both threatened and attracted by it.

It has been argued by the left for example that regulation through purchasing will allow or encourage governments to further abdicate their own responsibility to regulate.[931] Apart from the fact that we have already seen that state regulation is becoming increasingly problematic anyway, this argument ignores the fact that the electorate remains completely at liberty to reject a government which is arguing from this position. In practice, specific questions will tend to dictate rational responses to whether ethical purchasing or state regulation is the most appropriate way to address a particular issue. For example, many of the choices that people make (such as whether or not to drive a car) are so influenced by the framework in which these choices are made (such as no cycle lanes or public transport) that there are only limited gains to be made by treating them in isolation.

The environmental movement can also be wary about the idea of ethically screened purchasing because it can look like legitimising or encouraging the very Western consumer societies whose avaricious rates of consumption lie at the heart of global ecological problems. However, it can equally be argued that ethical purchasing not only does not legitimise

consumption but actually provides mechanisms to systematically screen purchases against these very issues. 'Do I
really need this product?' or 'What are the alternatives to
making this purchase?' are just as valid screens as 'Is this
company investing in South Africa?' 'Alternatives' sections
appear in many of the texts in the reports in this book.
Furthermore, unless the ecological analysis demands that
consumption be reduced to a point where no exchanges of
goods or services take place between any individuals or
communities, the idea of screening purchases will not go
away.

Commentators on the political right vary as widely in their
response to ethical purchasing as those from other groups.
Some see it as a communist plot to undermine the capitalist
system whilst others have seen it as an argument in favour of
capitalism.[1892] Although it would be amusing to discuss the
idea that they are both right, the essence of the appeal of
ethical purchasing to business is as follows. Most people
working within industry, given the choice, would presumably
rather make huge profits without exploiting health and
environment excessively. It is simply that competition does
not allow them to do so. Now, assuming for the moment that
ethical purchasers can operate with accurate information, there
is no more level playing-field than that offered through a
system of this kind. Companies out-compete each other not
only on price and quality but also on being more ethical.
Some people are even beginning to talk about the idea of
'qualitative' or 'ethical' or 'green' growth. If ethical standards
can somehow be realistically measured then ethical growth, it
is argued, could supplement targets of economic growth which
are becoming increasingly subject to critical scrutiny.

Conclusions

Ethical Purchasing Theory argues that socialism is in crisis
because of the effective collapse of the ability of nation states
to regulate industry. It argues that capitalism is also in crisis
because the same collapse of state regulation is also beginning
to reveal just how damaging to the environment and human
and animal rights unregulated global free-markets can be.
The key analyses in Ethical Purchasing Theory are not new
and draw on both doctrines. It takes the idea from socialist
theory that there are deep structural flaws in capitalism, and it
combines it with the doctrine of 'consumer (or purchaser)
sovereignty' from classic capitalist economic theory. This
combination creates a potential mechanism for the regulation

of industries that is democratic, multicultural, non-violent, internationalist and, perhaps most importantly, immediately available.

This mechanism should not be seen as a substitute for nation-state or international regulation but an additional tool for governments, public authorities, individuals and groups who are all being 'disempowered' by the internationalisation of production. Individual circumstances will usually dictate which method of regulation is appropriate to which problem. We believe that the potential of ethical purchasing really is this significant, and that by understanding this analysis it can begin to be widely used to address global issues, not in the haphazard way in which it is now operating, but in a rational and systematic fashion. Of course the resources required to deal with the volumes of information that this scale of practice demands would be enormous. But the revolution in information technology is already with us, and if we are not asking these questions and evaluating ethical information on this scale, we cannot have an economic system that will not systematically damage the environment and human and animal rights.

This fusion of socialist and capitalist theories does not mean that arguments are over. In reality there are a whole lot more just beginning, such as how this mechanism can be used most effectively and what its ends should be. This is because ethical purchasing does not offer a utopia or a fixed set of goals, but it offers instead, a means of achieving any number of, as yet, undefined ends.

"...When the consumer finally begins to exercise the virtually untapped power of citizen action - consumers will take their logical place at the head of the economic process..."
Ralph Nader

Chapter 3

Food

Baby Food & Baby Milk

It is a less than comforting thought that of the twelve baby food manufacturers featured in this report, nine have been criticised for various irresponsible marketing practices. And all of the companies which make baby milk have been found to be violating one or more requirements of the WHO/UNICEF baby-milk marketing code.

Food & Drink In most respects food and drink specifically designed for babies is subject to the same regulations as any other food product. The only significant difference is that baby foods are not permitted to contain colourings, artificial sweeteners or flavour enhancers.

Unfortunately, the baby food business is all too similar to the rest of the food industry when it comes to nutrition versus profits. In April 1991, the Food Commission published a study of commercial baby food products in which it found that parents were spending a significant amount of their money on water and thickening agents. These give the appearance of quantity but add little to the nutritional quality of the product. For this reason many of the food products did not comply with the European Society for Paediatric Gastroenterology's minimum recommended levels of protein or calories or both.[576]

Drinks designed for babies have not escaped criticism either. Both Milupa and SmithKline Beecham have paid compensation for dental problems caused by their products. (See the Companies Section for more details.)

Baby Milk Products attempting to simulate breastmilk have been on the market since the late nineteenth century, and have been a focus for controversy ever since.

Concerns over 'bottle baby disease' in the Third World, and the aggressive promotional activities of the companies, led to the drawing up of the WHO/UNICEF International Code of Marketing of Breastmilk Substitutes in 1981. At the World Health Assembly in the same year, 118 countries voted for this to become the new voluntary code of practice adopted as a minimum requirement for all countries. Today, International Baby Food Action Network (IBFAN) groups continue to lobby for worldwide adoption of the code, and to monitor all companies producing breastmilk substitutes.

1. **Adequate labelling**
   - clear information stating that breastfeeding is superior and that the product should only be used with the advice of a health worker
   - clear directions on usage and health warnings
   - no pictures of babies or other illustrations which 'idealise' the product.
2. **No promotion to the public**
   - no point of sale advertising, sample giving, special displays, discount coupons etc.
3. **No gifts to mothers or health workers.**
4. **Educational materials**
   - should clearly state the facts, including the hazards of inappropriate feeding and the unnecessary use of formula in many cases.
5. **No promotion in healthcare facilities**
6. **No promotion to health workers**
7. **No free samples**
   - to pregnant women, mothers or members of their family
   - to maternity wards or hospitals.
8. **No promotion of soft foods before nutritionally necessary**

(Source: Breaking the Rules 1991.[2])

Baby Milk Action (the group co-ordinating the Nestlé boycott in this country) claims that over 99% of mothers are able to breastfeed. The Code exists to ensure that any woman who wishes to breastfeed will not be dissuaded by company promotions undermining the message that 'breast is best'. See the 'Nescafé Boycott' section of the Instant Coffee report for more details about 'bottle baby disease' and the marketing of baby milk.

Bottlefeeding and the Environment

The environmental impact of commercial baby milk is similar to many other food products. What is different is that it is, in most cases, easily replaced by a truly natural and renewable resource. Baby milk requires land to raise cattle or grow soya beans. Electricity is used in processing which often requires very high temperatures. It is packaged in a variety of substances, including tin, paper and plastic, most of which is not recycled. Once produced and packaged it has to be transported all over the world. Ecuador, for example, imports baby milks from the USA, Ireland, Switzerland and Holland. Baby Milk Action also maintains that recent concerns over dioxins in breastmilk should not encourage mothers to bottle feed. It argues that any dioxins found in breastmilk will have caused much more damage whilst the baby is still in the womb. Also, since dioxins are created by chemical and industrial processes, an increase in bottle feeding would only increase the concentrations of dioxins in the environment.[120]

The Alternatives Food for babies can be produced by liquidising or sieving (preferably organic) fruit and vegetables. Also the Food Commission recommends using highly nutritious foods such as smooth peanut butter, mashed baked beans and fruit with natural yoghurt.[576] There are many baby food recipe books both for the meat-eater and the vegetarian, such as *The Best Healthy Baby Cookbook* by Carol Hunter (Thorsons), and *Vegetarian Baby* by Sharon Yntema (Thorsons).

Instead of sweetened and flavoured baby drinks, babies which need extra liquids can just drink ordinary water which has been boiled and cooled.[587]

Commercial baby milks should only be used when breastfeeding is either not possible or not chosen by the mother. The so-called follow-up milks which are sold for babies from four to six months have been described by the World Health Assembly as "not necessary".[14]

For further information about any issue concerning baby milk contact Baby Milk Action, 23 St Andrew's Street, Cambridge CB2 3AX. Tel: 0223 464420.

Best Buys

Baby food: Baby Organix, Johanus and Thursday's Child are all organic and are therefore Best Buys.

Baby drinks - None of the companies which make baby drinks has a clean record. Since these products can be easily replaced with (cooled, previously boiled) water, we are not recommending a Best Buy.

Baby milk - For those who need to bottle feed, the difference in the formulations of baby milks mean that a doctor should recommend which one is most suitable for each individual. We are therefore not recommending a Best Buy for this product either.

(This article was first published in July 1992.)

Brand Name	South Africa	Oppressive Regimes	Trade Union Relations	Wages & Conditions	Land Rights	Environment	Irresponsible Marketing	Nuclear Power	Armaments	Animal Testing	Factory Farming	Other Animal Rights	Political Donations	Boycott Call	Company Group
Food & Drink															
Baby Organix															Captiva Brands International
Baby Ribena	■	■		■	◢		■			◢			CON		SmithKline Beecham
Boots	■	■		◢	■		■				■ CON		■		The Boots Co
Cow & Gate			◢			■				■					V B Nutricia
Delrosa	■	■	◢	◢			■				■ BUI/CPS				Reckitt & Colman
Farley's	■	■		◢	■		■				■ CON				The Boots Co
Granose			◢	◢	■						■				Archer-Daniels-Midland
Heinz			◢		◢		◢			■					H J Heinz
Johanus															Caradoc Ltd
Liga rusks		■			■					■			■		BSN
Milupa	■	◢			■					■					Altana Industrie
Olvarit			◢		■					■					V B Nutricia
Robinsons	■	■	◢		◢						■ BUI/CPS				Reckitt & Colman
Thursday's Child															Thursday Cottage
Milk															
Aptamil	■	◢			■					■					Altana Industrie
Boots	■	■		◢	■		■				■ CON		■		The Boots Co
Cow & Gate			◢		■								■		V B Nutricia
First					■										Valio M K
Forward					■										Valio M K
Junior Milk	■	■		◢	■		■				■ CON		■		The Boots Co
Milumil	■	◢			■										Altana Industrie
Milupa	■	◢			■										Altana Industrie
Ostermilk	■	■		◢	■		■				■ CON		■		The Boots Co
Ostersoy	■	■		◢	■		■				■ CON		■		The Boots Co
Progress	◢	■			■		■				■ USA				American Home Products
SMA	◢	■			■		■				■ USA				American Home Products
Wysoy	◢	■			■		■				■ USA		■		American Home Products

Biscuits

This report covers biscuits and some crackers and crispbreads. With more than 1,000 brands on the UK market it has been necessary, for reasons of space, to put only biscuit manufacturers' names on the Table. These names are well known and appear prominently on the packets. For example, Hob Nobs are clearly marked 'McVities', and Wagon Wheels are clearly marked 'Burtons'.

The Market

One company, McVities, produces five of the top ten biscuit brands, giving its parent company, United Biscuits, nearly half of all sales in 1990. Northern Foods, BSN and Wittington are the other major biscuit companies. Concentration of ownership is a marked trend which began most significantly in the 1950s. In 1957 there were 157 UK biscuit companies but by 1989 this number had fallen to just 16.[1053]

Hob-Nobbing with the Conservative Party

There is a peculiarly strong link between the biscuit industry and the Conservative Party. United Biscuits was the highest donor to the Conservative Party in 1990 with £112,000 and Allied Lyons the second highest with £110,000. In the year to March 1990, Wittington Investments gave £100,000 to the Conservative Party, the fourth highest donation that year, through one of its subsidiaries, George Weston Holdings.

What's in a Biscuit?

Britain is the third highest consumer of biscuits in the world after Finland and Holland, and on average we each eat five packets of biscuits a month.[1418] With such an excessive habit it is interesting to know exactly what we are consuming. Sweet biscuits usually contain refined flour, processed sugar, saturated fats, salt and additives. Though not all biscuits are manufactured to taste sweet, even biscuits designed to be eaten with cheese may contain a small amount of sugar. Long-term sugar consumption has been indirectly linked to the increase in obesity, diabetes, heart disease, dermatitis and gallstones.[23] The table below shows the fat and sugar content of a variety of biscuits.

Total Sugar and Fat Content per 100g

	sugar	fat
Sweet		
Jaffa Cakes	57g	11g
Wafer filled	46g	30g
Chocolate coated	43g	28g
Ginger Nuts	36g	15g
Cream sandwiches	30g	26g
Chocolate digestives	29g	24g
Semi-sweet	22g	17g
Plain digestive	14g	21g
Plain		
Rye crispbread	3g	2g
Water biscuits	2g	13g
Wholemeal crackers	2g	11g

(Source: Parents for Safe Food, 1990)

Sugar and Fat Content

For more information on the health debate surrounding fats and sugar, see the reports on Butter & Margarine and Sugar. Generally, manufacturers are decreasing the use of additives in biscuits in response to consumer pressure. However, the following additives (which have been identified as 'hazardous'[1418]), may be found in certain biscuits: artificial colours E102, E110, E132; caramel E150. See one of the E numbers guide books such as 'Additives, Your Complete Survival Guide',[33] for more information.

Some biscuits contain animal fats and/or gelatine (made from leftover animal gristle and bone) yet the contents of a brand are not always consistent. Hob Nobs, for example do contain animal fats yet the chocolate Hob Nobs do not.

Chocolate Biscuits

Cocoa, the main ingredient in chocolate has been criticised by environmentalists because of the dangerous pesticides used on the cocoa bean.[586] It is also a health and safety issue for cocoa plantation workers. For more information on this subject, see the Chocolate report.

Biscuits

Organic Biscuits The purchase of organic food, food produced without chemicals, encourages a system of farming which is better for the environment, for workers and for consumers. It is becoming increasingly widespread in the UK and organic biscuit brands are now available. Doves Farm and 'Mitchell Hill Healthy Life' (Simmers) both produce a range of organic biscuits.

Packaging Biscuits are predominantly wrapped in plastics (often laminated or metalised). These are non-biodegradable and presently unrecyclable. However, biscuits can often be bought loose on market stalls.

For the concerned consumer, baking your own biscuits is undoubtedly the best way of avoiding unnecessary packaging and knowing exactly what goes into your snack. (See the reports on Flour, Butter & Margarine and Sugar.

Best Buys We have not discovered any criticisms of the suppliers of Bahlsen, Doves Farm, Jordans cereal bars, Paterson-Bronte, Prewetts and Rakusen crackers. Doves Farm biscuits, cookies and crackers are all made with organic flour and are therefore the clear Best Buy.

Of the most widely available brands, Elkes and Fox's biscuits come out best.

(This report was first published in October 1991.)

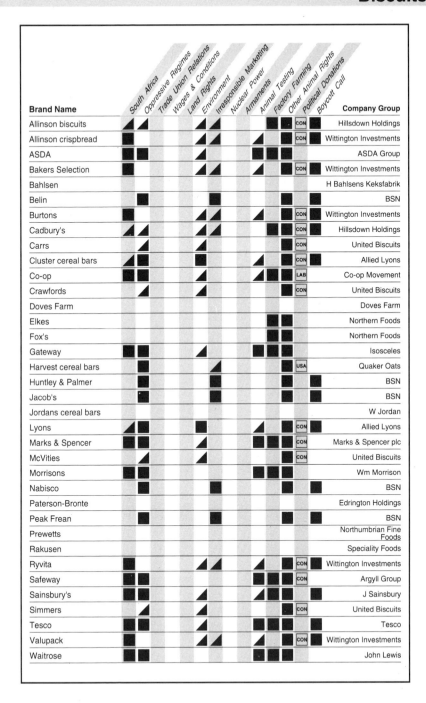

Brand Name	South Africa	Oppressive Regimes	Trade Union Relations	Wages & Conditions	Land Rights	Environment	Irresponsible Marketing	Nuclear Power	Armaments	Animal Testing	Factory Farming	Other Animal Rights	Political Donations	Boycott Call	Company Group
Allinson biscuits									■	■		CON	■		Hillsdown Holdings
Allinson crispbread	■									■		CON	■		Wittington Investments
ASDA	■	■						■	■	■					ASDA Group
Bakers Selection	■									■		CON	■		Wittington Investments
Bahlsen															H Bahlsens Keksfabrik
Belin		■							■				■		BSN
Burtons	■									■		CON			Wittington Investments
Cadbury's									■	■		CON			Hillsdown Holdings
Carrs										■		CON			United Biscuits
Cluster cereal bars										■		CON	■		Allied Lyons
Co-op	■	■							■	■		LAB			Co-op Movement
Crawfords										■		CON			United Biscuits
Doves Farm															Doves Farm
Elkes									■	■					Northern Foods
Fox's									■	■					Northern Foods
Gateway	■	■							■	■	■				Isosceles
Harvest cereal bars		■										USA			Quaker Oats
Huntley & Palmer		■								■			■		BSN
Jacob's		■								■			■		BSN
Jordans cereal bars															W Jordan
Lyons		■								■		CON	■		Allied Lyons
Marks & Spencer	■	■						■	■	■		CON			Marks & Spencer plc
McVities										■		CON			United Biscuits
Morrisons	■	■						■	■	■					Wm Morrison
Nabisco		■								■			■		BSN
Paterson-Bronte															Edrington Holdings
Peak Frean		■								■			■		BSN
Prewetts															Northumbrian Fine Foods
Rakusen															Speciality Foods
Ryvita		■								■		CON	■		Wittington Investments
Safeway	■	■						■	■	■		CON			Argyll Group
Sainsbury's	■	■							■	■			■		J Sainsbury
Simmers										■		CON			United Biscuits
Tesco	■	■						■	■	■					Tesco
Valupack	■									■		CON			Wittington Investments
Waitrose	■	■						■	■	■					John Lewis

Bread

The greater part of the bread market is controlled by just two big food companies: Ranks Hovis McDougall (Tomkins) and Wittington Investments.

Because of the sheer number of independent bakers, we have not covered them in this report. However, they are likely to be supplied by one of the big flour companies: Wittington Investments, Tomkins and Dalgety (see the Flour report).

Commercial Baking

Until very recently the flour most commercial bakers chose to use was a combination of 'hard' wheat from North America and softer European wheat.

When flour is mixed with water to make dough, its protein content is converted to gluten, an elastic substance capable of retaining gas, so allowing the baked product to rise. Since bread requires a stronger structure than cakes and biscuits, it needs a hard flour with a higher protein content which is therefore able to retain more gas. However, many would argue that this scenario is merely highly attractive to the baker who in effect is able to sell the consumer a bigger proportion of air. Because of import levies charged on American and Canadian wheat it is now more attractive for UK bakers to use home-grown wheat. Fortunately for them there is now a process which can use 'softer' wheat to produce bread equally cheaply.

The Chorleywood Bread Process (CBP)

Invented about twenty years ago CBP allows the lengthy fermentation stage to be replaced by a few minutes of intense mechanical dough mixing. The process requires more water to maintain the consistency of the loaf, so the baker get a quicker, cheaper production and the consumer gets a loaf with a higher percentage of water. About seventy five per cent of bread is made this way.

Further speed and cost-cutting came for the commercial baker with the government approval of genetically-engineered yeast in March 1990. Although it was endorsed as safe by three advisory committees, the yeast's possible effects on health and the environment are unknown. The government refused public access to the information on which the decision was made, and there were no plans to label the new ingredient.[575, 786]

The month after permission was given, Allied Bakeries (Wittington) said they did not plan to use the new yeast, whilst British Bakeries (Tomkins) declined to comment. If companies are using the genetically-engineered yeast the lack of labelling means that the consumer has no way of avoiding products containing it.[575]

Genetically-Engineered Yeast

Where bread is concerned definitions are less rigid than they are for flour (see the Flour report). Brown bread, for example, may be nothing more than white bread dyed brown with food colourings. Wholemeal must contain the whole grain but it can also have additives such as vitamin C.[1418]

Bread Types

Chemical additions to bread are supposedly made to improve the product. As with modern baking methods the advantages are often for the baker rather than the consumer.

Additives which can still be found in bread are sometimes harmless. Vinegar (E260) is added to delay mould growth, and ascorbic acid/vitamin C (E300) to produce a lighter loaf. However, the safety of others has been questioned. Calcium propionate (E282), another mould delayer, is reported to cause headaches and skin rashes amongst workers handling the chemicals.[33] Caramel (E150) is used as a colorant in brown bread, to make the loaf look more nutritious. Caramel has been shown to cause ill-effects in human volunteers[452] and was classified as 'unquestionably a hazard to many people' in 'Additives: Your Complete Survival Guide'.[33]

Additives

Organic Producers

The majority of organic cereal used in bread production is imported from the USA and mainland Europe; however, the acreage of organic land in the UK is expected to increase at about fifty per cent a year, so the reliance on imports will be lessened.[1144]

The advantages of buying organic bread are fourfold for the ethical consumer. Firstly, buying organic produce helps to support a sustainable system of agriculture. Secondly, organic produce contains no pesticides. Thirdly, there are strict rules on other ingredients. The Soil Association standards state that no gluten powder, bleaching agents, flour improvers, emulsifiers, colorants, preservatives or any other chemical additives can be included in any symbol-bearing products. Fourthly, the companies that produce organic bread have been subject to less criticism than the mainstream producers.

Below are details of the companies that we know about, but there are probably others whose products are equally as good. Companies which produce organic flour appear in the Flour report.

Doves Farm's products include organic wheat flours and organic bread.

Shipton Mill produces organic bread and cake-making flours.

Whole Earth organic bread is only sold in the South of England but the company plans to extend its availability.

The Soil Association has published five regional guides to the outlets of all sorts of organic produce. The regions are divided thus: Scotland & Borders, Midlands & North, Wales & Borders, West Country and South & East (including London). Each guide costs £2.50 and is available from the Soil Association, 86 Colston Street, Bristol BS1 5BB. Tel: 0272 290661

Best Buys

We have discovered no criticisms of Doves Farm, Shipton Mill and Whole Earth. Their brands are also organic, making them definite Best Buys for bread.

If your choice is limited to organic bread from one of the larger companies, then Warburtons is the best option, since there is no organic Starbake brand as far as we know.

Buying from a small local baker is also a possibility if it uses one of the Best Buy organic flours (see the Flour report).

(This article was first published in February 1991.)

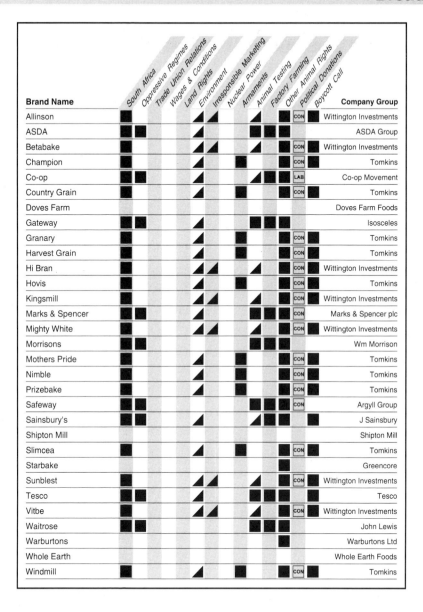

Brand Name	South Africa	Oppressive Regimes	Trade Union Relations	Wages & Conditions	Land Rights	Environment	Irresponsible Marketing	Nuclear Power	Armaments	Animal Testing	Factory Farming	Other Animal Rights	Political Donations	Boycott Call	Company Group
Allinson	■					◢	◢			◢		■	CON	■	Wittington Investments
ASDA	■	■				◢				■	■	■			ASDA Group
Betabake	■					◢	◢			◢		■	CON	■	Wittington Investments
Champion	■					◢			■			■	CON	■	Tomkins
Co-op	■	■				◢				◢	■	■	LAB		Co-op Movement
Country Grain	■					◢			■			■	CON	■	Tomkins
Doves Farm															Doves Farm Foods
Gateway	■	■				◢				■	■	■			Isosceles
Granary	■					◢			■			■	CON	■	Tomkins
Harvest Grain	■					◢			■			■	CON	■	Tomkins
Hi Bran	■					◢	◢			◢		■	CON	■	Wittington Investments
Hovis	■					◢			■			■	CON	■	Tomkins
Kingsmill	■					◢	◢			◢		■	CON	■	Wittington Investments
Marks & Spencer	■	■				◢				■	■	■	CON		Marks & Spencer plc
Mighty White	■					◢	◢			◢		■	CON	■	Wittington Investments
Morrisons	■	■								■	■	■			Wm Morrison
Mothers Pride	■					◢			■			■	CON	■	Tomkins
Nimble	■					◢			■			■	CON	■	Tomkins
Prizebake	■					◢			■			■	CON	■	Tomkins
Safeway	■	■								■	■	■	CON		Argyll Group
Sainsbury's	■	■				◢				◢	■	■		■	J Sainsbury
Shipton Mill															Shipton Mill
Slimcea	■					◢			■			■	CON	■	Tomkins
Starbake												■			Greencore
Sunblest	■					◢	◢			◢		■	CON	■	Wittington Investments
Tesco	■	■				◢				■	■	■		■	Tesco
Vitbe	■					◢	◢			◢		■	CON	■	Wittington Investments
Waitrose	■	■								■	■	■			John Lewis
Warburtons												■			Warburtons Ltd
Whole Earth															Whole Earth Foods
Windmill	■					◢			■			■	CON	■	Tomkins

Breakfast Cereals

The first cornflake was introduced into this country in 1922. Since then the words 'Kellogg's' and 'cornflakes' have been almost synonymous. In 1989, that other well-known name, Nestlé, got in on the act when it formed a joint venture with the US company, General Mills.

Other companies play a relatively small part compared to these two, but thankfully there are a number of small, ethical companies producing organic cereals.

We have only put each company's best-known brand on the Table. Their other brands are listed in 'Breakfast Cereal Brands'.

Advertising Sugar

Numerous irritating television commercials not only set out to persuade health-conscious adults but also impressionable younger viewers to enjoy their wares. Some of the companies in this report are amongst those which have been criticised, by Parents for Safe Food and the Food Commission as well as others, for advertising sugar-laden products to children.

In its section on advertising to children the IBA code states that, "No product or service may be advertised ... which might result in harm to them physically, mentally or morally, and ... which takes advantage of the natural credulity and sense of loyalty of children."

Sugar Puffs are advertised to children by children at peak children's viewing times, and have a sugar content of over 50%. Government medical reports state unequivocally that sugar causes tooth decay, and other commentators have recognised the addictive nature of sugar consumption and other physical problems that can be caused by sugar.[1342] Clearly there is a discrepancy somewhere.

Unrepentant, Quaker's Marketing Director claimed, "It is wrong to suggest to mothers that pre-sweetened breakfast cereals are harming their children's health. The popularity of Sugar Puffs helps mums ensure their children do actually eat a breakfast."[660]

Although most critics of these products and their advertising argue for stricter controls on the timing and content of commercials, it is clear that the willingness of companies to flout the present rulings are partly to blame for the damage to children's health.

Sugar content of breakfast cereals

Brand	sugar as % of weight
Sugar Puffs	57
Frosties	42
Ricicles	40
Honey Smacks	39
Coco Pops	32
Rice Krispies	11
Cornflakes	7
Weetabix	6
Shredded Wheat	1

Source: Parents for Safe Food: The Safe Food Handbook
(Ebury Press 1990)

Pesticides

Agrochemical farming methods have serious environmental as well as health implications. Modern varieties of wheat require artificially high levels of nitrates and phosphates which may leach into rivers and lakes causing toxic algal blooms.[409] Insecticides wipe out the food supplies of other wildlife, and the huge farm machinery used means bigger fields and less hedgerows. Again, choosing organic cereals will be one way of discouraging these practices.

Organic cereals also solve the problem of wholegrain cereals containing more pesticides than refined ones (see the Flour report).

Packaging

For some reason Kelloggs has stopped making its packets with recycled cardboard. Many other cereal manufacturers have followed suit.[1140] Some companies do, however, use recycled cardboard and usually say so on their products.

Another noticeable change for the worse is the inner packaging which appears to have switched from waxed paper to plastic in recent years.

Breakfast Cereals

Best Buys

We have not discovered any criticisms of the companies which own the Allinson, Doves Farm, Jordans, Kallo, Mornflakes, Suma and Whole Earth brands. All of these, except Allinson, include at least one organic variety and will mainly be found in health food shops.

Of the mainstream brands, Weetabix and the rest of the cereals owned by the same company (see Breakfast Cereal Brands) come out the best.

Breakfast Cereal Brands

Doves Farm
Cornflakes, Bran Flakes, Wheelies.

Kellogg Company
(Kellogg's) All-Bran, Bran Buds, Bran Flakes, Coco Pops, Common Sense Oat Bran Flakes, Cornflakes, Country Store, Crunchy Nut Cornflakes, Frosties, Fruit 'n' Fibre, Golden Crackles, Golden Oatmeal Crisp, Honey Nut Loops, Honey Smacks, Nutri-Grain, Puffa Puffa Rice, Raisin Splitz, Rice Krispies, Ricicles, Smacks, Special K, Start, Sultana Bran, Toppas, Variety Packs.

Nestlé/General Mills
Cheerios, Cinnamon Toast Crunch, Cocoa Puffs, Coco Shreddies, Crisp Rice, Fincken Flakes, Force Flakes, Frosted Shreddies, Golden Grahams, Honey Nut Cheerios, Lucky Charms, Shredded Wheat, Shreddies, Wheetflakes.

Quaker Oats
Harvest Crunch, Oat Krunchies, Puffed Wheat, Quaker Oats, QuakeAwake, Sugar Puffs.

Weetabix
Alpen, Branfare, Country Mills, Cruesli, Fruit & Nut Bran, Oat & Wheat Bran, Ready Brek, Weetabix, Weetaflakes, Weetos.

Whole Earth Foods
Cornflakes, Wheat Puffs.

Wittington Investments
Ryvita Bran-enriched Cornflakes & Sunblest Cornflakes

(This article was first published in August 1990.)

Brand Name	South Africa	Oppressive Regimes	Trade Union Relations	Wages & Conditions	Land Rights	Environment	Irresponsible Marketing	Nuclear Power	Armaments	Animal Testing	Factory Farming	Other Animal Rights	Political Donations	Boycott Call	Company Group
Allinson															Ryecroft Foods Ltd
ASDA	■	■		◣				■	■	■					ASDA Group
Cheshire										◣					Koninlijke Wessanen
Co-op	■	■		◣				◣	■	■			LAB		Co-op Movement
Doves Farm															Doves Farm Foods
Gateway	■	■		◣				■	■	■					Isosceles
Granose		◣		◣	◣							■			Archer-Daniels-Midland
Grape Nuts	◣	■						■		■			USA	■	Philip Morris
Holland & Barrett										■			CON		Lloyds Chemists
Hollymill	◣						◣								Health & Diet Company
Jordans															W Jordan & Son
Kallo Puffed Rice															Kallo Foods Ltd
Kelkin										■					Wardell Roberts
Kelloggs	■	◣	◣	◣				◣					CON USA	■	Kellogg Company
Marks & Spencer	■	■		◣				■	■	■			CON		Marks & Spencer plc
Mornflakes															Morning Foods
Morrisons	■	■						■	■	■					Wm Morrison
Ryvita	■				◣	◣		◣		■		CON		■	Wittington Investments
Safeway	■	■						■	■	■			CON		Argyll Group
Sainsbury's	■	■		◣				◣	■	■			■		J Sainsbury
Shredded Wheat	■	■	◣	◣		■		■		■					Nestlé/General Mills
Sugar Puffs		■		◣						■		USA			Quaker Oats
Suma															Suma Wholefoods
Tesco	■	■		◣				■	■	■			■		Tesco
Waitrose	■	■						■	■	■					John Lewis
Weetabix				◣											Weetabix Ltd
Whole Earth															Whole Earth Foods

Butter & Margarine

The Milk Machine   Vegans have for a long time recognised the ethical implications of the consumption of milk and dairy products. The life of a modern dairy cow is rarely a natural one. To provide a constant supply of milk the dairy cow is usually impregnated every year (usually by artificial insemination) beginning at the age of two.[199] She is then milked for ten months of the year, and for six or seven of those months she will be pregnant again with her next calf.[1666] The calves are usually taken away from her after a few days and she produces ten times as much milk as her calf would have drunk. To achieve these unnaturally high yields her diet may be supplemented with concentrated protein pellets, often containing animal offal. Professor John Webster at the Department of Animal Husbandry, Bristol University has estimated that the amount of work done by today's high yielding dairy cow is equivalent to a human jogging for six hours every day.[1669]

A profitable spin-off from dairy farming is its links with the meat industry. Over 60% of beef cattle in the UK are reared from the calves of the dairy herd. One in three calves, about half a million, are exported to be reared in veal crates on the continent. Here they will live in crates 5ft x 2ft and will be fed on a milk-substitute gruel which makes them anaemic, keeping their flesh white.[1669] Other calves may be reared as bulls or as replacement dairy cows. Unhealthy calves will be slaughtered and used as pet food.[1666]

Margarines and spreads that do not contain any animal or dairy products include: Suma, Whole Earth, Vitaquell, Vitelma, Granose and Meridian.

Margarine   Margarine is a highly processed food product. The fat is extracted from either plant or animal material. The oil is then washed, bleached, filtered, deodorised and decoloured. It may then be hardened (by hydrogenation) which, in effect, makes the fat more saturated. Water is added next and an emulsifier to stop the mixture separating. E additives such as colours, flavours, anti-oxidants and preservatives may also then be added.

Like butter, margarine must by law be at least 80% fat and no more than 16% water, and must contain the added vitamins A and D which occur naturally in butter.

One problem of buying margarines and other spreads containing vegetable oils is that the working conditions under which these oils are produced are an unknown factor. Both palm and coconut oil are produced as cash crops, often on plantations in Malaysia, Indonesia and West Africa, but the lack of informative labelling does not allow you to avoid products which contain these oils. Of the named oils, soya is produced mainly in the USA, Brazil, China and Argentina and sunflower in Russia, Eastern Europe and Argentina.[1139]

Country of Origin

Dairy spreads, such as Clover, are a blend of cream and vegetable oils, basically butter with oil added to make it more spreadable. Typically they contain 75% fat.
Fat spreads, such as Krona and Summer County, are made from animal and/or vegetable oils and contain about 70% fat.
Reduced-fat spreads, such as Mello, usually contain about 60% fat and 35% water.
Low-fat spreads, such as Outline and Shape, are usually about 40% fat and 55% water. A recent addition to these spreads is the introduction of very low-fat spreads which are only 25% fat but 60% water.

Other Spreads

A report in 1984 by the government's Committee on Medical Aspects of Food Policy recommended the nation cut down on fats generally and, specifically, saturated fats. Most health educators agree that we should eat food that is low in total fat content and substitute polyunsaturated fats for saturated fats to reduce the risk of heart disease.
Saturated fats include: animal/milk fat, coconut oil, palm oil and hydrogenated vegetable oil.
Polyunsaturated fats include: sesame, sunflower, soya, safflower, corn, walnut and fish oils.
We therefore need to know not only how much fat a product contains but also the proportions of saturated and unsaturated fats. Unfortunately, manufacturers do not have to declare either of these things on their packets though some choose to do so voluntarily.
Additives used in individual margarines and other spreads vary and should be checked for health risks in E number guide books such as 'Additives - Your Complete Survival Guide'.[33]

Health Risks

(This article was first published in February 1990)

Brand Name	South Africa	Oppressive Regimes	Trade Union Relations	Wages & Conditions	Land Rights	Environment	Irresponsible Marketing	Nuclear Power	Armaments	Animal Testing	Factory Farming	Other Animal Rights	Political Donations	Boycott Call	Company Group
Spreads															
Clover					■					◿					Milk Marketing Board
Delight	■	■	◿		■	◿			■	■			■		Unilever
Gold				◿	◿				■	■	CON				Unigate
Golden Crown	◿	■			■			■		USA	■				Philip Morris
Outline	■	■	◿		■			■	■	■	■				Unilever
I can't believe it's not butter!	■	■	◿		■			■	■	■	■				Unilever
Mello	◿	■			■				■	USA	■				Philip Morris
Whole Earth															Whole Earth Foods
Shape				◿	◿	◿			■	■	CON				Unigate
Willow					■					◿					Milk Marketing Board
Own Brands															
ASDA	■	■		◿				■	■	■					ASDA Group
Co-op	■	■		◿				◿	■	■	LAB				Co-op Movement
Gateway	■	■		◿				■	■	■					Isosceles
Marks & Spencer	■	■						■	■	■	CON				Marks & Spencer plc
Morrisons	■	■						■	■	■					Wm Morrison
Safeway	■	■						■	■	■	CON				Argyll Group
Sainsbury's	■	■		◿				◿	■	■			■		J Sainsbury
Tesco	■	■		◿				■	■	■			■		Tesco
Waitrose	■	■						■	■	■					John Lewis

Best Buys We have not discovered any criticisms of An Bord Bainne, therefore its Kerrygold brand is the butter best buy. Margarine and Other Spreads best buys are the Meridian, Suma, Vitaquell, Vitelma and Whole Earth brands.

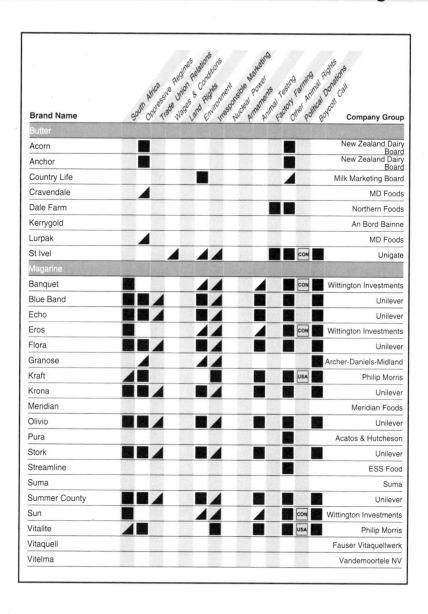

Brand Name	South Africa	Oppressive Regimes	Trade Union Relations	Wages & Conditions	Land Rights	Environment	Irresponsible Marketing	Nuclear Power	Armaments	Animal Testing	Factory Farming	Other Animal Rights	Political Donations	Boycott Call	Company Group
Butter															
Acorn	■										■				New Zealand Dairy Board
Anchor	■										■				New Zealand Dairy Board
Country Life				■							◢				Milk Marketing Board
Cravendale	◢														MD Foods
Dale Farm										■	■				Northern Foods
Kerrygold															An Bord Bainne
Lurpak	◢														MD Foods
St Ivel				◢	◢	◢				■	■	CON	■		Unigate
Margarine															
Banquet	■			◢	◢		◢			■	CON		■		Wittington Investments
Blue Band	■	■	◢	■	◢			■		■			■		Unilever
Echo	■	■	◢	■	◢			■		■			■		Unilever
Eros	■			◢	◢		◢			■	CON		■		Wittington Investments
Flora	■	■	◢	■	◢			■		■			■		Unilever
Granose		◢		◢	◢						■				Archer-Daniels-Midland
Kraft	◢	■			■					■		USA	■		Philip Morris
Krona	■	■	◢	■	◢			■		■			■		Unilever
Meridian															Meridian Foods
Olivio	■	■	◢	■	■			■		■			■		Unilever
Pura										■					Acatos & Hutcheson
Stork	■	■	◢	■	◢			■		■			■		Unilever
Streamline										■					ESS Food
Suma															Suma
Summer County	■	■	◢	■	■			■		■			■		Unilever
Sun	■			◢	◢		◢			■	CON		■		Wittington Investments
Vitalite	◢	■			■			■		■		USA	■		Philip Morris
Vitaquell															Fauser Vitaquellwerk
Vitelma															Vandemoortele NV

Cat & Dog Food

Mars (with Pedigree and Whiskas) and Dalgety (with Spillers and Winalot) between them they account for about 80% of the UK market for tinned pet food. For space reasons only one brand each from Mars, Dalgety and BP feature on the Tables for tinned options; others are listed in 'Other Brands'.

The Meat Industry

Generally, pet food is made from raw materials which are classified 'unfit for human consumption', or which are surplus to requirements, often effectively by-products from a company's other operations. The use of meat and slaughterhouse by-products may subsidise today's cruel factory farming system. Furthermore, farm slurry and sewage is a major source of river pollution.

Looking at the worldwide implications of the meat industry, some farm animals are fed on grain which may have been imported from countries where people are badly nourished. In 1984 for example, when we were relieving our consciences with Live Aid, the UK imported animal feed from Ethiopia. This might still be a problem if pets were fed directly on grain, but it requires about nine pounds of grain to produce just one pound of meat. Most commentators would also agree that changing patterns of food consumption in the West will not be enough to tackle the root problems of unequal food distribution. Each year, the UK spends nearly £1 billion on cat and dog food, several times that received by our best-known relief and development agencies.

Packaging

Most UK pet 'owners' still buy steel cans. Over two billion are thrown away annually, with the consequent costs to the environment of their creation and disposal. Recycling rates are still pitifully low, although they vary from region to region. Alternatives to the can, especially for the 'premium' products, may use two or more materials, making recycling difficult. The cardboard used for dry foods is most easily recycled.

Vegetarian Cats and Dogs

Vegetarian pet owners, or those concerned about factory farming, may choose to feed their pets a meat-free diet. Dogs are omnivorous and may be fed a vegetarian diet. However, it should be noted that cats cannot live on a vegetarian diet, and will likely seek to supplement it if an owner attempts to enforce one. Vegecat and Vegekit (which apparently provide cats with the necessary protein supplements), and Vegedog are vegan products made in the US and distributed in the UK by Katz Go Vegan (whose contact address is: the Vegan Society, Box 161, 7 Battle Road, St Leonards-on-Sea, East Sussex TN37 7AA).

Alternatives

Cats could be allowed to fend for themselves, as in the Mediterranean, though this will to some extent depend where you live. You could feed your pet scraps. Home-made recipes can be obtained from the Vegan Society, certain pet care manuals or, for example, 'The Complete Herbal Handbook for Cats and Dogs' by Juliette de Bairacli Levy, who advocates raw meat since it most closely replicates a natural diet.

Best Buys

Dog food: For tins, Happidog (vegetarian) is the Best Buy, followed by the (non-vegetarian) Brandy, Butcher's Tripe, Champion Chunks, Healthmeal and Laughing Dog brands. For complete dried food, Happidog is the Best Buy. Brandy, Champion, Gilpa, Laughing Dog, Vitalin and Wafcol are next best. For semi-moist, the choice is between, Bounce, Frolic and Minced Morsels. For mixers/ biscuits, Laughing Dog, Nature-Meal and Wafcol are best.
Cat Food: Brandy, Clever Cat and Nature-Cat are Best Buys for tins. For semi-moist, Delikat is best and for dried food, the choice is between Brekkies, Kit-e-Kat and Meowmix.

Other Brands

Tinned Dog Food

Dalgety:	Choice, Goodlife, Kennomeat, Top Dog, Winalot Prime
Mars:	Cesar, Mr Dog, Pal, Pedigree Chum
BP:	Duo, Gala, Gold Star, Red Heart

Tinned Cat Food

Dalgety:	Bonus, Choosy, Purrfect, Savour
Mars:	Kit-e-Kat, Sheba, Whiskas
BP:	Cats Choice, Gala

(This article was first published in September 1989.)

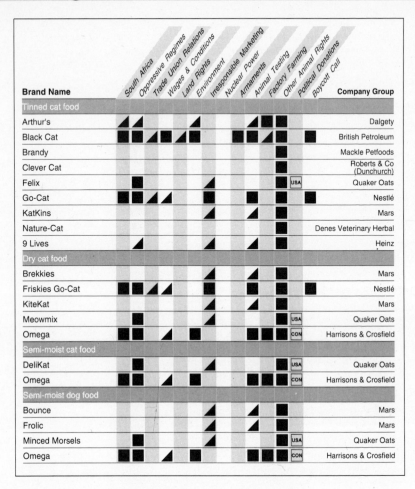

Brand Name	South Africa	Oppressive Regimes	Trade Union Relations	Wages & Conditions	Land Rights	Environment	Irresponsible Marketing	Nuclear Power	Armaments	Animal Testing	Factory Farming	Other Animal Rights	Political Donations	Boycott Call	Company Group
Tinned cat food															
Arthur's	◤	◤		◤		◤			◤	■	■				Dalgety
Black Cat	■	■	◤	■	◤	■		■	■	◤	■		■		British Petroleum
Brandy										■					Mackle Petfoods
Clever Cat										■					Roberts & Co (Dunchurch)
Felix	■					◤				■ (USA)					Quaker Oats
Go-Cat	■	■	◤	◤		■		■		■			■		Nestlé
KatKins				◤		◤				■					Mars
Nature-Cat										■					Denes Veterinary Herbal
9 Lives	◤			◤		◤				■					Heinz
Dry cat food															
Brekkies				◤						■					Mars
Friskies Go-Cat	■	■	◤	◤		■		■		■			■		Nestlé
KiteKat				◤		◤				■					Mars
Meowmix	■				◤					■ (USA)					Quaker Oats
Omega	■	■	◤	■				■	■	■ (CON)					Harrisons & Crosfield
Semi-moist cat food															
DeliKat	■			◤						■ (USA)					Quaker Oats
Omega	■	■	◤	■			■	■	■ (CON)						Harrisons & Crosfield
Semi-moist dog food															
Bounce				◤		◤				■					Mars
Frolic				◤		◤				■					Mars
Minced Morsels	■			◤						■ (USA)					Quaker Oats
Omega	■	■	◤	■			■	■	■ (CON)						Harrisons & Crosfield

Brand Name	South Africa	Oppressive Regimes	Trade Union Relations	Wages & Conditions	Land Rights	Environment	Irresponsible Marketing	Nuclear Power	Armaments	Animal Testing	Factory Farming	Other Animal Rights	Political Donations	Boycott Call	Company Group
Tinned dog food															
Award		◤			◤		◤			■					Heinz
Bonus Dog	◤	◤			◤		◤			■	■				Dalgety
Bounce					◤		◤			■					Mars
Brandy										■					Mackle Petfoods
Butch	■	■	◤	■	◤	■			■	◤	■		■		British Petroleum
Butchers Tripe										■					F W Baker
Champion Chunks										■					Mackle Petfoods
Chunky		■			◤					■			USA		Quaker Oats
Happidog															Happidog Petfoods
Healthmeal										■					Denes Veterinary Herbal
Laughing Dog										■					Roberts & Co (Dunchurch)
Complete dry dog food															
Brandy										■					Mackle Petfoods
Champion										■					Mackle Petfoods
Frolic							◤	◤		■					Mars
Gilpa										■					Gilbertson & Page
Happidog Supermeal															Happidog Petfoods
Laughing Dog										■					Roberts & Co (Dunchurch)
Omega	■	■		◤	■				■	■	■		CON		Harrisons & Crosfield
Pedigree Chum					◤		◤			■					Mars
Spillers Dog Diet	◤	◤			◤			◤		■	■				Dalgety
Vitalin										■					Kennel Nutrition
Wafcol										■					Armitage Brothers
Mixers/Biscuits															
Biscrok							◤	◤		■					Mars
Buffet Treats	■	■	◤	◤		■			■	■			■		Nestlé
Butch	■	■	◤	■	◤	■			■	◤	■		■		British Petroleum
Gold Star	■	■	◤	■		■			■	◤	■		■		British Petroleum
Laughing Dog										■					Roberts & Co (Dunchurch)
Markies							◤	◤		■					Mars
Nature-meal										■					Denes Veterinary Herbal
Nuckles	■	■	◤	■	◤	■			■	◤	■		■		British Petroleum
Omega	■	■		◤	■				■	■	■		CON		Harrisons & Crosfield
Pedigree Chum					◤		◤			■					Mars
Smackers					◤		◤			■					Mars
Spillers Bonio	◤	◤			◤			◤		■	■				Dalgety
Wafcol										■					Armitage Brothers
Winalot	◤	◤			◤			◤		■	■				Dalgety

Chocolate

The cacao tree, from which we get the cocoa bean, came originally from Central America, and is now grown in tropical climates the world over. From Brazil and Ecuador to Singapore and even China, cacao trees spread their strange branches. But it is in Africa and mainly the Ivory Coast and Ghana that most of the world's cocoa is grown. Both these countries rely very heavily on the product, which accounts for nearly half their exports. Nigeria, Malaysia and Brazil are also significant suppliers of beans, but they are much less dependent on the crop.

The dependency of countries such as the Ivory Coast on cocoa was originally forced on them by the colonial powers in the nineteenth century, but even since 'independence' the expansion of cocoa plantations has continued.

The large chocolate companies have themselves never been directly involved to any great extent with the growing of cocoa. Through a system of tying farmers to loans with conditions attached about who they can buy from and sell to, the companies still enjoy a virtual monopoly and often pay well below the market rate for their cocoa. Lappé and Collins in Food First describe the situation:

"Over fifty per cent of Nestlé's turnover derives from products using milk, cocoa or coffee as raw materials and yet Nestlé owns not a single cow nor an acre of coffee nor cocoa production estates. It doesn't need to. It can control production more effectively and with less risk by dominating the local commodity markets and by monopolising supplies to the producers."[573]

Pesticides A report in the Food Magazine in 1989 drew attention to the hazards from pesticides faced by workers on cocoa plantations, especially in Brazil.[586] Working conditions on some large estates are appalling, with workers receiving no training in the safe use of toxic chemicals and spraying with inadequate safety gear. The scale of the problem is unknown, but many thousands are likely to be suffering the effects. Although the problems are worst in Brazil, other countries such as Malaysia also practice similar methods of intensive production, and those which do not, such as Ghana and the Ivory Coast are under increasing pressure from the companies and the World Bank to follow suit.

There is evidence that minute traces of pesticides are coming into this country in cocoa beans. Although the chocolate manufacturers do not actually own any cocoa plantations, they are definitely in an influential position and should be pressurising growers not to follow the intensive chemical-based route.

Consumers can vote against intensive chemical use by choosing chocolate products which use organic cocoa. Green & Black's uses cocoa solids in its chocolate that have been certified organic by Nature et Progres, the French equivalent of the Soil Association, while Mascao chocolate is looking to increase its organic content.

Fair Trade

The price paid for cocoa can be erratic, with price speculation and overproduction on world markets meaning cocoa producers rarely receive a fair price for their produce. The cocoa-growing countries' plight is made worse still by the overall decline in the real price of cocoa over the last decade. The Mascao and Green & Black's chocolates brands both come from organisations which give the cocoa producers fairer prices. Mascao is made using cocoa from a Bolivian co-operative, and sugar from small-scale growers in the Philippines. It is produced and distributed by the European Fair Trade Association. Green & Black's cocoa is produced in Togo, where producers are paid a contract price agreed for three years in advance that is between £150 and £250 per tonne above the world price for cocoa beans.

Packaging

It has to be said that chocolates are one of the most ridiculously overpackaged products around, especially things like Easter Eggs which probably contain more card and plastic than chocolate.

Bars of chocolate nowadays come in two sorts of wrapping. The 'traditional' one now consists of aluminium foil plus a paper wrapper (e.g. KitKat). The latest fashion is 'flow-wrapping' (like Mars bars now) which uses pearlised film, made of polypropylene. In terms of energy use in manufacture there probably is not much to choose between the two sorts - but aluminium and paper are at least theoretically recyclable. Polypropylene gives off toxic fumes when burnt, and does not naturally degrade otherwise.

Health

The health risks associated with eating chocolate are the same as for those of its ingredients - sugar, fat and cocoa (which contains caffeine). Information on these subjects appears in the reports on Sugar, Butter & Margarine and Coffee.

Further information about the global and personal implications of chocolate production and consumption can be found in the new WEN book "Chocolate Unwrapped - The Politics of Pleasure" (Available for £9.99 - including P&P - from WEN, Aberdeen Studios, 22 Highbury Grove, London N5 2EA)

Chocolate Brands

Cadbury-Schweppes
Dairy Milk, Fruit & Nut, Whole Nut, Bournville, Fry's Chocolate Cream, Crunchie, Flake, Double Decker, Caramel, Fudge, Boost, Wispa, Roses, Milk Tray, Biarritz, Buttons, Time Out, Twirl, Creme Eggs

Ferrero
Ferrero, Rocher, Kinder, Raffaello, Fresco Mint

Huhtamaki Oy
Leaf, Hellas, Lo

Lindt
Lindt, Chocoletti, Lindor

Mars
Mars, Twix, Snickers, Bounty, Minstrels, Maltesers, M&Ms, Ripple, Galaxy, Milky Way, Topic, Tracker, Balisto

Nestlé
Aero, Yorkie, Milky Bar, Dairy Crunch, Caramac, Drifter, Kit Kat, After Eight, Black Magic, Dairy Box, Lion Bar, Match Makers, Munchies, Rolo, Smarties, Quality Street, Secret, Toffee Crisp, Vice Versa, Walnut Whip

James Finlay
Paynes, Just Brazils, Just Mints, Poppets, Toms Holly Bar, Yankie Bar

Philip Morris
Suchard, Toblerone, Milka, Cote D'Or, Lila Pause, Marabou Dime, Bitz, Logger, Waifa, Chocolate Orange, All Gold, Moonlight, Spartan, Velvet Milk, Carousel, Neapolitan, Mint Crisp, Pyramint.

(This article was first published in September 1989.)

Best Buys

We have not discovered any criticisms of the companies which own the following chocolate brands: Dorchester Chocolates, Ferrero, Green & Black's, Lindt, Mascao, Plamil and Ritter Sport. Of these, Green & Black's and Mascao stand out because of their commitment to fair trade and organic cocoa production. These can both be obtained in whole food shops or from their distributors Whole Earth Foods Ltd and Traidcraft respectively.
For those wanting to avoid milk products in chocolate Plamil and Dorchester Chocolates offer vegan alternatives.

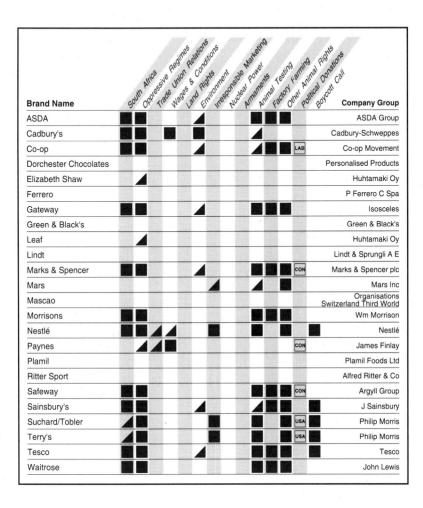

Brand Name	South Africa	Oppressive Regimes	Trade Union Relations	Wages & Conditions	Land Rights	Environment	Irresponsible Marketing	Nuclear Power	Armaments	Animal Testing	Factory Farming	Other Animal Rights	Political Donations	Boycott Call	Company Group
ASDA	■	■			◣			■	■	■					ASDA Group
Cadbury's	■	■	■		■			◣							Cadbury-Schweppes
Co-op	■	■			◣			◣	■		[LAB]				Co-op Movement
Dorchester Chocolates															Personalised Products
Elizabeth Shaw	◣														Huhtamaki Oy
Ferrero															P Ferrero C Spa
Gateway	■	■			◣			■	■	■					Isosceles
Green & Black's															Green & Black's
Leaf	◣														Huhtamaki Oy
Lindt															Lindt & Sprungli A E
Marks & Spencer	■	■			◣			■	■	■	[CON]				Marks & Spencer plc
Mars					◣			◣		■					Mars Inc
Mascao															Organisations Switzerland Third World
Morrisons	■	■						■	■	■					Wm Morrison
Nestlé	■	■	◣	◣		■		■		■		■			Nestlé
Paynes	◣	◣	■							[CON]					James Finlay
Plamil															Plamil Foods Ltd
Ritter Sport															Alfred Ritter & Co
Safeway	■	■						■	■	■	[CON]				Argyll Group
Sainsbury's	■	■			◣			◣	■			■			J Sainsbury
Suchard/Tobler	◣	■			■			■		[USA]	■				Philip Morris
Terry's	◣	■			■			■		[USA]	■				Philip Morris
Tesco	■	■			◣			■	■	■					Tesco
Waitrose	■	■						■	■	■					John Lewis

Cooking Oil

Refined oils go through a series of processes which can involve the use of high temperature pressing and petroleum-based solvents to extract the oil. Treatment with caustic soda, bleaching to remove colour and deodorization may also take place. Temperatures can rise to 470ºF (243ºC), which results in the loss of nutrients, vitamins and enzymes.[1254]

Unrefined oils are pressed from the seed, nut or grain and then filtered through cotton or paper. Even this process can generate temperatures up to 86ºF (30ºC), so the term cold-pressed used on some labels is not strictly correct. These oils retain more vitamin E, lecithin and carotene, and strong flavour and odour. Once opened, however, they are prone to rancidity.[1254]

Saturated or Unsaturated?

Most saturated fats come from animal sources, but coconut and palm oil are also high in saturates and may be included in blended vegetable oils which do not have to be labelled with each oil used.[1418]

Much argument and research has occurred over the relative healthiness of poly and monounsaturated fats. At the moment monounsaturates are out in front but polyunsaturates still have their supporters. Some research has suggested that a high intake of polyunsaturates could be linked to some types of cancer,[1254] whilst monounsaturates are praised because they may lower blood cholesterol.[1418] Below is a list of the different oils and their predominant fat type.

> **Saturated fat:** palm, coconut.
> **Polyunsaturated fat:** corn, grapeseed, pine seed, pumpkin, safflower, sesame, soya bean, sunflower, walnut.
> **Monounsaturated fat:** almond, groundnut/peanut, hazelnut, olive, rapeseed.[1709]

If a refined oil has gone through the gruelling processes described earlier, then it is unlikely to contain any pesticide residues.[1418] But since the nutritional value of a refined oil has been reduced, a 'cold-pressed' or unrefined oil may seem more attractive. However since the least refined oils will have more chance of pesticide residues, unrefined organic oils might seem to be the answer. Both Meridian Foods and Suma in this report have some organic oils including sunflower, safflower and olive oils.

(This article was first published in April 1991.)

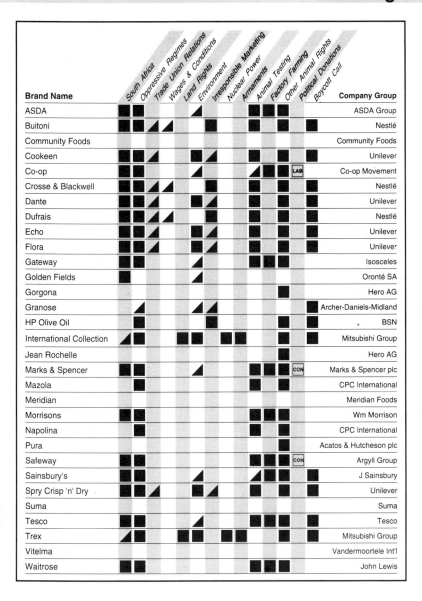

Brand Name	South Africa	Oppressive Regimes	Trade Union Relations	Wages & Conditions	Land Rights	Environment	Irresponsible Marketing	Nuclear Power	Armaments	Animal Testing	Factory Farming	Other Animal Rights	Political Donations	Boycott Call	Company Group
ASDA	■	■		◤				■	■	■					ASDA Group
Buitoni	■	■	◤	◤		■			■		■		■		Nestlé
Community Foods															Community Foods
Cookeen	■	■	◤		■	◤		■		■			■		Unilever
Co-op	■	■			◤		◤			■	■		LAB		Co-op Movement
Crosse & Blackwell	■	■	◤	◤		■			■		■		■		Nestlé
Dante	■	■		◤	■	◤		■		■			■		Unilever
Dufrais	■	■	◤			■			■		■		■		Nestlé
Echo	■	■		◤	■	◤		■		■			■		Unilever
Flora	■	■		◤	■	◤		■		■			■		Unilever
Gateway	■	■		◤				■	■	■					Isosceles
Golden Fields	■			◤											Oronté SA
Gorgona											■				Hero AG
Granose			◤		◤	■							■		Archer-Daniels-Midland
HP Olive Oil		■			■					■			■		BSN
International Collection	◤			■	■		■ ■			■			■		Mitsubishi Group
Jean Rochelle											■				Hero AG
Marks & Spencer	■	■		◤				■	■	■			CON		Marks & Spencer plc
Mazola		■								■					CPC International
Meridian															Meridian Foods
Morrisons	■	■						■	■	■					Wm Morrison
Napolina		■							■	■					CPC International
Pura											■				Acatos & Hutcheson plc
Safeway	■	■						■	■	■			CON		Argyll Group
Sainsbury's	■	■		◤			◤		■	■			■		J Sainsbury
Spry Crisp 'n' Dry	■	■	◤		■	◤		■					■		Unilever
Suma															Suma
Tesco	■	■		◤				■	■	■			■		Tesco
Trex	◤	■		■	■		■ ■			■			■		Mitsubishi Group
Vitelma															Vandermoortele Int'l
Waitrose	■	■						■	■	■					John Lewis

Best Buys

Best Buys are the unrefined, organic brands of Suma and Meridian. Additionally, we have not discovered any criticisms of the companies that produce the Community Foods and Vitelma cooking oil brands.
Of the more widely available brands, Pura comes out the best.

Crisps & Savoury Snacks

On average every man, woman and child in the United Kingdom eats three packets of savoury snacks every week.[962] The main crisp and snack manufacturers' brands are listed on the Table. A full list of crisp and snack brands for each company appears in the 'Other Brands' list.

Healthy Eating? Like much of the food industry, the snack people have not been slow to climb aboard the health bandwagon with lower fat crisps, crisps fried in their skins for extra fibre or even the addition of vitamins and minerals.

However most crisp companies still include additives in their products which have been banned by the government in foods 'specially formulated for babies and young children'. This is in spite of the evidence that more children in the UK eat crisps than in any other European country.[1454] Although the government ban only covers foods 'specifically described by manufacturers as baby food',[33] the behaviour of most companies on this issue certainly seems in breach of the spirit, if not the letter, of the law. How many of the snack adverts currently on television actually feature, or are aimed at, young children?

Irresponsible Marketing The continued use of restricted additives is clearly an issue of corporate responsibility - especially when you consider that some manufacturers can produce a perfectly good product without them (e.g.. Hedgehog). The following additives are banned for use in products 'for babies and young children' and can be found in crisps and savoury snacks.

621 - aka Monosodium Glutamate

E320 - aka BHA (butylated hydroxianisole)

E321 - aka BHT (butylated hydroxitoluene)

Saccharin

Monosodium Glutamate, the most commonly used, is a flavour enhancer, which makes even the cheaper flavourings seem appetising. It is toxic to hypersensitive people, causing flushing and chest pain, and it is banned from 'baby food' because of its nerve stimulant properties and because it has been shown to cause cellular brain damage in new born animals.[33]

E320 and E321 are described in 'Additives - Your Complete Survival Guide' as, "perhaps the most serious chronic hazard from food additives". They are suspected carcinogens and possibly cause birth defects.[33]

Saccharin is a less common ingredient in these products but yet another suspected carcinogen.[33]

Companies selling at least one savoury snack product containing any of these restricted ingredients include: Bahlsen, Bensons Crisps, Dalgety, D & S (Food Products), Pepsico, Seabrook Investments, Unichips and Wittington Investments.[425]

Environment

As a highly processed product, crisps (and their counterparts) can be accused of using too much energy with few beneficial results. Several different processes are needed to produce all the 'extruded', 'fried pellet' and 'sheeted snacks', but the scale of energy usage is clear from the following description of basic crisp production.

Specially grown potatoes are blasted with water and caustic soda to remove their skins, then sliced, fried in vegetable oil, covered in artificial flavours, colours and antioxidising agents, and finally packaged in various plastic wrappings. The end product consists of thirty per cent oil, a good deal of air, a small amount of potato and a few additives - all this costs five hundred per cent more than the raw materials prior to processing.[106]

When it comes to the environment there is also the question of packaging; most snacks of this kind are packaged in non-biodegradable plastic films, perhaps metallised, and although their production is not generally described as wasteful of energy,[621] they are a problem when it comes to waste.

Plastics can be recycled but they need to be separated by type of plastic due to different chemical characteristics, so even with plastics separated in household waste a further sorting must take place before they can be safely used. For a consumer to tell plastic types apart for sorting, labelling is necessary, and as yet this is not common practice in the crisps industry.

The final environmental question about these products must be, do the ends justify the means? Is it necessary to buy a product which is inferior in nutrition, higher in price, and leaves a more hazardous waste product than the organic material from which it originates?

(This article was first published in April 1990.)

Crisps & Savoury Snacks

Other Brands

Bensons Crisps
Cheese Straws, Coggies, Dragon, Hand Fried, Hoggit, La Mexicana, Mammoth Bites, Nuggets, Oops, Thin Jims, Wickettes

Dalgety
Crunchy Fries, Ghostbusters, Golden Lights, Primes, Rileys, Ringos, Snake Bites, Teenage Mutant Hero Turtles, Thunder Cats, Wheat Crunchies

D & S (Food Products) Ltd
Cornettes, Crackles, Croutons, Indian Poppadums, Tortilla Chips

Desilu Dresses Ltd
Beefy Bites, Cheesy Feet, Dinosaurs, Hot Lips Tomato, Smith Weston

Pepsico Inc
Bacon Fries, Cheese Moments, Cheetos, Chester Cheetah, Chip Sticks, Crinkles, Farmhouse Jackets, Frazzles, Ruffles, Salt'n'Shake, Scampi Fries, Square Crisps, Tuba Loop

Portfolio Foods Ltd
Animates, Hit Man, Krunchie Krackers, Macho Man, On Yums, Quarter Backs, Tangy Toms Tomato, Terrors, Transform-A-Snack, Undertaker, Yankee Stars

Unichips SpA
Beano Dandy, Country Taste, Tuckers

United Biscuits
Baker's Street, Brannigans, Frisps, Jumbo Jaws, KP World Snacks, Oriental Kitchen, Roysters, Solos, Space Raiders

Wittington Investments
Burger'n'Chips, Cheese Pleesors, Chicken'n'Chips, Fish'n'Chips, Huggy Bear, Pizza Pleesors, Snipp Snapps

Best Buys

We have not discovered any criticisms of the companies that manufacture the Bensons, D & S, Hedgehog, Highlander, Oatsters, Seabrook, Stackers, Supa Dupas and Vita Crisp brands. See the 'Other Brands' list for more brands made by these companies. Of all these brands, the Hedgehog and Hoggit brands manufactured by Bensons Crisps stand out because they use organic potatoes.

Brand Name	South Africa	Oppressive Regimes	Trade Union Relations	Wages & Conditions	Land Rights	Environment	Irresponsible Marketing	Nuclear Power	Armaments	Animal Testing	Factory Farming	Other Animal Rights	Political Donations	Boycott Call	Company Group
ASDA	■	■		◺					■	■	■				ASDA Group
Bensons															Bensons Crisps plc
Co-op	■	■		◺						◺	■		LAB		Co-op Movement
D & S															D & S (Food Products) Ltd
Discos		◺		◺							■		CON		United Biscuits
Gateway	■	■		◺					■	■	■				Isosceles
Golden Wonder	◺	◺		◺					◺	■					Dalgety
Groovers	◺	◺		◺					◺	■					Dalgety
Hedgehog															Bensons Crisps plc
Highlander															Unichips S A
Hula Hoops		◺		◺							■		CON		United Biscuits
KP		◺		◺							■		CON		United Biscuits
Krunchie Puffs											■				Portfolio Foods Ltd
Marks & Spencer	■	■		◺					■	■	■		CON		Marks & Spencer plc
Monster Munch	◺	◺		◺	◺				■		■		USA	■	PepsiCo Inc
Morrisons	■	■													Wm Morrison
Nik Naks	◺	◺		◺					◺	■	■				Dalgety
Oatsters															W Jordan (Cereals)
Phileas Fogg		◺		◺							■		CON		United Biscuits
Potato Puffs	■			◺	◺				◺		■		CON		Wittington Investments
Pringles	◺	■		◺					■	◺			■		Procter & Gamble.
Quavers	◺	■		◺	◺				■		■		USA		PepsiCo Inc
Real McCoys		◺		◺							■		CON		United Biscuits
Safeway	■	■							■	■	■		CON		Argyll Group
Sainsbury's	■	■		◺						◺	■	■	■		J Sainsbury
Seabrook															Seabrook Investments
Sharwoods	■					◺	■				■		CON	◼	Tomkins
Skips		◺		◺							■		CON		United Biscuits
Smiths	◺	■		◺	◺				■		■		USA	■	PepsiCo Inc
Stackers															Bahlsen
Supa Dupas															Desilu Dresses Ltd
Tesco	■	■		◺					■	■	■		■		Tesco
Tudor	◺	■		◺	◺				■		USA		■		PepsiCo Inc
Twiglets		■				■			■		■				BSN SA
Vitacrisps															Unichips SA
Waitrose	■	■							■	■	■				John Lewis
IWalkers	◺	◺		◺	◺				■		USA		■		PepsiCo Inc
Wotsits	◺	◺		◺					◺	■	■				Dalgety
X L															Bensons Crisps plc

Flour

Ranks Hovis McDougall (Tomkins) and Dalgety dominate the sales of branded flours, but there are a number of specialist organic millers whose products are becoming more and more well known.

Flour Types White flour is made without the wheatgerm and bran parts of the grain. Wheatgerm is yellowish in colour and is said to mar the whiteness of the flour. Also the heat produced by the metal rollers when grinding the flour tends to turn wheatgerm rancid. Brown flour also has both wheatgerm and bran removed but the wheatgerm is toasted and then replaced. This process makes the wheatgerm more digestible and slows down its rancid properties.

Wholemeal flour must contain endosperm, wheatgerm and bran. The processing of white and brown flour removes some of the important vitamins and minerals which must be present according to the law. Iron, thiamin, niacin and calcium carbonate are therefore replaced.[1418]

Pesticides All products made with agrochemically-grown cereals leave the health conscious on the horns of a dilemma. Highly processed white and brown flour have most of the valuable fibre content removed and often have to be fortified to comply with minimum standards of nutrition. However, when wheat is sprayed in the fields and the store room, it is the bran that absorbs the chemicals. So products made with non-organic wholemeal flour may contain more harmful pesticide residues than less nutritious white bread.

(This article was first published in February 1991.) Luckily, there is the organic alternative. Doves Farm, Shipton Mill, Pimhill, Marriages, Jordans and The Watermill, Little Salkeld all produce organic flours and appear as Best Buys for this report.

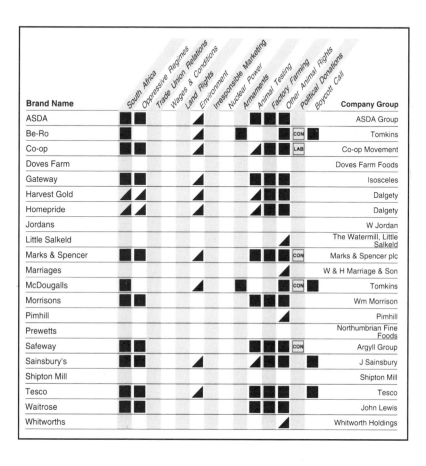

Brand Name	South Africa	Oppressive Regimes	Trade Union Relations	Wages & Conditions	Land Rights	Environment	Irresponsible Marketing	Nuclear Power	Armaments	Animal Testing	Factory Farming	Other Animal Rights	Political Donations	Boycott Call	Company Group
ASDA	■	■			◢			■	■	■					ASDA Group
Be-Ro	■				◢			■				CON	■		Tomkins
Co-op	■	■			◢			◢	■	■		LAB			Co-op Movement
Doves Farm															Doves Farm Foods
Gateway	■	■			◢			■	■	■					Isosceles
Harvest Gold	◢	◢			◢			◢	■	■					Dalgety
Homepride	◢	◢			◢			◢	■	■					Dalgety
Jordans															W Jordan
Little Salkeld										◢					The Watermill, Little Salkeld
Marks & Spencer	■	■			◢			■	■	■	CON				Marks & Spencer plc
Marriages										◢					W & H Marriage & Son
McDougalls	■				◢			■				CON	■		Tomkins
Morrisons	■	■						■	■	■					Wm Morrison
Pimhill										◢					Pimhill
Prewetts															Northumbrian Fine Foods
Safeway	■	■						■	■	■	CON				Argyll Group
Sainsbury's	■	■			◢			◢	■	■			■		J Sainsbury
Shipton Mill															Shipton Mill
Tesco	■	■			◢			■	■	■			■		Tesco
Waitrose	■	■						■	■	■					John Lewis
Whitworths										◢					Whitworth Holdings

Best Buys

We have not discovered any criticisms of Doves Farm, W Jordan or Shipton Mill. Their flours are also organic and are therefore Best Buys. The Watermill, W & H Marriage and Pimhill all receive marks for making animal feeds but their flours are also organic so they would be next best. Buying organic produce, where possible, helps to support a sustainable system of agriculture. The best choice from the mainstream producers would be Whitworths.

Ice Cream & Lollies

This report examines companies manufacturing and marketing ice cream, ice lollies, sorbets and frozen desserts. Lyons Maid has recently been bought by Nestlé, the company being boycotted by health campaigners for its irresponsible marketing of breastmilk substitutes in the Third World.

Manufacture The manufacture of ice cream in the UK is governed by the 1967 Ice Cream Regulations, which state that any product described as ice cream must contain a minimum of 5% fat and 7% non-fat milk solids (NFMS).[589] This legislation is a hangover from the Second World War, when rationing of milk and cream spurred ice cream manufacturers to experiment with non-dairy fats.

The fats used vary according to the type of ice cream. For dairy ice cream it must be milk fat, butter, cream or anhydrous milk fat (butter with all the water removed). Fats used in standard ice cream vary according to whichever are cheapest on the world market. Most commonly these are highly saturated ones such as hydrogenated palm and coconut.[589]

The constituents of 'standard' ice cream require emulsifiers to stop the water separating out into droplets. Emulsifiers, normally mono and di-glycerides (E471), may be synthesised from the slaughterhouse by-products, glycerine and tallow. Stabilisers prevent the water reforming as ice crystals and commonly used stabilisers include: seaweed extracts carrageenan (E471) and sodium alginate (E401); seed gums guar (E412) and locust bean (E410); gelatine and cotton by-products such as sodium carboxymethyl cellulose (E466). Added colour is mainly used in the cone, and typically in use are carcumin (E100), annatto (E160b), sunset yellow (E110), and carmoisine(E122).[33] Felicity Lawrence's 'Additives: Your Complete Survival Guide' awards these last three its worst rating: "Avoid - unquestionably a hazard to many people".[33] Typically lollies are sweetened with both sugar and saccharin, the latter to keep costs down.[583] Saccharin is one of the additives banned by the government for use in products 'for babies and young children'.[33] Although the ban only covers foods especially described by the manufacturer as 'baby food', lollies are clearly a product targeted at young children. For more information on the corporate responsibility issues involved here see the Crisps report.

Margaret Thatcher's first task as a food scientist with Allied Lyons in the 1950s was to formulate a soft ice cream mixture that could hold even more added air.[589] Since then, much has been written on the subject of what poor value soft ice cream represents. Although some added air is deemed necessary to give a soft texture, typical cornet ice cream is 50% air and 33% water, the remainder a mixture of skimmed milk, hydrogenated vegetable fat, sugar, and additives.[589] With modern soft ice cream machines designed to be 'self-pasteurising', health regulations only require that the machine be cleaned out every six weeks. Yet soft ice cream is one of the most frequently sampled sources of microbial contamination, and as many as a third of samples from mobile vans have been found to be contaminated.[589]

Alternatives

There is a huge number of small producers, often just a single farm, supplying local markets. Since there are more than 800 of these, and no list is available, we have not included them in this report, although they are very likely to be Best Buys. There is also now a considerable range of soya-based desserts on the market for those allergic to the products of, or unsympathetic to the methods of, the dairy industry (for more details see the Butter & Margarine report). Soya ice cream is available from wholefood shops.

Best Buys

Ice Cream Tubs and Blocks: We have discovered no criticisms of the companies which own the Berrydales, Cricket St Thomas, Dayvilles, Leopardi, My Way, New England, Newbury Fayre, N'Ice Day, Sunrise Ice Dream, Thayers and Treats brands. Of these brands Berrydales, N'Ice Day and Sunrise Ice Dream are soya-based. All these brands are Best Buys.
Ice Creams and Lollies: Boston Crunch, Carob Ice, Thayers and Treats all come from companies of which we have found no criticisms. Of these Carob Ice is the only soya-based product. All these brands are Best Buys.

(This article was first published in July 1992.)

Brand Name	South Africa	Oppressive Regimes	Trade Union Relations	Wages & Conditions	Land Rights	Environment	Irresponsible Marketing	Nuclear Power	Armaments	Animal Testing	Factory Farming	Other Animal Rights	Political Donations	Boycott Call	Company Group
Ice Cream Tubs & Blocks															
ASDA	■	■		◣			■	■	■						ASDA Group
Co-op	■	■		◣		◣	■	■					[LAB]		Co-op Movement
Creamery Fayre											■				Hazlewood Foods
Cricket St Thomas															Cygnus Venture Partners
Dairy Tops	■				◣	◣	◣				■		[CON]	■	Wittington Investments
Dale Farms										■	■				Northern Foods
Dayville's															Dayville Holdings Ltd
Gateway	■	■		◣			■	■							Isosceles
Haagen Dazs	■	■	◣	◣	◣		◣		■				■		Grand Metropolitan
Leopardi															Cygnus Venture Partners
Loseley			■		■					■	■		[BUI]	■	Booker
Lyons Maid	■	■	◣	◣		■	■	■	■					■	Nestlé
Marks & Spencer	■	■		◣			■	■	■	[CON]					Marks & Spencer plc
Marietta's	■				◣	◣	◣						[CON]	■	Wittington Investments
Morrisons	■	■					■	■							Wm Morrison
My Way															Cygnus Venture Partners
New England															Cygnus Venture Partners
Newbury Fayre															Cygnus Venture Partners
Opal Sorbet					◣		◣	■							Mars Inc
Safeway	■	■					■	■	■	[CON]					Argyll Group
Sainsbury's	■	■		◣		◣	■	■					■		J Sainsbury
Sara Lee	◣	■		◣		■			■						Sara Lee Corp
St Ivel			◣		◣	◣				[CON]	■				Unigate
Tesco	■	■		◣			■	■	■				■		Tesco
Thayers															Thayers Real Dairy Ice Cream
Treats															Treats Ice Cream
Waitrose	■	■					■	■							John Lewis
Walls	■	■	◣			■	◣	■	■				■		Unilever
Weight Watchers			◣				◣	◣	■						Heinz
Ice Cream & Lollies															
Boston Crunch															Cygnus Venture Partners
Lyons Maid	■	■	◣	◣		■		■					■		Nestlé
Mars						◣		◣	■						Mars Inc
Mr Freeze			◣												Huhtamaki Oy
Ski Bar										■	■				Northern Foods
Thayers															Thayers Real Dairy Ice Cream
Treats															Treats Ice Cream
Walls	■	■	◣			■	◣	■		■			■		Unilever

Brand Name	South Africa	Oppressive Regimes	Trade Union Relations	Wages & Conditions	Land Rights	Environment	Irresponsible Marketing	Nuclear Power	Armaments	Animal Testing	Factory Farming	Other Animal Rights	Political Donations	Boycott Call	Company Group
Soya Tubs & Blocks															
Berrydales															Berrydales
Elysia											■				Hero AG
Ice Delight	▲			▲	▲						■				Archer-Daniels-Midland
Loseley	■			■						■	■	BUI	■		Booker
N'Ice Day															Dayville Holdings Ltd
Soycreme	▲			▲	▲						■				Archer-Daniels-Midland
Sunrise Ice Dream															Soya Health Foods
Sweet Sensation	▲			▲	▲						■				Archer-Daniels-Midland
Soya Ices															
Carob Ice															Soya Health Foods
So Good	▲			▲	▲						■				Archer-Daniels-Midland
Yoga	▲			▲	▲						■				Archer-Daniels-Midland
Yogice	▲			▲	▲						■				Archer-Daniels-Midland

Walls (Unilever), Lyons Maid (Nestlé), Treats and Mars each produce so many branded products that we have listed them below, not on the Table.

Lyons Maid (Nestlé)
Soft Ice Cream: Lyons Maid, Bertorelli, Midland Counties, Mister Softee, Tonibell.
Lollies: Apple Maid, Big Squeeze, Clarkes, Coconut Flake, Fab, Favourite Centres, Funny Bunny, Juice Bars, Marble, Merlin's Brew, Mint Crisp, Mivvi, Mr Men, Nobbly Bobbly, Orange Maid, Panda, Sensation, Shazzam, Super Sprint, Teenage Mutant Hero Turtle, Toffee Crumble, Totem Pole, Triple Choc, Turkish Delight, Twange, Zoom.
Choc Ices: Ace, Classico, Figaro.
Tubs & Blocks: Caramel Swirl, Encore, Finesse, Fruit Harvest, Gold Seal, Hostess, Lyons Maid, Napoli, Tropical Sensation.

Mars
Lollies: Opal Fruits.
Ice Cream Bars: Bounty, Galaxy Dove, Milky Way, Snickers, Topic, Twix.

Treats
Cones: Grandioso.
Lollies: Bananarama, Black Forest, Candipop Toffee, Festival, Golden Surprise, Humpty Dumpty, Jazza, Juicy Lucy, Refresher, Screwdriver, Snocreme, Sorrento, Space Commander, Space Destroyer, Split Screwball, Strika, Superstar.

Walls (Unilever)
Cones: Cornetto.
Lollies: Boomy, Calippo, Dynamie, Feast, Freaky Foot, Funny Face, Max the Lion, Mini Milk, Orange Frutie, Pzazz, Red Alert, Scribbler, Sparkles, Strawberry Split, Tangle Twist.
Choc Ices: Winner, Chunky.
Ice Cream Bars: Blue Ribbon, Cadbury's Dairy Milk Ice Cream, Fresta, Kick, Magnum, Sky.
Tubs & Blocks: Blue Ribbon, Cadbury's Choc Combination, Carissima, Cream of Cornish, Dream, Elite, Gino Ginelli, Romantica, Royale, Sonata, Too Good to be True, Vienetta.

Jam & Other Spreads

This report covers jam, marmalade, honey, nut butter, syrup, chocolate and carob spreads, yeast extract, cheese spreads (but not soft cheese) and sandwich spreads (but not paté).

Jam and Marmalade
These are mainly created by simply boiling fruit with sugar in a sealed vat. Fresh or frozen fruit is used because dried fruit is preserved with sulphite which discolours and leaves an unpleasant taste, necessitating the use of colorants and flavourings.

Sugar is the main ingredient of most jams. Ordinary and extra jams must contain 60% sugar, and reduced sugar jams between 30% and 55%. The latter are known as fruit spreads and can only be described as 'jam' if labelled as suitable for diabetics. Although it is not strictly an additive, refined sugar was thought bad enough for a mention in 'Additives - Your Complete Survival Guide', in which it was rated 'avoid - unquestionably a hazard to many people'. (For more details see the Sugar report.)

The additives that may be present in <u>non-organic</u> jam include the following sweeteners, which are banned by the UK government from foods 'specially prepared for babies and young children'.[33] These are:

420 sorbitol
421 manitol
acesulfame potassium
aspartame
hydrogenated glucose syrup
isomalt
saccharin
sodium saccharin
thaumatin
xylitol

To meet organic standards, jams labelled as organic must have no colorants, anti-oxidants, preservatives or artificial flavourings.

Honey

Although honey is about 75% sugar to begin with, some brands may also have sugar added. To avoid this possibility, consumers might want to choose an unblended product from a single flower type or a single country of origin. However, among the UK's leading suppliers are Mexico and China, both on our list of Oppressive Regimes.

According to the Organic Consumer Guide,[1335] there are some organic brands, and though they cannot guarantee each individual flower, there are some regions that are mainly free from chemicals (and bees usually travel no more than three miles from the hive). The Soil Association has now licensed a honey as organic. It comes from Zambia and is distributed by Suma.

Peanut Butter

Although some of the peanuts grown in developing countries are locally consumed, most are cash crops, and in many developing countries (such as Sudan) peanut production has led to widespread soil erosion.

Another problem associated with peanuts is aflatoxin. This is a potent carcinogen, produced by mould growth, often found in crops exposed to damp. Careful screening can virtually eliminate its presence. Alternatively, Whole Earth claims to eliminate fungal growth by planting maize in rotation, and ploughing green beans back into the soil.

Other Spreads

Cheese Spread may contain up to 60% water, gelatine and gums. It is generally made from leftover cheese, mixed with fat, additives, spices and flavourings.

Syrup is made entirely from sugar, and it is therefore not surprising to find the market dominated by sugar companies; Tate & Lyle and British Sugar (Wittington Investments), control 75% and 10% of the market respectively.

Packaging

Most jams come in glass jars. The sensible answer to the resource-use and landfill questions would be to re-use jars. The only company we know to have a policy in this area is Whole Earth which uses at least 50% recycled glass.

Many of the other spreads come packaged in layers of different materials, making recycling very difficult.

Best Buys

Jam & Marmalade - We have not discovered any criticisms of the companies which own the following brands. These are therefore Best Buys: Dorothy Carter, Duerr, Elsenham, Meridian, Scotts, Stute, Suma, Sunwheel, Tiptree and Whole Earth. Whole Earth, Meridian and Duerr supply organic products.

Cheese Spreads - Primula is the Best Buy.

Chocolate and Carob Spreads - We have not discovered any criticisms of the companies selling the following brands: ChocoCrunch, Nutella, Plamil and Stute. Plamil supplies carob spreads.

Honey - Equal Exchange is the Best Buy since it is a fair trade brand. Hedgehog, Martlet, Stute, Suma, Tiptree and West Country are also supplied by companies of which we have found no criticisms.

Nut Butters - Again, Equal Exchange is the Best Buy. Meridian and Whole Earth supply organic brands and are also Best Buys.

Sandwich Spreads - Of the brands featured, Hazlewood and Shippams come out best.

Syrup - Over all, Wittington comes out marginally better than Tate & Lyle.

Yeast Extract - Community Foods, Meridian and Natex are Best Buys.

(This article was first published in June 1991.)

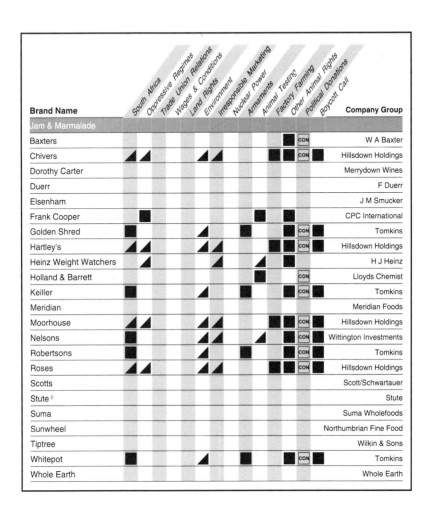

Brand Name	South Africa	Oppressive Regimes	Trade Union Relations	Wages & Conditions	Land Rights	Environment	Irresponsible Marketing	Nuclear Power	Armaments	Animal Testing	Factory Farming	Other Animal Rights	Political Donations	Boycott Call	Company Group
Jam & Marmalade															
Baxters										■	CON				W A Baxter
Chivers	◢	◢		◢	◢				■	■	CON	■			Hillsdown Holdings
Dorothy Carter															Merrydown Wines
Duerr															F Duerr
Elsenham															J M Smucker
Frank Cooper		■					■		■						CPC International
Golden Shred	■			◢		■			■	■	CON	■			Tomkins
Hartley's	◢	◢		◢	◢				■	■	CON	■			Hillsdown Holdings
Heinz Weight Watchers	◢				◢				■						H J Heinz
Holland & Barrett							■				CON				Lloyds Chemist
Keiller	■			◢		■			■	■	CON	■			Tomkins
Meridian															Meridian Foods
Moorhouse	◢	◢		◢	◢				■	■	CON	■			Hillsdown Holdings
Nelsons	■			◢	◢	◢			■	■	CON	■			Wittington Investments
Robertsons	■			◢		■			■	■	CON	■			Tomkins
Roses	◢	◢		◢	◢				■	■	CON	■			Hillsdown Holdings
Scotts															Scott/Schwartauer
Stute															Stute
Suma															Suma Wholefoods
Sunwheel															Northumbrian Fine Food
Tiptree															Wilkin & Sons
Whitepot	■			◢		■			■	■	CON	■			Tomkins
Whole Earth															Whole Earth

Jam & Other Spreads

Brand Name	South Africa	Oppressive Regimes	Trade Union Relations	Wages & Conditions	Land Rights	Environment	Irresponsible Marketing	Nuclear Power	Armaments	Animal Testing	Factory Farming	Other Animal Rights	Political Donations	Boycott Call	Company Group
Honey															
Cheshire										◣					Koninklijke Wessanen
Equal Exchange															Equal Exchange Trading
Gales	■	■	◣	◣		■		■		■	■		■		Nestlé
Hedgehog															Bensons Crisps
Martlet															Merrydown Wine
Ratcliffe	■	■	◣	◣		■		■		■	■		■		Nestlé
Shippam										■					Whitman Corp
Stute															Stute
Suma															Suma
Tiptree															Wilkin & Sons
West Country															Merrydown Wine
Nut Butter															
Duerr															F Duerr
Equal Exchange															Equal Exchange Trading
KP		◣			◣					■	CON				United Biscuits
Meridian															Meridian Foods
Sun Pat	■	■	◣	◣		■		■		■	■		■		Nestlé
Whole Earth															Whole Earth
Chocolate & Carob															
Cadbury's	◣	◣			◣	◣			■	■	CON		■		Hillsdown Holdings
ChocoCrunch															Scott/Schwartauer
Nestlé	■	■	◣	◣		■		■		■	■		■		Nestlé
Nutella															P. Ferrero & C SpA
Plamil															Plamil Foods
Stute															Stute
Sun Pat	■	■	◣	◣		■		■		■	■		■		Nestlé
Syrup															
Fowler's Treacle	■	■	◣	CON	◣	◣		■	■		CON				Tate & Lyle
Lyle's	■	■	◣	■	◣	◣		■	■		CON				Tate & Lyle
Silver Spoon	■				◣	◣			◣		■	CON	■		Wittington Investments

70

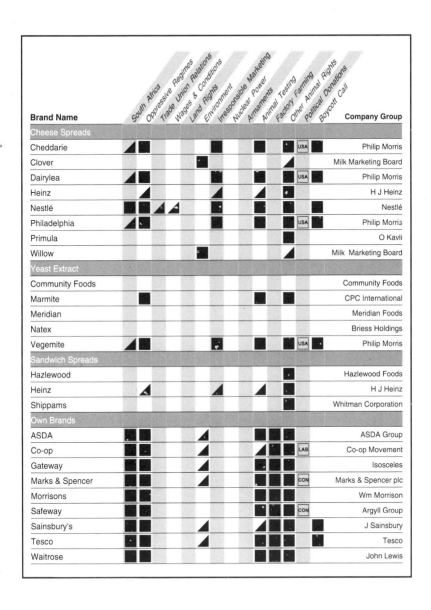

Brand Name	South Africa	Oppressive Regimes	Trade Union Relations	Wages & Conditions	Land Rights	Environment	Irresponsible Marketing	Nuclear Power	Armaments	Animal Testing	Factory Farming	Other Animal Rights	Political Donations	Boycott Call	Company Group
Cheese Spreads															
Cheddarie	◩	■			■			■		▪	USA	■			Philip Morris
Clover				■					◢						Milk Marketing Board
Dairylea	◩	■			■			■		■	USA	■			Philip Morris
Heinz		◢			◢			◢		▪					H J Heinz
Nestlé	■	▪	◢	◢		■	▪		■		▪		■		Nestlé
Philadelphia	◩	▪			■			■		■	USA	■			Philip Morris
Primula										■					O Kavli
Willow				■					◢						Milk Marketing Board
Yeast Extract															
Community Foods															Community Foods
Marmite		■						■		■					CPC International
Meridian															Meridian Foods
Natex															Briess Holdings
Vegemite	◩	■				▪		■		■	USA	▪			Philip Morris
Sandwich Spreads															
Hazlewood										▪					Hazlewood Foods
Heinz	◢				◢			◢		■					H J Heinz
Shippams										■					Whitman Corporation
Own Brands															
ASDA	■	■		◢				■	■	■					ASDA Group
Co-op	■	▪		◢			◢	■	■	■	LAB				Co-op Movement
Gateway	■	■						■	■	■					Isosceles
Marks & Spencer	■	■		◢				■	■	■	CON				Marks & Spencer plc
Morrisons	■	■						■	■	▪					Wm Morrison
Safeway	■	■						■	▪	■	CON				Argyll Group
Sainsbury's	■	■		◢			◢	■	■			■			J Sainsbury
Tesco	▪	■		◢				■	■	▪		■			Tesco
Waitrose	■	■						■	■	▪					John Lewis

Sauces, Pickles & Mustards

This report covers brown sauce, tomato ketchup, sweet pickle and piccalilli, chutneys, mustards and condiment sauces (e.g. cranberry, mint, horseradish). It does not cover pickled vegetables, such as pickled onions.

The Companies

As with most food products the market is dominated by a handful of multinationals, which all leave something to be desired where ethical consumerism is concerned, and which turn up many times in this book. Nestlé and BSN have both been criticised for their irresponsible marketing of breast milk substitutes, Hillsdown and Dalgety both have major factory farming interests, and Unilever receives marks in eight of the fourteen categories.

Fortunately, there are some brands which are quite widely available in health food shops and some major stores. We have not discovered any criticisms of the suppliers of these brands.

The Market

Heinz is by far the most popular brand of tomato sauce, followed by Daddies and Crosse & Blackwell. The sweet pickle market is dominated by Branston (Nestlé), Haywards and Heinz, whilst Sharwoods' mango chutney is the best seller for chutneys. The Bicks brand of relishes has half that market, whilst Colmans and Crosse & Blackwell lead the condiments market.[1058]

Sugar

Although sauces and pickles only form a tiny part of most people's diet and are therefore nutritionally unimportant, they do contain relatively large amounts of sugar. Tomato ketchup, for example, is about 25% sugar. There is more sugar in sweet pickles than any single type of vegetable. Sugar is added to these products to give them flavour and the right sort of consistency.[1418] (See the Sugar report for more details on sugar and health.)

Best Buys

(This article was first published in February 1993.)

The Burnham, Gordons, Nazirs, Pataks, Suma, Tiptree and Whole Earth brands are Best Buys. To our knowledge, only the Whole Earth range is organic.

72

Brand Name	South Africa	Oppressive Regimes	Trade Union Relations	Wages & Conditions	Land Rights	Environment	Irresponsible Marketing	Nuclear Power	Armaments	Animal Testing	Factory Farming	Other Animal Rights	Political Donations	Boycott Call	Company Group
ASDA	■	■		◤						■	■	■			ASDA Group
Baxters											CON				W A Baxter
Beetop											■				Hazlewood Foods
Benedicta	■	■	◤			■	◤		■		■		■		Unilever
Bicks		■													McCormick & Co
Branston	■	■	◤	◤		■				■			■		Nestlé
Burnham															Wilkin & Sons
Colmans	■	■	◤				◤				BUI CPS				Reckitt & Colman
Co-op	■	■		◤				◤		■	■	LAB			Co-op Movement
Crofters (Gateway)	■	■		◤						■	■	■			Isosceles
Crosse & Blackwell	■	■	◤	◤		■			■				■		Nestlé
Daddies		■				■				■			■		BSN
Gordons															Charles Gordon Associates
Grey Poupon		■				■				■			■		BSN
Hartley's	◤	◤		◤	◤					■	■	CON	■		Hillsdown Holdings
Haywards	◤	◤		◤	◤					■	■	CON	■		Hillsdown Holdings
Hazlewoods											■				Hazlewood Foods
Homepride	◤	◤		◤				◤		■	■				Dalgety
Heinz		◤				◤		◤		■					H J Heinz
HP		■				■				■			■		BSN
Ideal Sauce		◤				◤		◤		■					H J Heinz
Lea & Perrins		■				■				■			■		BSN
Maille		■				■				■			■		BSN
Marks & Spencer	■			◤				■		■	■	CON			Marks & Spencer plc
Morrisons	■	■								■	■	■			Wm Morrison
Nazirs															Nazirs Ltd
Ocean Spray	■			◤			■				CON	■			Tomkins
OK Sauce	■	■	◤	◤						■	BUI CPS				Reckitt & Colman
Pan Yan	■	■	◤	◤		■			■		■		■		Nestlé
Pataks															Pataks (Spices) Ltd
Ratcliffes	■	◤		■			◤			■					Croda International
Safeway	■	■								■	■	CON			Argyll Group
Sainsbury's	■	■		◤				◤		■	■		■		J Sainsbury
Sharwoods	■			◤			■				CON	■			Tomkins
Suma															Suma
Tesco	■	■		◤						■	■		■		Tesco
Tiptree															Wilkin & Sons
Waitrose	■	■								■	■	■			John Lewis
Whole Earth															Whole Earth

Sugar

The sugar market in Britain is dominated by two companies - Tate & Lyle and Wittington Investments (Silver Spoon). Tate & Lyle specialises in cane sugar and Wittington in beet sugar. Sugar made from beet holds a two-thirds share of the sugar market in Britain.

The Sugar Industry

Cane Sugar

Cane sugar is grown in tropical countries around the world, especially the Caribbean. As a legacy from the colonial era, many countries, like Mauritius, Jamaica and Cuba, are still reliant on the sugar crop for their survival - a dependency often fuelled by their need for foreign exchange to pay off foreign debts.

These days countries have to compete on the world market where prices are, on average, ever diminishing. Conditions for sugar workers can be dire - many are paid at rates below subsistence level. Oxfam has frequently had to intervene to support sugar workers who, they have said, are often "among the poorest and most oppressed sectors of society".[1553]

The Sugar Protocol of the Lomé Convention is an attempt on the part of the members of the European Community to take some responsibility for the problems of their former colonies. In it they promise to import some 1,3 million tonnes of cane at a guaranteed price (unchanged since 1985-6).

Beet Sugar

Widescale sugar beet farming began in Britain in the 1920s following shortages experienced during World War One. Beet farming now falls under the ambit of the Common Agricultural Policy, the stated aim of which is to maintain a steady flow of EC-produced sugar onto the domestic market. The Community pays its farmers more than five times the world market price on a fixed quota of production. The system encourages farmers to overproduce in order to ensure they never fall below quota.[558]

Europe currently generates, each year, some 3-4 million tonnes of sugar surplus to domestic requirements, which is then dumped on the world market.[1553] According to a recent OECD study, these kind of sugar policies have cut world sugar prices by between 5-10%.[549]

The ethical consumer buying sugar may wish to consider which mode of production to support - i.e. cane or beet. Ordinarily, locally grown produce like beet would have preference over imports from the point of view of energy saving and transport costs. However, as explained by Belinda Coote in Oxfam's book 'The Hunger Crop', there are a number of considerations, which may mean that some consumers might want to choose cane-produced sugar over beet.[1553]

Cane versus Beet

As we have already explained, world prices for sugar are in decline largely due to overproduction in the developed world. Attempts to shift dependency from this single cash crop are hampered in countries whose foreign debt demands they make export earnings. Countries that try to diversify may be checked by lack of capital and the fact that world prices of all cash crops are in decline.

Oxfam is in favour of consumers supporting cane sugar: "While conditions are bad for sugar workers in many producer countries, they would be a great deal worse if Europe stopped importing their cane sugar".

In this report all brands of sugar are derived from cane, with the exception of Silver Spoon and some Whitworth's products which come from beet.

There are some importers which try to secure fairer returns for cane sugar producers. Traidcraft offers fair trade sugar from Mauritius and the Philippines. Production for the latter supports a project on the island of Negros helping sugar workers create alternative work opportunities. Billingtons pays a premium to its suppliers in Mauritius, since all the processing and packaging of the raw sugar takes place there.[1545]

Fair Trade

On average it is estimated that we each consume 100lb of sugar every year.[1418] White sugar's benefits are purely calorific, since the refining process removes the few nutrients that raw whole sugars can boast.[1342] Excess sugar consumption can lead to obesity and consequent risks of heart disease and high blood pressure.

Sugar and Health

Janet Pleshette in 'Overcoming Addictions' also argues that high levels of sugar consumption over a long period of time may lead to diabetes.[1342]

Sugar has been cited in an official report as being "the most important dietary factor in the cause of dental caries".[661] Bacteria, living on the plaque on our teeth, can turn sugar into acid seconds after it enters the mouth. The acid attacks the enamel coating of the tooth leading eventually to decay. The acid may still persist for up to two hours.[726]

Both a government committee and the World Health Organisation have recommended that consumption be reduced to 10% of total dietary energy, from the present average of about 18-25%. WHO goes further and says that consumption of sugars could safely fall to zero because they "contribute no nutrients and are not essential for human health".[815]

After seeing the Sugar Bureau's advert promoting sugar as 'natural and safe', Action and Information on Sugars commented: "Sugar is not safe...Neither is it natural. Its a highly refined, chemically treated product and is effectively prohibited from claiming directly it is natural by guidelines on food advertising issued by MAFF [in 1989]."[673]

Alternatives

Given the many health problems associated with sugar it makes sense to try to cut down consumption. Professor John Yudkin, in his book on sugar called "Pure, White and Deadly",[1391] argues that in our consumption of such products we abuse the evolutionary role of our natural sweet tooth. In the past, our ancestors would satisfy their cravings for sweetness by eating fruit and sweet vegetables, and in so doing obtained necessary nutrients such as vitamin C.[1391]

To those wanting to reduce or cease consumption of sugar, the advice from nutritionists is to phase it out gradually.[1391]

Best Buys

We have not discovered any criticisms of the companies owning the Traidcraft and Prewetts brands of cane sugar. Of these, Traidcraft stands out, because of the company's fair trading policy.

Billingtons' cane sugar also seems a good option, as it comes ready-packaged from Mauritius, so giving the producers a price above the EC rate.

(This article was first published in February 1992.)

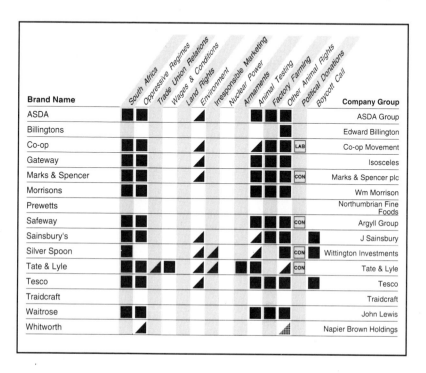

Brand Name	South Africa	Oppressive Regimes	Trade Union Relations	Wages & Conditions	Land Rights	Environment	Irresponsible Marketing	Nuclear Power	Armaments	Animal Testing	Factory Farming	Other Animal Rights	Political Donations	Boycott Call	Company Group
ASDA	■	■				◤		■	■	■					ASDA Group
Billingtons											■				Edward Billington
Co-op	■	■				◤		◤	■	■			LAB		Co-op Movement
Gateway	■	■				◤		■	■	■					Isosceles
Marks & Spencer	■	■				◤		■	■	■			CON		Marks & Spencer plc
Morrisons	■	■						■	■	■					Wm Morrison
Prewetts															Northumbrian Fine Foods
Safeway	■	■						■	■	■			CON		Argyll Group
Sainsbury's	■	■		◤			◤	■	■			■			J Sainsbury
Silver Spoon	◣			◤	◤		◤		■		CON	■			Wittington Investments
Tate & Lyle	■	■	◤	■	◤	◤		■	■		◤	CON			Tate & Lyle
Tesco	■	■				◤		■	■	■			■		Tesco
Traidcraft															Traidcraft
Waitrose	■	■						■	■	■					John Lewis
Whitworth		◤								◢					Napier Brown Holdings

Tinned Fruit & Vegetables

Origin Unlike fresh produce, tinned food manufacturers are not obliged to detail the country of origin on the label, though you may find with some tinned fruit that this information is given on the label or the tin itself.

Vegetables
Generally, vegetables are imported fresh or grown and canned in the UK. Peas, green beans, carrots and potatoes are mainly grown in this country, though potatoes are sometimes imported from the Netherlands, Belgium and Luxemburg.[1859] Tomatoes are freighted in from Italy and sweetcorn from North America, France, Israel and Italy.[1859] The more exotic the vegetable, the more energy is likely to have been used to bring it to your table. For example okra may originate in India, Zambia or Kenya. Often these exotic vegetables are canned abroad and the finished product imported.[425]

Fruit
80% of tinned fruit is imported, mainly from Greece, Italy and Spain.[1860] However, pears, apricots and peaches may be South African, and many citrus fruits are sourced in Israel.[1860] Most pineapples originate in Kenya, followed by Thailand, the Philippines, Swaziland and South Africa.[1860]
Pineapple plantations in the Philippines in particular have been criticised as blackspots for the use of dangerous pesticides,[1729] and poor working conditions,[1545] and encroaching on tropical rainforests.[418] The ethical pineapple seems a rare bloom indeed: Traidcraft introduced tinned pineapple rings from Tanzania in its 1990/91 catalogue, but has since withdrawn this line and has no plans to reintroduce it. The Co-op imports pineapple grown and canned in Botswana. Exporting the finished product also places more revenue in the hands of the producers.
India, Israel, Kenya and the Philippines are on our list of Oppressive Regimes.

Beans
Raw haricot beans are imported from the USA and prepared and canned in the UK for baked beans.

Additives

Vegetables
These usually contain only sugar and salt. Peas are the exception to this as they commonly contain the following azo dyes: tartrazine (E102), sunset yellow (E110), Brilliant Blue FCF (133) and Green S (142). Tartrazine has received much

publicity over the years in connection with hyperactivity in children, skin rashes, asthma etc,[33, 296] though all fourteen azo dyes used in convenience food have had questions raised about their suitability.[33]

Baked Beans

These contain sugar, salt and often modified starch, a bulking agent requiring the use of 'stabilisers' and hydrolysed vegetable protein, a 'flavour enhancer'. Artificial sweeteners may also be added.

Fruit

Usually only a sugar syrup is used, except in the case of pie fillings when colourings may be included.

See the Sugar report for more details about the health effects of sugar consumption.

No amount of testing of individual additives can predict the combined effects of ingestion of a 'cocktail' of E numbers. At present we know of no research being carried out to establish the effects of their interaction.

Environment

Cans represent a considerable waste of energy and resources, as they are not refillable or reusable. In effect, they have the shortest useful life of any food container,[106] as we are advised not to store food in the can once opened due to the risk of contamination with metal oxides.

Several local authorities claim that steel cans are recovered from domestic refuse using magnets and then sent for recycling. Supermarkets are introducing tin can banks, but still the great steel beast largely remains in our landfill sites.

Best Buys

Vegetables: Prize Winner, Suma, Triangle Foods and Valfrutta are the Best Buys. These are followed by a number of second bests: Danoxa, Dominic, Orchard Pride, Riverdene, Simpsons, SPL, Talpe and Wardour. Triangle Foods' range includes organic beans such as chick peas.

Baked Beans: Whole Earth and Triangle Foods supply baked beans with no added sugar and are Best Buys. Whole Earth do an organic variety.

Fruit: As yet we can recommend only the Co-op as a Best Buy for pineapples. Australian Gold, Premier Gold, Prize Winner, S&B and Valfrutta can be regarded as Best Buys for other fruit.

(This article was first published in May 1992.)

Tinned Fruit & Vegetables

Brand Name	South Africa	Oppressive Regimes	Trade Union Relations	Wages & Conditions	Land Rights	Environment	Irresponsible Marketing	Nuclear Power	Armaments	Animal Testing	Factory Farming	Other Animal Rights	Political Donations	Boycott Call	Company Group
Tinned Vegetables															
Batchelors	■	■	◢		■	◢			■		■			■	Unilever
Chesswood	■				◢		■				CON	■			Tomkins
Crosse & Blackwell	■	■	◢	◢		■			■		■			■	Nestlé
Danoxa										■					Albert Fisher
Dominic										■					JLI Group
Farrows	■	■	◢		■	■			■		■			■	Unilever
Gerber Pride		◢								■					Quadriga Holdings
Green Giant	■	■	◢	◢		■	◢		■					■	Grand Metroplitan
Hartley's	◢	◢			◢	◢				■	■	CON	■		Hillsdown Holdings
John West	◢	■	◢		■	◢		■			■			■	Unilever
Morton	◢	◢			◢	◢				■	■	CON	■		Hillsdown Holdings
Napolina		■					■			■					CPC International
Newforge		■			■					■	■	BUI	■		Booker
Orchard Pride										■					Laxgate Ltd
Princes	◢			■	■		■	■			■			■	Mitsubishi Group
Prize Winner															Riviana Foods
Riverdene										■					Martin Mathew
Royal Norfolk	◢	◢			◢	◢				■	■	CON	■		Hillsdown Holdings
Simpsons										■					Simpson Ready Foods
Smedley's	◢	◢			◢	◢				■	■	CON	■		Hillsdown Holdings
SPL										■					SPL Ltd
Suma															Suma
Talpe										■					Albert Fisher
Triangle Foods															Triangle Foods
Valfrutta															Consorzio Cooperativo
Wardour										■					Waissel's Ltd
Baked Beans															
Crosse & Blackwell	■	■	◢	◢		■			■		■			■	Nestlé
Hartley's	◢	◢			◢	◢				■	■	CON	■		Hillsdown Holdings
Heinz		◢			◢		◢			■					H J Heinz
HP		■			■					■			■		BSN
Royal Norfolk	◢	◢			◢	◢				■	■	CON	■		Hillsdown Holdings
Smedley's	◢	◢			◢	◢				■	■	CON	■		Hillsdown Holdings
Princes	◢	■		■	■		■	■			■				Mitsubishi Group
Triangle Foods															Triangle Foods
Whole Earth															Whole Earth

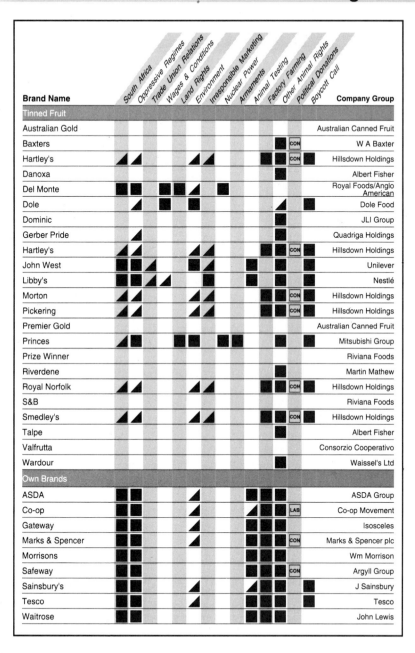

Brand Name	South Africa	Oppressive Regimes	Trade Union Relations	Wages & Conditions	Land Rights	Environment	Irresponsible Marketing	Nuclear Power	Armaments	Animal Testing	Factory Farming	Other Animal Rights	Political Donations	Boycott Call	Company Group
Tinned Fruit															
Australian Gold															Australian Canned Fruit
Baxters											■		CON		W A Baxter
Hartley's	◢	◢		◢	◢					■	■		CON	■	Hillsdown Holdings
Danoxa											■				Albert Fisher
Del Monte	■	■		■	■	◢		■							Royal Foods/Anglo American
Dole		◢		■	■					◢		■			Dole Food
Dominic											■				JLI Group
Gerber Pride		◢									■				Quadriga Holdings
Hartley's	◢	◢		◢	◢					■	■		CON	■	Hillsdown Holdings
John West	■	■	◢		■	◢		■		■	■			■	Unilever
Libby's	■	■	◢	◢		■			■		■			■	Nestlé
Morton	◢	◢		◢	◢					■	■		CON	■	Hillsdown Holdings
Pickering	◢	◢		◢	◢					■	■		CON	■	Hillsdown Holdings
Premier Gold															Australian Canned Fruit
Princes	◢	■			■	■		■			■			■	Mitsubishi Group
Prize Winner															Riviana Foods
Riverdene											■				Martin Mathew
Royal Norfolk	◢	◢		◢	◢					■	■		CON	■	Hillsdown Holdings
S&B															Riviana Foods
Smedley's	◢	◢		◢	◢					■	■		CON	■	Hillsdown Holdings
Talpe											■				Albert Fisher
Valfrutta															Consorzio Cooperativo
Wardour											■				Waissel's Ltd
Own Brands															
ASDA		■	■		◢				■	■	■				ASDA Group
Co-op		■	■		◢				◢	■			LAB		Co-op Movement
Gateway		■	■		◢				■	■	■				Isosceles
Marks & Spencer		■	■		◢				■	■	■		CON		Marks & Spencer plc
Morrisons		■	■						■	■					Wm Morrison
Safeway		■	■						■	■	■		CON		Argyll Group
Sainsbury's		■	■		◢				◢	■	■	■			J Sainsbury
Tesco		■	■		◢				■	■	■	■			Tesco
Waitrose		■	■						■	■	■				John Lewis

Yogurt

This report covers dairy and soya yogurt and fromage frais.

Bio-yogurts

The bacteria present in <u>all</u> yogurt, Lactobacillus bulgaricus and Streptococcus thermophilus, do not always survive the journey through the human gut. Therefore a range of bio-yogurts have appeared on the market to satisfy the consumer desire for a yogurt which might aid digestion by promoting the growth of beneficial microflora in the human gut. Bio-yogurts must additionally contain bifidus and Lactobacillus acidophilus. Although a study published in the Food Magazine found these present within the limits to comply with the legal requirements for a bio-yogurt, in Onken Bioghurt and Chambourcy yoghurt actif the bifidus content was not high enough to have a beneficial effect.[587] Jane Thomas, a spokesperson for Busses Farm, told ECRA that the live bacterial content of its yogurt cannot be guaranteed after it leaves the manufacturing plant as it is dependent on the conditions of transport and storage. Dr Valeria Marshall, of Oxford Polytechnic's Centre for Sciences of Food & Nutrition, suggests that although bio-yogurts are helpful if your digestion has been upset by illness and antibiotics, for them to enhance a healthy digestion they would need to be 'of human origin'.

Dairy Farming

Soya, sheep and goats' yogurts have been included in this report to aid consumers who feel strongly about the intensive farming methods currently employed by the dairy industry. For more details about the dairy industry see the Butter & Margarine report.

Milk Supply

Although 97% of the milk consumed in the UK is sold through the Milk Marketing Boards, organic dairy producers are now establishing their own network. The Farmers' Dairy Company was recently established by Busses Farm employees as a co-operative through which organic dairy farmers can sell their products in mainstream shops.

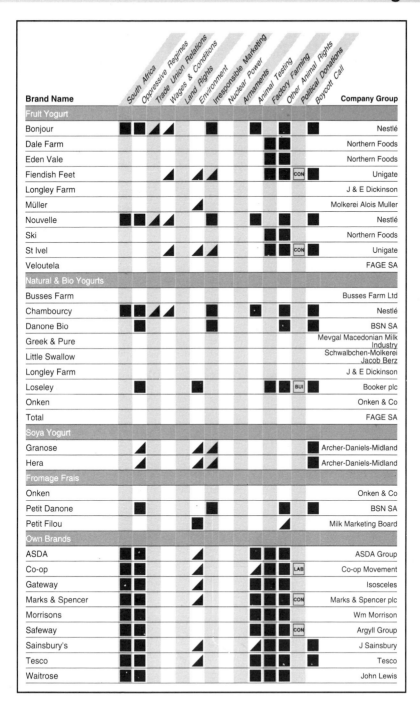

Brand Name	South Africa	Oppressive Regimes	Trade Union Relations	Wages & Conditions	Land Rights	Environment	Irresponsible Marketing	Nuclear Power	Armaments	Animal Testing	Factory Farming	Other Animal Rights	Political Donations	Boycott Call	Company Group
Fruit Yogurt															
Bonjour	■	■	◤	◤		■		■	■					■	Nestlé
Dale Farm										■	■				Northern Foods
Eden Vale										■	■				Northern Foods
Fiendish Feet				◤	◤	◤				■	■		CON	■	Unigate
Longley Farm															J & E Dickinson
Müller				◤											Molkerei Alois Muller
Nouvelle	■	■	◤	◤		■		■	■					■	Nestlé
Ski										■	■				Northern Foods
St Ivel				◤	◤	◤				■	■		CON	■	Unigate
Veloutela															FAGE SA
Natural & Bio Yogurts															
Busses Farm															Busses Farm Ltd
Chambourcy	■	■	◤	◤		■		·	■					■	Nestlé
Danone Bio		■				■		·						■	BSN SA
Greek & Pure															Mevgal Macedonian Milk Industry
Little Swallow															Schwalbchen-Molkerei Jacob Berz
Longley Farm															J & E Dickinson
Loseley		■			■					■	■		BUI	■	Booker plc
Onken															Onken & Co
Total															FAGE SA
Soya Yogurt															
Granose			◤		◤	◤							■		Archer-Daniels-Midland
Hera			◤		◤	◤							■		Archer-Daniels-Midland
Fromage Frais															
Onken															Onken & Co
Petit Danone		■				·			■					■	BSN SA
Petit Filou				■								◤			Milk Marketing Board
Own Brands															
ASDA	■	·		◤				■	■	■					ASDA Group
Co-op	■	■		◤			◤	■	■			LAB			Co-op Movement
Gateway	·	■		◤					■	■					Isosceles
Marks & Spencer	■	■		◤				■	■	■		CON			Marks & Spencer plc
Morrisons	■	■							■	■					Wm Morrison
Safeway	■	■						■	■	■		CON			Argyll Group
Sainsbury's	■	■				◤		◤	■	■		■			J Sainsbury
Tesco	■	■		◤				■	■	■	·		■		Tesco
Waitrose	·	■						■	■	■					John Lewis

Additives   **Sweeteners:** These are commonly fruit puree and syrups, and sugar. Which? magazine, surveying nineteen yogurts in 1989 found that brands aimed at children were highly sweetened - up to 15% sugar by weight.[1698]

Preservatives: Potassium sorbate (E202) is used in some fruit yogurts, particularly longlife ones, and Additives, Your Complete Survival Guide, cautions that it 'affects the livers of rats in very low doses...also forms mutagenic compounds with nitrates...a definite hazard to specific groups of people.'[33]

Alternatives   There are many local producers which are likely to have a clean record on the issues we cover but which we have not covered in this report. Goats' or ewes' milk, used in some greek yogurts such as Total and Greek & Pure, is unlikely to be obtained from animals linked to intensive farming in the same way as British dairy cattle, so readers concerned with animal welfare may find them a viable alternative. Evelyn Findlater, in her book 'Making Your Own Home Proteins' suggests those suffering from eczema, asthma, migraine, stomach ulcers and hay fever may find symptoms alleviated by switching from cows' to goats' milk produce.[1137]

Some consumers may wish to try making their own yogurt, which is a relatively simple process requiring no equipment more expensive than a thermos flask. Many books are available detailing these processes.

Best Buys   **Fruit yogurts:** We have discovered no criticisms of the companies which own the Longley Farm and Veloutela brands. These are therefore Best Buys.

Natural and Bio Yogurts: We have no criticisms of the companies which own the Busses Farm, Onken, Little Swallow, Longley Farm, Total, and Greek & Pure brands. Those who wish to encourage organic agriculture may favour the first two, as these are made from organic milk and carry the Soil Association logo.

Fromage Frais: Onken is the Best Buy.

(This article was first published in September 1992.)

Small farms supplying a local market are also highly likely to be considered Best Buys.

Chapter 4

Drink

Beer & Cider

The UK beer industry is dominated by four large breweries:
Bass, Courage (Fosters), Allied-Lyons/Carlsberg and
Whitbread which, between them, control 74% of the market.[521]
Guinness and Scottish & Newcastle also have a substantial
role. The main brands made by these six appear on the Table,
while the 'Other Beer Brands' list has some of their lesser-
known brands. Quite often a drinks brand will be made by one
company under licence from another. All company groups
involved in these aspects of supplying brands in the UK will be
listed, where we have the information, with the licensor's
name appearing first under 'Company Group' on the Table.

Real Ale The remainder of the beer market is made up of brewers
ranging in size from fair-sized regional brewers with a few
hundred pubs to 'micro-brewers' making only a barrel or two a
week. The 'Small Brewers' list gives the names of many of
these independent brewers, who may be in your locality.
Many smaller breweries would no longer exist were it not for
the efforts of CAMRA, the Campaign for Real Ale. One of the
most successful consumer campaigns ever, CAMRA claims to
have stemmed the tide of 'keg' (pasteurised and pressurised)
beer in favour of a more traditional and better tasting product.
Even the large nationals now produce one or two real ales of
varying quality. Membership of CAMRA costs £10 from
CAMRA, 34 Alma Road, St Albans, Herts AL1 3BW.

Imports and Most good beer does not travel very well, so foreign beers are
Overseas usually brewed here under licence rather than imported. There
Brands is a vast complicated web of licensing deals criss-crossing the
globe - so the companies involved with brands in the lists
given here only apply to the UK and not elsewhere.
There is however a growing trend for 'premium' (expensive)
beers to be directly imported in bottles or cans. An ever-
growing range of beers is now becoming available.

Alcohol has been used as a mood-altering drug for thousands of years. In Sweden the real cost of drinking - taking into account illness, time off work and other social problems - has been calculated as £67 for a £20 bottle of whisky.[728] Concern at the scale of social problems associated with alcohol has led the Scandinavian countries to control the alcohol business with high prices through state-owned monopolies. Norway now has compulsory health warnings on bottles, and France has recently enacted legislation to ban most sorts of advertising for alcoholic drinks.[222]

There is no doubt that alcohol misuse is related to serious health problems. Alcohol Concern, the UK pressure group, estimate that 28,000 people die each year from alcohol related causes.[770]

Whilst there may be some truth in the argument that alcohol abuse is a symptom rather than a cause of a deeper social malaise, there is no doubt that advertising does not help. Much advertising for beer and lager seems to be aimed at younger and younger people. And UK research has shown one in five fifteen year olds to be drinking more than the health guidelines recommended for adults.[588]

Some research has claimed that alcohol may actually help to prevent heart disease. Three or four drinks a day for three or four days a week was shown to help - but neither more nor less drinking had the same beneficial effect.[856] These findings are, not surprisingly, controversial. The only guidelines for health that are generally agreed are the limits set by the health authorities of 14 units of alcohol per week (21 for men). (A unit is one glass of ordinary wine, one pub-measure of spirits or a half-pint of average-strength beer.)

Alcohol

Modern drinks production is a highly complex affair, and a huge range of chemical additives may be used. Nowhere, though, is there any legislation requiring labelling of ingredients, as with food, so it is hard to find out exactly what we might be drinking. Beers might contain, in addition to hops, malt and sugar, such ingredients as hydrochloric acid, caustic soda, plaster of paris, dimethylpolysiloxane or sulphites.[582] Sulphites are known to provoke asthma attacks in up to ten per cent of sufferers, and have to be labelled in the US. The effects of these chemical cocktails are uncertain - it may be that they are responsible for more hangovers than the alcohol itself. In the absence of any ingredients labelling, the best that consumers can do is to hope that by choosing organic or traditionally-produced drinks (real real ale?) they might be

Additives

avoiding the worst excesses. Buying organic drinks also encourages a less environmentally-damaging farming system. It has also been argued that, in any case, the adverse effects of alcohol are likely to far outweigh any potential effects of any other unknown additives.

Fishy Goings On

Isinglass, a substance derived from fish, is commonly used as 'finings', to clarify beers and other drinks. It is mainly used in cask-conditioned real ales. As a general rule, vegans would avoid real ale, and all the beers of Bass, Scottish & Newcastle and Guinness use animal derivatives.[65] Canned and keg lager is the least likely to contain animal derivatives - Carslberg and Heineken are in the clear here. We cannot list all the animal free brands here - see the Vegan Society's Animal Free Shopper for a full listing if you are interested. It costs £4.50 from The Vegan Society.

Packaging

Beer and cider comes in every sort of packaging conceivable. Definitely the greenest is beer and cider on draught - glasses and barrels all get washed and reused. A small proportion of beers come in returnable glass bottles - mostly those sold in pubs.

One-trip containers are the norm for the take-home trade. Such is the power of supermarkets and other distributors, that responsible companies launching new organic brands cannot get them distributed in returnable containers. Glass and aluminium are the two main choices, although there are more and more PET plastic bottles in supermarkets. In energy terms, PET containers are probably the most efficient - choose them in preference if there is a plastics recycling scheme near you. Otherwise, in the choice between glass and aluminium, glass wins out both on energy terms and in the mining of basic ingredients. Bauxite mining for aluminium causes severe environmental destruction, and aluminium is the most energy intensive of all common metals in its production.[243]

Alternatives

There are plenty of alternatives to the mainstream beer and cider brands available - see the 'Organics' and 'Small Brewers' sections. Home brewing is also an option. There are plenty of books on the subject, and you don't have to use commercial kits.

Beer

Best Buys to take home are the organic brews - Lincoln Green, Original Flag Porter and Saxon as we have not discovered any criticisms of the companies that make them. The Golden Promise brand is also worth considering. Details of how to obtain them appear in the 'Organics' section.

For draught, there are over a hundred small breweries of which we have found no criticisms. Which one you choose will depend upon where you live. Bear in mind that most real ales will not be strictly vegan/vegetarian though.

Of the major national brands Grolsch and Ruddles come out best. Red Stripe, and brands owned by Scottish & Newcastle may also be worth considering.

Cider

Organic brands Avalon and Dunkertons are best all round again, and can be obtained from the suppliers listed in the 'Organics' section.

Mainstream cider companies seem to be an altogether more ethical bunch than beer brewers, with even the worst, Bulmers, comparing favourably to the better national brewers. We have not discovered any criticisms of the following cider-makers: Aspall, Gaymer Group, Inch's, Merrydown, Taunton's, and Westons.

Best Buys

(This article was first published in December 1991.)

Brand Name	South Africa	Oppressive Regimes	Trade Union Relations	Wages & Conditions	Land Rights	Environment	Irresponsible Marketing	Nuclear Power	Armaments	Animal Testing	Factory Farming	Other Animal Rights	Political Donations	Boycott Call	Company Group
ASDA															ASDA Group plc
Bass															Bass plc
Beamish															Fosters
Becks													CON		Brauerei Beck & Co/ Scottish & Newcastle
Boddingtons													CON		Whitbread
Breaker															Bass
Brew XI															Bass
Budweiser															Anheuser Busch / Fosters
Carling Black Label															Bass
Carlsberg													CON		Allied Lyons / Carlsberg
Castlemaine XXXX													CON		Allied Lyons / Carlsberg
Charrington															Bass
Co-op													LAB		Co-op Movement
Coors													CON		Adolph Coors / Scottish & Newcastle
Courage Best															Fosters
Double Diamond													CON		Allied Lyons / Carlsberg
Flowers													CON		Whitbread
Fosters															Fosters
Gateway															Isosceles
Grolsch															Grolsch
Guinness															Guinness
Harp													CON		Guinness / Scottish & Newcastle
Heineken													CON		Heineken / Whitbread
Hofmeister															Gebr. Marz / Fosters
Holsten Pils															Holsten Brauerei / Fosters
John Smiths															Fosters
Jupiler													CON		Interbrew / Scottish & Newcastle
Kaliber															Guinness
Kestrel													CON		Scottish & Newcastle
Kronenbourg 1664															B S N /Fosters
Labatts													CON		John Labatt / Allied Lyons / Carlsberg
Lamot															Bass
Löwenbrau													CON		Allied Lyons / Carlsberg
Marks & Spencer													CON		Marks & Spencer
McEwans													CON		Scottish & Newcastle
Miller													USA		Philip Morris / Fosters
Mitchells & Butlers															Bass
Molson													USA		Molson Co / Philip Morris / Fosters
Morrisons															William Morrison

Brand Name	South Africa	Oppressive Regimes	Trade Union Relations	Wages & Conditions	Land Rights	Environment	Irresponsible Marketing	Nuclear Power	Armaments	Animal Testing	Factory Farming	Other Animal Rights	Political Donations	Boycott Call	Company Group
Murphy's	■			■					◣				CON		Heineken / Whitbread
Newcastle Brown									◣				CON		Scottish & Newcastle
Red Stripe									◣				CON		Charles Wells
Ruddles															Grolsch
Safeway	■	■							■	■	■		CON		Argyll Group
Sainsbury	■	■		◣					◣	■	■			■	J Sainsbury
Skol	◣	■		■					◣		■		CON		Allied Lyons / Carlsberg
Stella Artois				■					◣				CON		Interbrew / Whitbread
Stones	■	■		◣	◣				◣						Bass plc
Swan	◣	■		■					◣		■		CON		Allied Lyons / Carlsberg
Tartan									◣				CON		Scottish & Newcastle
Tennent's	■	■		◣	◣				◣						Bass plc
Tesco	■	■		◣					■	■	■			■	Tesco
Tetley	◣	■		■					◣		■		CON	■	Allied Lyons / Carlsberg
Theakston's	■	■							◣				CON		Scottish & Newcastle
Toby Bitter	■	■		◣	◣										Bass plc
Waitrose	■	■							■	■	■				John Lewis
Watney's	■	■	◣	◣	◣	◣	■		◣		■				Fosters
Webster's	■	■	◣	◣	◣	◣	■		◣		■				Fosters
Whitbread								■	◣				CON		Whitbread
Worthington	■	■		◣	◣				◣						Bass plc
Yorkshire								■	◣				CON		Whitbread
Younger's									◣				CON		Scottish & Newcastle

Allied Lyons/Carlsberg

ABC Best Bitter, Alloa's, Allsopps, Ansells, Archibald Arrol's, Arrol's, Aylesbury, Benskins, Burton, Cockleroaster, Dartmoor, Davenports, Deakin's Downfall, Entire, Falcon, Friary Meux, Greenalls, Hobec, Holts, Ind Coope, John Bull, Klassiek, Long Life, Nicholson's, Oranjeboom, Plant's Progress, Royal Dutch Post Horn, Shipstone's, St Christopher, Taylor Walker, Three Horses, Trent, Tuborg, Walker, Wrexham

Scottish & Newcastle

Home, Matthew Brown, Newcastle Exhibition, Pilsner Urquell

Bass

Allbright, Charger, Hemeling, Highgate, Moosehead, Schlitz, Springfield, Steinlager

Fosters Brewing Group

AKA, Bulldog, Colt 45, Directors, Ekstreme, Magnet Old, Norwich Anglian, Truman, Wadworths 6X, Watneys, Wilsons

Whitbread

Bentley's, Castle Eden, Chesters, Fremlins, Gold Label, Higsons, Hoegaarden, Kaltenberg, Mackeson, Newquay Steam, Tooheys, Trophy, Welsh Bitter, Wethereds, White Label

Brand Name	South Africa	Oppressive Regimes	Trade Union Relations	Wages & Conditions	Land Rights	Environment	Irresponsible Marketing	Nuclear Power	Armaments	Animal Testing	Factory Farming	Other Animal Rights	Political Donations	Boycott Call	Company Group
Applewood															Taunton Cider
Aspall															Aspall's Cider
ASDA	■	■		◢					■	■	■				ASDA Group
Autumn Gold															Taunton Cider
Brody															Taunton Cider
Bulmers			◢	◢											HP Bulmer
Co-op	■	■		◢				◢	■	■			LAB		Co-op Movement
Copperhead															Gaymer Group
Crispen			◢	◢											HP Bulmer
Desert Gold			◢	◢											HP Bulmer
Diamond Blush															Taunton Cider
Diamond White															Taunton Cider
Drum															Taunton Cider
Dry Blackthorn															Taunton Cider
Fres															Taunton Cider
Gateway	■	■		◢					■	■	■				Isosceles
Gaymers Olde English															Gaymer Group
Ice Dragon															Gaymer Group
Inch's															Inch's Cider Ltd
'K'															Gaymer Group
Max			◢	◢											HP Bulmer
Marks & Spencer	■	■		◢					■	■	■		CON		Marks & Spencer
Merrydown															Merrydown Wine
Moonstone															Taunton Cider
Morrison's	■	■							■	■	■				William Morrison
Newquay Steam							■		◢				CON		Whitbread
Red Rock															Taunton Cider
Safeway	■	■							■	■	■		CON		Argyll Group
Sainsbury	■	■		◢				◢	■	■			■		J Sainsbury
Scrumpy Jack			◢	◢											HP Bulmer
Special Vat															Taunton Cider
Strongbow			◢	◢											HP Bulmer
Symonds			◢	◢											HP Bulmer
Taunton															Taunton Cider
Tesco	■	■		◢					■	■	■		■		Tesco
Waitrose	■	■							■	■	■				John Lewis
Westons															H Weston & Sons Ltd
Woodpecker			◢	◢											HP Bulmer

The list below comes from CAMRA's 1993 Good Beer Guide's Independent Brewers section. We have not discovered any criticisms of the companies unless the letters 'B' or 'C' appear beside the name. 'B' indicates Brewers Society members, and therefore members of BIBRA as of April 1992. 'C' indicates political donations to the Conservative Party in the last five years. Parent companies or significant stakeholders are also noted.

Small Brewers

Adnams & Co	B	
Ann Street Brewery	B	
Archers Ales		
Arkell's Brewery	B	
Ash Vine Brewery		
Aston Manor Brewery		
Ballard's Brewery		
Banks & Taylor Brewery		
Bank's	B	C^{1076}
(Wolverhampton & Dudley)		
Bateman & Son, George	B	
Bathams (Delph) Ltd		
Beer Engine		
Belhaven Brewery	B	
(Control Securities)		
Berrow Brewery		
Big Lamp Brewery		
Blackawton Brewery		
Black Sheep Brewery		
S A Brain	B	
W H Brakspear & Sons	B	
(Whitbread owns 15%)		
Branscombe Vale Brewery		
British Oak Brewery		
Broughton Brewery		
Bullmastif Brewery		
Bunces Brewery		
Burton Bridge Brewery		
Burtonwood Brewery		
Bushy's Brewery		
Butcombe Brewery		
Butterknowle Brewery		
Cain & Co, Robert		
(Faxe Jyske, Denmark)		
Caledonian Brewing	B	
Camerons	B	C^{1076}
(Wolverhampton & Dudley)		
Chainmaker Beer		
Chiltern Brewery		
Clark & Co Ltd, H B		
Coach House Brewing		
Commercial Brewery		
Cook's Brewery		
Cotleigh Brewery		

Cropton Brewery		
Crouch Vale Brewery		
Crown Brewery	B	
(Guinness)		
Daleside Brewery		
Dent Brewery		
Donnington Brewery		
Earl Soham Brewery		
Eldridge Pope	B	C^{1087}
Elgood & Sons Ltd	B	
Everards Brewery	B	C^{1076}
Exe Valley Brewery		
Exmoor Ales		
Featherstone Brewery		
Federation Brewery		
Felinfoel Brewery	B	
Forbes Ales		
Franklin's Brewery		
Fuller, Smith, Turner	B	C^{1076}
Gale & Co, George	B	
Gibbs Mew plc	B	
Goacher, P & D J		
Goldfinch Brewery		
Goose Eye Brewery		
Greene King plc	B	
Guernsey Brewery	B	
(Ann Street Brewery)		
Hadrian Brewery		
Hall & Woodhouse	B	C^{1084}
Hambleton Ales		
Hampshire Brewery		
Hanby Ales		
Hanson's Brewery	B	C^{1076}
(Wolverhampton & Dudley)		
Hardington Brewery		
Hardys & Hansons	B	C^{1076}
Harvey & Son (Lewes)	B	
Harviestoun Brewery		
Heritage Brewery		
Hesket Newmarket Brewery		
Hilden Brewery		
Holden's Brewery	B	
Holt plc, Joseph	B	
Hook Norton Brewery	B	

Hop Back Brewery		
Hoskins & Oldfield		
Hoskins Brewery plc		
Hughes Brewery, Sarah		
Hull Brewery		
Hyde's Anvil Brewery	B	
Island Brewery		
Isle of Man Breweries	B	
Jennings Bros	B	
Jolly Roger Brewery		
Judge's Brewery		
Kelham Island Brewery		
Keystone Brewing		
King & Barnes	B	
Larkins Brewery		
J W Lees & Co	B	
Linfit Brewery		
Lions Original Brews		
Lloyds Country Beers		
Longstone Brewery		
Maclay & Co	B	
Malton Brewery		
Mansfield Brewery	B	
Marston Moor Brewery		
Marston, Thompson		
& Evershed	B	
(Whitbread owns 32%)		
Mauldons Brewery		
McGuinness, Thomas		
McMullen & Sons	B	C[1087]
Mill Brewery		
Mitchell's of Lancaster	B	C[1078]
Mole's Brewery		
Moorhouse's Brewery		
Morland & Co	B	C[1076]
(Greene King owns 43.4%)		
Morrell's Brewery	B	
Nethergate Brewery		
Nix Wincott Brewery		
North Yorkshire Brewing		
Oak Brewing Co		
Old Brewery,		
Old Luxters Farm		
Old Mill Brewery		
Orkney Brewery		
Otter Brewery		
Packhorse Brewing		
Palmer, J C & R H	B	
Parish Brewery		
Pilgrim Brewery		
Plassey Brewery		
Poole Brewery		
Preston Brewing		
Randall Ltd, R W	B	
Randalls Vautier	B	
Redruth Brewery	B	
Reepham Brewery		
Reindeer Trading Co		
Ridley & Sons, T D	B	
Ringwood Brewery		
Rising Sun		
Frederic Robinson	B	C[1076]
Robinwood Brewers		
Ross Brewing		
Rudgate Ales		
Ryburn Brewery		
Samuel Smith	B	
Scotties Brewery		
Selby Brewery	B	
Shepherd Neame	B	C[1076]
Smiles Brewing		
Springhead Brewery		
St Austell Brewery	B	C[1078]
Stocks Brewery		
Summerskills Brewery		
Timothy Taylor	B	C[1076]
Thompson's Brewery		
Daniel Thwaites	B	C[1076]
Titanic Brewery		
Tollemache &	B	
Cobbold Brewery		
Traquair House		
Tring Brewery		
Trough Brewery		
Uley Brewery		
Ushers Brewery		
Vaux Breweries	B	C[1076]
Wadworth & Co	B	
Ward & Co, S H	B	
(Vaux Breweries Ltd)		
Charles Wells	B	C[1076]
West Coast		
West Highland		
Whitby's Brewery		
Wickwar Brewing		
Wiltshire Brewery		
(Chainmaker Beer Co)		
Wolverhampton	B	C[1076]
& Dudley Breweries		
Wood Brewery		
Woodforde's Norfolk Ales		
Worldham Brewery		
Wortley Brewery		
Wychford Brewery		
Wye Valley Brewery		
Yates Brewery		
Young & Co's Brewery	B	

Organics

Beer:
Saxon Strong Ale (Ross Brewing Co.)
Golden Promise Bitter (Caledonian Brewing Company Ltd)
Original Flag Porter (Flag Brewery)
Lincoln Green Lager (Lincoln Green Lager Ltd)

Ciders:
Avalon Vineyard
Dunkertons Cider Co

Some or all of the above can be obtained from the following distributors:

Vintage Roots, Sheeplands Farm, Wargrave Road, Wargrave, Berkshire RG10 8DT. (0734) 401222.

Vinceremos, Unit 10, Ashley Ind. Estate, Wakefield Rd, Ossett, West Yorks. (0924) 276393.

The Organic Wine Co. PO Box 81, High Wycombe, Bucks HP13 5QN. (0494) 446557.

Organics, 290 Fulham Place Rd, London SW6 6HP. (071) 381 9924.

Rodgers Fine Wines, 37 Ben Bank Rd, Silkstone Common, Barnsley, South Yorks. S75 4PE. (0226) 790794.

Haughton Fine Wines, Chorley, Nantwich, Cheshire CW5 8JR. (0270) 74 537.

Coffee

This report covers only instant coffees and not ground varieties or beans.

Around 48 million tonnes coffee is grown every year in around 25 countries mainly in Africa and Latin America. These sources could not be more varied. In Latin America, especially Colombia and Brazil, coffee is typically grown in large single-crop intensive plantations which have been carved out of the fragile forests. The soil is often quickly exhausted, massive amounts of chemicals are used, and the plantations spread to take in more and more land. This highly concentrated coffee production can cause extensive pollution problems. Rivers in Colombia down stream from where the beans are washed are more acidic and have more organic pollutants than anywhere else in the country.

On the other side of the world, coffee is often grown under quite different conditions. In African countries such as Rwanda, Burundi and Kenya most coffee is grown by smallholders. Typically a smallholding would have no more than a hundred coffee trees, and subsistence foods would be grown alongside. The coffee beans are sold through a co-operative or a state agency, but the bureaucracy can be slow and payments often late. Yields per acre are low on such smallholdings, but so too are the chemical inputs, and the quality of the coffee is often high.

Development analysts often highlight the important role coffee plays in the 'dependency culture' which plagues economic relations between the rich West and African and Latin American countries. Often massively in debt, these countries are encouraged to grow more cash crops for export, to get the foreign currency to pay off the debts. Not only can this take valuable land out of food production in countries that have serious malnutrition problems, but it also offers a precarious livelihood in return.

There is little we can do as consumers to influence this sort of structural problem - although it would be making an important statement to avoid coffee (where labelled) from oppressive regimes. These countries have political structures **least likely**

to mitigate against the dislocation that large scale export
cropping can cause. Fair Trade arrangements would obviously
not be so detrimental. Countries among ECRA's list of thirty-
nine regimes with an important role in coffee production are:
Brazil, Colombia, El Salvador, Guatemala, Haiti, Honduras
and Kenya.

The Nestlé Boycott

*"I saw mother after mother in the paediatric wards, head in hands, crying
beside the cribs where their babies lay, malnourished, dehydrated, sick
from **Bottle Baby Disease.** It doesn't need to happen. A decade ago we
knew the truth about irresponsible marketing of infant formula. Allowing
the companies to continue these practices is an inexcusable outrage of
humanity, if not outright criminality."*
Janice Mantell, Action for Corporate Accountability (USA)

Every 30 seconds, a baby dies from unsafe bottle feeding. Nestlé holds
about 50% of the world's breastmilk substitute market and is being
boycotted for continued breaches of the 1981 WHO Code regulating the
marketing of breastmilk substitutes.

Without breastfeeding babies don't get the benefit of passive immunity
normally passed on in the mothers' milk. The risk of contracting serious
diseases from bottle feeding is therefore high, but it is further compounded
by the fact that, in the Third World, many people don't have access to a
clean water supply with which to make up the formula, and poverty can
lead to mothers over-diluting the formula to make it go further. Water-
borne diseases fed straight to vulnerable babies cause what is now a
common condition in many parts of the world - diarrhoea, vomiting,
respiratory infections, malnutrition, dehydration and commonly death -
known as Bottle-Baby disease.

The companies know this happens. A Code drawn up in 1972 to regulate
the supply of free samples of breastmilk substitutes was adopted by the
World Health Organisation in 1981. After a long boycott campaign, Nestlé
and other companies eventually agreed to abide by the Code, and the
boycott was called off in 1984.

However reports have continued to come in from around the world that the
Code is **still** being violated by babymilk companies, and Nestlé in
particular has become the focus of criticism being by far the largest
supplier of babymilk to Third World countries. The boycott campaign was
re-launched in 1988, and is now active in over 80 countries.

BABY MILK ACTION are coordinating the UK boycott campaign and
they can be contacted at 23, St. Andrew's Street, Cambridge, CB2 3AX

Caffeine For information on caffeine see the Tea report.

Fair Trade There are some instant coffee producers who stand out for an ethical consumer, most notably the fair trade organisations Traidcraft, Equal Exchange and Oxfam. Their aim is to source products from community-based groups in countries seeking justice for their rural poor through active development policies, and where possible from local processors and packers. Nicaraguan and Tanzanian coffee are good examples.
Franz Niehoff's Natural Organic Coffee is also worth mentioning, as one of its two suppliers is a Mexican cooperative which previously had no direct access to the coffee market, and which has been able to get higher prices as a result. Additionally, its arabica beans are certified as organic to Demeter standards.[1829]

Best Buys Best by far are the Traidcraft, Oxfam and Equal Exchange coffees, available from wholefood shops, Oxfam shops and many other outlets, and of course by mail-order.
Niehoff's Natural Organic Coffee is another good option and is available in wholefood shops or from its UK distributor Community Foods.
If you cannot find these then the King Cup, Grandos and Vendona brands all come from companies of which we have discovered no criticisms. These are of course a less positive choice.

(This article was first published in May 1989.)

Brand Name	South Africa	Oppressive Regimes	Trade Union Relations	Wages & Conditions	Land Rights	Environment	Irresponsible Marketing	Nuclear Power	Armaments	Animal Testing	Factory Farming	Other Animal Rights	Political Donations	Boycott Call	Company Group
Alta Rica	■	■	◢	◢		■			■	■			■		Nestlé
ASDA	■	■		◢					■	■	■				ASDA Group
Blend 37	■	■	◢	◢		■			■				■		Nestlé
Brim	◢	■				■			■		USA		■		Philip Morris
Café Hag	◢	■				■			■		USA		■		Philip Morris
Camp		■													McCormick & Co Inc
Cap Colombie	■	■	◢	◢		■			■	■			■		Nestlé
Choice	■	■		■	◢				■	■			■		Unilever
Co-op	■	■		◢				◢	■	■	LAB		■		Co-op Movement
Elevenses	■	■	◢	◢		■			■	■			■		Nestlé
Equal Exchange															Equal Exchange Trading Ltd
Fireside Choice	▨	▨				▨	▨						▨		Gold Crown Group
Gateway	■	■		◢					■	■	■				Isosceles
Gold Blend	■	■	◢	◢		■			■	■			■		Nestlé
Golden Stream	▨	▨				▨	▨						▨		Gold Crown Group
Grandos															Kord GmbH
Kenco	◢	■				■			■		USA		■		Philip Morris
King Cup															Brash Brothers
Lyons	◢	■				■		◢			CON		■		Allied Lyons
Mantunna	▨	▨				▨	▨						▨		Gold Crown Group
Marks & Spencer	■	■		◢					■	■	CON		■		Marks & Spencer
Master Blend	◢					■			■		USA		■		Philip Morris
Maxwell House	◢					■			■		USA		■		Philip Morris
Mellow Birds	◢					■			■		USA		■		Philip Morris
Moccona	◢		◢			■				■					Sara Lee Corp
Morrisons	■	■							■	■	■				Wm Morrison
Natural Organic Coffee															Franz Niehoff
Nescafé	■	■	◢	◢		■			■		■		■		Nestlé
Nescoré	■	■	◢	◢		■			■		■		■		Nestlé
Oxfam															Oxfam
Red Mountain	■	■		■	◢				■	■			■		Unilever
Safeway	■	■							■	■	CON		■		Argyll Group
Sainsbury's	■	■		◢				◢	■	■			■		J Sainsbury
Tesco	■	■		◢					■	■			■		Tesco
Traidfair															Traidcraft
Vendona	■														S. Daniels
Waitrose	■	■							■	■	■				John Lewis

Fruit Juice

In recent years a commodities market in fruit juices has grown up, much like the markets for tea and coffee. You can just imagine it: great lumps of frozen, highly concentrated orange juice being bought and sold by frantic dealers with stripey shirts and cordless telephones. These people of course never actually see any real orange juice, apart from at the breakfast table, but they make a living out of it nonetheless.

Most 'manufacturers' of fruit juice use these frozen juice-concentrates, bought on the world market from perhaps several different countries. Once they get their hands on these blocks of frozen concentrate, they are then thawed, blended to a standard quality, diluted down and packaged. Hence the ubiquitous phrase, 'a blend of pure fruit juice from more than one country'.

Probable Country of Origin

According to the trade, 75% of the UK's orange juice comes from Brazil,[132] a country where many suffer from vitamin C deficiency.[119] Israel also produces orange juice[135] and most of the grapefruit juice,[134] whilst pineapple juice may come from South Africa,[135] Kenya or the Philippines.[134] All of these countries appear on our list of Oppressive Regimes. Apple juice may originate solely from the UK (as does Copella) and, if so, will be labelled as such.

Pure Juice?

Anything labelled as pure fruit juice must, by law, contain 100% pure juice; no additives (preservatives and colourings) and at the same strength as when the fruit was originally squeezed.

However, according to a Ministry of Agriculture survey in February 1991, most leading brands of orange juice which claim to be pure and unsweetened in fact contained additives or extra sugar. Only five of the twenty one brands tested were found to be pure juice - Del Monte, De L'Ora, St Ivel Real, Waitrose and Stute. Of these only Stute appears in our Best Buys. Of the other brands in this report, Assis, Express, Just Juice and Sun Pride all failed the aforementioned tests on purity.[576]

(This article was first published in March 1989.)

We have not discovered any criticisms of the parent companies of the Assis, Copella and Stute brands. These brands are therefore Best Buys. If none of these is available, the brands owned by Northern Foods - Dale Farms, Eden Vale and Express - would be next best.

Best Buys

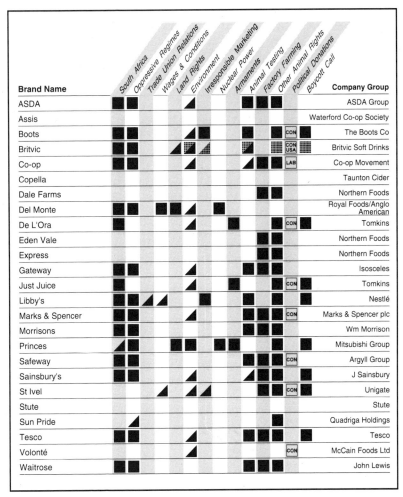

Brand Name	Company Group
ASDA	ASDA Group
Assis	Waterford Co-op Society
Boots	The Boots Co
Britvic	Britvic Soft Drinks
Co-op	Co-op Movement
Copella	Taunton Cider
Dale Farms	Northern Foods
Del Monte	Royal Foods/Anglo American
De L'Ora	Tomkins
Eden Vale	Northern Foods
Express	Northern Foods
Gateway	Isosceles
Just Juice	Tomkins
Libby's	Nestlé
Marks & Spencer	Marks & Spencer plc
Morrisons	Wm Morrison
Princes	Mitsubishi Group
Safeway	Argyll Group
Sainsbury's	J Sainsbury
St Ivel	Unigate
Stute	Stute
Sun Pride	Quadriga Holdings
Tesco	Tesco
Volonté	McCain Foods Ltd
Waitrose	John Lewis

The rating columns (left to right): South Africa, Oppressive Regimes, Trade Union Relations, Wages & Conditions, Land Rights, Environment, Irresponsible Marketing, Nuclear Power, Armaments, Animal Testing, Factory Farming, Other Animal Rights, Political Donations, Boycott Call.

Soft Drinks

The average Briton consumes around 133 litres of soft drinks - the equivalent of 400 cans - every year. This report looks at carbonated and concentrated soft drinks brands, i.e. fizzy drinks and squashes, and sparkling fruit juices.

Third World   The spread of Coca-Cola and Pepsico operations is truly global. Coca-Cola distributes its branded products in over 155 countries. In Mexico, Coca-Cola and Pepsico control 77% of the soft drinks market, while in Brazil, Coca-Cola alone has 55% of the market.[1164] Soft drinks have been described as making the "most extensive dietary impact of foreign corporations in the developed world". They are usually priced just within the reach of the poorest in these countries and may represent, via their glossily advertised images, symbols of an enviable Western lifestyle.[573]

Because of the relative poverty of many people in the Third World, staple foods may be neglected in preference to soft drinks. In 1969 it was reported that babies in Zambia had become malnourished because their mothers fed them Coke and Fanta, believing it was the best thing they could give their children. Around that time 54% of the seriously malnourished children admitted to the children's hospital at Ndola had 'Fantababy' written on their progress charts. The Zambian government subsequently banned Fanta advertisements "because of their influence on the poor".[573]

A study at the Nutrition Institute in Rio de Janeiro found high levels of consumption of Coke, Fanta and Pepsi in its survey of school children between 6-14 years old. All the children showed signs of vitamin deficiency whilst the poorest of them also showed protein/calorie malnutrition.[573]

A Mexican priest wrote, in 1974, that Mexican villagers believed soft drinks should be consumed every day, leading to lower consumption of natural products such as fruit. Some families were even seen to be selling their natural products in order to buy soft drinks.[573]

Secret Ingredients?   While the recipes for Coca-Cola, Pepsi and many soft drinks are closely guarded secrets, the ingredients we do know about do not give much cause for comfort.

Sugar: Cola drinks usually contain about 10% sugars - some 13 lumps in a 330ml can. Ribena contains approximately 15% sugars - 15 lumps in a 250ml carton. These proportions seem the norm for most soft drinks (except of course the 'diet' varieties). See the Sugar report for details about sugar and health.

Saccharin: This has to carry a health warning in the US, as it has been linked to the development of bladder cancer in laboratory animals.[726] The Food Commission undertook a survey in 1991 of soft drinks brands and found a number of them, not just those labelled 'diet' drinks, contained saccharin as well as sugar. They found this a worrying trend given that MAFF research in 1990 found 1 in 6 children between the ages of two and five were consuming more than 2.5mg of saccharin per kg of bodyweight, which was then the UK maximum acceptable daily intake (and is still that of EC and WHO recommendations).[583]

Caffeine: A standard can of cola may contain between 40-60mg of caffeine, while a cup of coffee can have between 86-99mg. See the Tea report for more details about caffeine and health.

Tartrazine (E102): is among a number of coal tar dyes used as an orange colouring in some soft drinks (especially concentrates). It has been linked to hyperactivity in children as well as asthma and rashes. Manufacturers have begun removing it from drinks.[1418]

Benzoates: The most commonly used preservatives in soft drinks. They have been found to provoke asthma and skin rashes in some people.[1418]

Packaging

Soft drinks come in four different types of packaging: glass or plastic (PET) bottles, and steel or aluminium cans.

'Returnables' schemes for either glass or PET bottles would be the packaging ideal, but unfortunately these are rather thin on the ground in the UK. In some European countries soft drinks manufacturers are using returnable packaging, but opposition from British supermarkets means this is unlikely to happen here in the immediate future.[381]

In the absence of these, using recycling facilities, for any of the forms of packaging, will be one way of reducing environmental impact. Although it is constantly changing, energy analysts currently tend to prefer PET over glass, over steel over aluminium. However, we are yet to come across a convincing cradle to grave analysis of the environmental impact of these forms of packaging.

(This article was first published in April 1993.)

Soft Drinks

Best Buys

The following brands are Best Buys: Amé, Bali Hi, Ben Shaw's, Calypso, Cawston Vale, Freshers, Gusto, Irn Bru, Jusoda, Lane's, Mato Taki, Old Jamaica, Orange Plus, Peach Blush, Pin Hi, PLJ, Pripp's Energy, Rock's, Rubicon, Schloer, St Clements, Strike Cola, Suncharm, Thorncroft, Ting, Tizer, V Cola, Vimto, Wells and Whole Earth.

Other Brands

Appletise	Cadbury-Schweppes/Coca-Cola
Bali Hi	J N Nichols (Vimto) plc
Britvic	Britvic Soft Drinks
Canada Dry	Cadbury-Schweppes/Coca-Cola
Cariba	Cadbury-Schweppes/Coca-Cola
Corona	Britvic Soft Drinks
C-Vit	SmithKline Beecham
Dexters	Grand Metropolitan
Fanta	Cadbury-Schweppes/Coca-Cola
Fizz Wizz	Britvic Soft Drinks
Freshers	J N Nichols (Vimto) plc
Giardini	H P Bulmer
Gini	Cadbury-Schweppes/Coca-Cola
Idris	Britvic Soft Drinks
Jusoda	A G Barr
Kia-Ora	Cadbury-Schweppes/Coca-Cola
Kiri	H P Bulmer
Lilt	Cadbury-Schweppes/Coca-Cola
Limon	Cadbury-Schweppes/Coca-Cola
Lucozade	SmithKline Beecham
Mato Taki	J N Nichols (Vimto) plc
Norfolk Punch	Grand Metropolitan
Old Jamaica	Benjamin Shaw & Sons Ltd
Orange Plus	J N Nichols (Vimto) plc
Pin Hi	J N Nichols (Vimto) plc
PLJ	Merrydown Wine
Princes' Jucee	Mitsubishi Group
Pripp's Energy	A G Barr
Purdey's	Grand Metropolitan
Quosh	Britvic Soft Drinks
Rio Riva	Hall & Woodhouse
Rose's	Cadbury-Schweppes/Coca-Cola
R. Whites	Britvic Soft Drinks
Schweppes	Cadbury-Schweppes/Coca-Cola
7-Up	Britvic/Pepsi
Shandy Bass	Britvic Soft Drinks
Sprite	Cadbury-Schweppes/Coca-Cola
St Clements	A G Barr
Strike Cola	A G Barr
Suncharm	Benjamin Shaw & Sons Ltd
Sunkist	Cadbury-Schweppes/Coca-Cola
Tizer	A G Barr
Top Deck	Britvic Soft Drinks
Ting	Benjamin Shaw & Sons Ltd
V Cola	J N Nichols (Vimto) plc

Brand Name	South Africa	Oppressive Regimes	Trade Union Relations	Wages & Conditions	Land Rights	Environment	Irresponsible Marketing	Nuclear Power	Armaments	Animal Testing	Factory Farming	Other Animal Rights	Political Donations	Boycott Call	Company Group
Amé															Greenbank Drinks Co
ASDA	■	■			◣		■	■	■						ASDA Group
Aqua Libra	■	■	◣	◣	◣		◣		■			■			Grand Metropolitan
Barraclough's	◣	■		■	■	■	■			◣		■			Mitsubishi Group
Ben Shaw's															Benjamin Shaw
Calypso															Cooke Bros
Carters										■					Hero AG
Cawston Vale															Cawston Group
Coca-Cola	■	■	■		■	◣		■			USA	■			Cadbury/Coca-Cola
Co-op	■	■			◣		◣	■			LAB				Co-op Movement
Gusto															Gusto
Irn-Bru															A G Barr
Isostar	■	■			◣	■		■							Sandoz AG
Lane's															G R Lane
Marks & Spencer	■	■			◣		■	■	■		CON				Marks & Spencer plc
Morrisons	■	■					■	■	■						Wm Morrison
One-Cal	■				◣			■			CON	■			Tomkins
Orangina	■	◣			◣										Pernod-Ricard/Bulmer
Panda							◣								Hall & Woodhouse
Peach Blush															Petty & Wood
Pepsi	■	■		◣	■	◣		■			CON USA	■			Britvic/Pepsi
Ribena	■	■			■	◣		■			CON				SmithKline Beecham
Robinson's	■	■	◣		◣			■			BUI CPS				Reckitt & Colman
Rock's															Rock's
Rubicon															Rubicon Products
Safeway	■	■					■	■	■		CON				Argyll Group
Sainsbury's	■	■			◣		◣	■	■				■		J Sainsbury
Sao Rico		◣			◣										H P Bulmer
Schloer															Merrydown Wine
Soda Stream	■	■		■		■		◣							Cadbury-Schweppes
Somerfield (Gateway)	■	■			◣		■	■	■						Isosceles
St Ivel				◣	◣	◣			■	■	CON	■			Unigate
Tango	■	■		◣	▨	◣		▨		▨	CON USA	▨			Britvic Soft Drinks
Tesco	■	■		◣	◣			■	■				■		Tesco
Thorncroft															Thorncroft Vineyard
Vimto	■														J N Nichols
Waitrose	■	■					■	■	■						John Lewis
Wells															Robinson Group
Whole Earth															Whole Earth

Tea & Herbal Tea

Even though tea consumption has been declining since 1968, the British still drink more tea than any other beverage apart from water and are the second largest per capita consumers of tea in the world after the Irish.

It was British companies that were responsible for the start of the global tea trade and they still hold a dominant position in the trading and marketing of tea throughout the world. Just four major diversified companies account for most of the tea sold in the UK - Unilever, Allied Lyons, Hillsdown Holdings and the CWS. The majority of companies on the Table are just tea blenders and packers buying tea on the world market. Unilever, James Finlay and George Williamson also own tea plantations in the Third World and account for a significant amount of the tea produced worldwide.[1164]

In the UK, 'black' tea like PG Tips and Typhoo is by far the most popular with herbal tea only, as yet, accounting for 2% of tea sales. Because 'black' tea has attracted many criticisms for the development and social problems it causes in the Third World, this article will concentrate on the 'black' tea industry.

The Unfair Tea Trade

Tea is a luxury crop grown primarily in the Third World for export to the West. The tea bush is thought to have originated in China in 2737 BC, but it wasn't until 1637 that Chinese tea came to England via the British East India Company which then had a monopoly on the trade.

Tea cultivation was spread in the 19th century by British colonialists to countries such as India, Sri Lanka and Kenya. Today tea is grown in 30 countries, mainly in Asia (India, China and Sri Lanka accounted for 57% of world production in 1989), followed by Africa, the USSR and South America.

In these countries, land that was used to grow food to meet peoples' needs was often expropriated by British companies. They established huge plantations or tea 'gardens'. Many of the peasants made landless by the plantations were forced to work on them. They became economically dependent on the plantations where they worked, lived and died. Many workers, like the Tamils in Sri Lanka, were 'imported' as workers and were stateless, voteless and subject to racist attacks from the indigenous Sinhalese. The problems of modern day Sri Lanka are clearly rooted in the tea trade.

Wages and conditions for plantation workers were poor from the beginning. In 1911, the Head of Government in Assam, spoke out against a labour system that "treated its workers like medieval serfs".[1507] In the 1970s and early 1980s, there was a great deal of media criticism of the wages and conditions of workers on plantations owned by Brooke Bond, James Finlay, George Williamson and the CWS, notably in India, Sri Lanka and Bangladesh. On many of their plantations, housing, sanitation, water supply and medical facilities fell short of minimum standards laid down by the countries' governments. (See the Companies section for individual details.) Although many plantations have now been nationalised or taken over by domestic elites or companies, this has made little difference to the wages and conditions of the workers. Tea pickers, mainly women, may be paid a basic wage of between 30p to £1 a day on completion of a minimum weight of tea leaves picked.[1628] In Bangladesh, which has one of the lowest wage rates in the world,[1507] tea pickers are paid a basic of 30p a day,[1472] whilst in Malawi, some daily plantation wages amount to the price of a loaf of bread.[1164] In Southern India, a tea picker may be paid 95p for picking the equivalent weight of 120 quarter pound packets of tea. Two thirds of plantation workers there are on the poverty line, spending more than 75% of their income on food.[1661] In 1989 in Sri Lanka, workers on all the mainly government-run tea plantations went on strike demanding a minimum wage of £39 a month instead of £23.[879]

There is, however, very little information published in the last five years about wages and conditions on specific plantations which may be owned by companies covered in this report.

Many companies claim that the low price of tea on the world market is to blame for low wages but even when tea prices are higher, plantation owners rarely choose to pass this on to their workers through higher wages. It is true that the price of tea on the world market has been declining for many years. Firstly, it has been suggested that the price is kept low by the handful of British multinational companies which buy most of the tea.[1164] They can shift their purchases from one national auction to another to obtain tea at its lowest price. This is made easier for companies like Unilever which own both tea sellers and buyers. Because of this monopolistic situation, tea is rarely

The Price of Tea

sold to the highest bidder and, as with the market for most primary commodities, the price set has little relationship to producers' production costs.

Secondly, demand for tea has been falling and there is often oversupply, both of which result in lower prices. The tea trade is not controlled by export quotas like the coffee market, so poor countries try to get as large a share of the rich nations' market as possible. And whilst the price of tea has been falling, the price of goods that Third World countries import (such as manufactured goods and pesticides) has been rising.

Countries or companies involved solely in the growing of tea thus get a low price for their tea. Tea growers get about 50% of the retail price of loose tea but only 15% of teabags. It is from the 'added value' of blending, packing and branding of tea that more money is to be made, especially with teabags. Companies such as Unilever and Finlay can make the most money out of tea since they grow, blend, pack and brand tea. China, India and Sri Lanka do export packaged and branded tea, but it is very difficult for them to break the tight grip that the multinationals have on branded tea sales throughout the western world.

Many countries are now trapped in producing export crops like tea because of debt. They are obliged to generate foreign exchange through exports just to pay back the interest on loans from western banks.

The Fair Tea Trade

Tea is a cheap drink for western consumers (about 1.5p a cup) because of the exploitation of tea workers in the Third World. The present tea trade does not offer an equitable share of the price of tea to tea workers in the Third World. Tea-buying consumers must take some of the responsibility for their continuing exploitation unless they decide to avoid 'black' tea or look to the alternative tea trade. Traidcraft was set up to trade with producers working for themselves and their local community, or countries with active rural development policies to help the poor. Their teas always carry information about the producer and the country of origin. WDM tea is packed in the country of origin so that the producers get the 'added value'. The Typhoo brand of tea has been relaunched as 'ethically approved'. The producer of the brands, Premier Brands (part of Hillsdown Holdings) is guaranteeing that its tea has been grown on plantations with high social and environmental standards. The tea is blended exclusively from approved estates and will bear a 'Caring for tea and our tea pickers' logo.

Premier Brands has assessed tea estates on 46 specific categories including tea quality, safety and hygiene and social aspects. The social criteria cover pay and working conditions, and health, education and housing benefits for the workers. Premier is now buying its tea directly from 75 approved estates in eight countries instead of at tea auctions. The chosen estates now have 'preferred supplier status' which ensures demand for part of their crop. The estates will be audited by Premier at least once a year. Whilst the Ethical Consumer welcomes this move, especially from a company whose parent is not renowned for its ethical behaviour, the initiative would have more weight if the estates were independently audited. This view is shared by the Fair Trade Foundation which wants Premier to apply for its Fairtrade Mark. Foundation member Christian Aid is encouraging its supporters to buy Typhoo as long as they write to Premier asking for more information about their criteria and urging the company to apply for the Fairtrade Mark.

Country of Origin

Many of the teas on sale in the UK are a blend of teas which come from wherever they may be bought cheapest. The main source of UK tea is Kenya, followed by India, Malawi, Sri Lanka, Indonesia and China. With the exception of Malawi, all these countries are on our list of Oppressive Regimes. However, no indication of countries of origin is usually given on the packets. Some packets do supply this information and they are usually 'premium' tea like Tetley Gold or 'speciality' teas like Assam and Darjeeling tea which is from India.

Tea and the Environment

Packaging

Tea packets are usually made from cardboard wrapped in cellophane. Loose tea is usually packaged in foil because research indicated that consumers were transferring tea to tea caddies. Unfortunately some companies have now started to use foil as a wrapping on the outside as well. Overpackaged tea is both a waste of resources and money. In their latest campaign against overpackaging, the Women's Environmental Network pointed out that about a quarter of a shopping bill is for the packaging.[1687] We could only find one brand whose packet was labelled as being "made using recycled board" and that was Yorkshire Tea.

Teabags

Teabags now account for 80% of UK tea sales. Many of these are individually tagged and wrapped. For the convenience of teabags, consumers pay a premium of 10-20% over loose tea prices. The unnecessary use of paper can be avoided by buying loose tea and a tea ball/egg.

Almost all teabags are now made from non-chlorine bleached paper following the controversy surrounding the creation of dioxins when paper is bleached by chlorine. (See the Tissue Paper report for more details.)

Pesticides

Some tea is grown with the use of chemical fertilizers and pesticides. Their application poses a hazard to tea workers and the environment and the tea itself may contain pesticide residues. The Tea Council says that the tea industry only uses non-persistent organophosphorous pesticides and that pesticides are only used on larger estates. These pesticides may pose less of a risk to the environment but they are still highly toxic and act on the nervous system. Furthermore, the size of tea estates is not indicated on the side of tea packets.[639] To discourage the use of pesticides consumers can buy organic tea. Ridgways and Lyons make organic teas which are labelled as such.

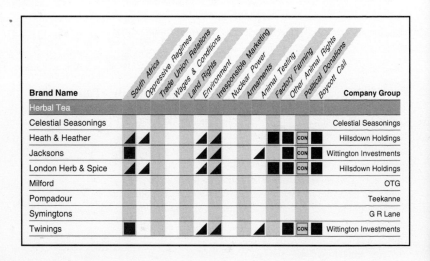

Brand Name	South Africa	Oppressive Regimes	Trade Union Relations	Wages & Conditions	Land Rights	Environment	Irresponsible Marketing	Nuclear Power	Armaments	Animal Testing	Factory Farming	Other Animal Rights	Political Donations	Boycott Call	Company Group
Herbal Tea															
Celestial Seasonings															Celestial Seasonings
Heath & Heather	◪	◪		◪	◪				■	■	CON	■			Hillsdown Holdings
Jacksons	■			◪	◪		◪		■	CON	■				Wittington Investments
London Herb & Spice	◪	◪		◪	◪				■	■	CON	■			Hillsdown Holdings
Milford															OTG
Pompadour															Teekanne
Symingtons															G R Lane
Twinings	■			◪	◪		◪		■	CON	■				Wittington Investments

Brand Name	South Africa	Oppressive Regimes	Trade Union Relations	Wages & Conditions	Land Rights	Environment	Irresponsible Marketing	Nuclear Power	Armaments	Animal Testing	Factory Farming	Other Animal Rights	Political Donations	Boycott Call	Company Group
Ahmad Tea															Ahmad Tea Ltd
ASDA	■	■		◣				■	■	■					ASDA Group
Ashbys	·														Paulig Ltd
Brooke Bond	■	■	◣			■	◣		■		■		■		Unilever
Co-op	■	■		◣			◣	■	■		LAB				Co-op Movement
Empsons															Brash Brothers
Fireside	▒	▒		▒				▒					▒		Gold Crown Group
Glengettie	◣	◣		◣	◣					■	■	CON	■		Hillsdown Holdings
Jacksons	■			◣	◣				◣			CON	■		Wittington Investments
Kardomah	◣	◣		◣	◣					■	■	CON	■		Hillsdown Holdings
King Cup															Brash Brothers
Luaka	◣					◣									Health & Diet
Lyons	◣	■			■			◣			■	CON	■		Allied Lyons
Macleods	◣	◣		◣	◣					■	■	CON	■		Hillsdown Holdings
Mantunna	▒	▒		▒				▒					▒		Gold Crown Group
Marks & Spencer	■·	■		◣				■	■	■		CON			Marks & Spencer plc
Melroses	◣	◣		◣	◣					■	■	CON	■		Hillsdown Holdings
Morrisons	■	■						■	■	■					Wm Morrison
Nairobi															Nairobi Coffee & Tea
Nambarrie	■			◣	◣			◣			■	CON	■		Wittington Investments
Namosa	■			◣	◣			◣			■	CON	■·		Wittington Investments
Old England															OTG
Paynes		◣	◣	■								CON			James Finlay
Ridgways	◣	◣		◣	◣					■	■	CON	■		Hillsdown Holdings
Safeway	■	■								■	■	■·CON			Argyll Group
Sainsbury's	■	■		◣				◣	■	■			■		J Sainsbury
Somerfield (Gateway)	■	■		◣				■	■	■					Isosceles
Tesco	■	■		◣				■·	■	■			■		Tesco
Tetley	◣	■			■			◣			■	CON	■		Allied Lyons
Traidfair															Traidcraft
Twinings		■		◣	◣			◣			■	CON	■		Wittington Investments
Typhoo	◣	◣		◣	◣					■	■	CON	■		Hillsdown Holdings
Vendona															S Daniels
Waitrose	■	■						■	■	■					John Lewis
WDM															Traidcraft
Williamson & Magor		◣										CON			George Williamson
Yorkshire Tea															Prospect Foods

Tea & Herbal Tea

Caffeine According to the Tea Council, tea is a healthy, natural drink containing traces of vitamins, minerals and fluoride. It aids digestion and helps kidney action and also contains caffeine "giving that 'uplift' or stimulus to mind and body".[457] Caffeine is, however, an addictive stimulant. Heavy doses can cause adverse health effects such as migraine, insomnia, palpitations and raised blood pressure. Too much caffeine can also overstimulate the kidneys and cause digestion problems.[1342] Weight for weight, tea contains more caffeine than coffee but less weight is used to make a cup of tea. A cup of average strength tea has 40mg of caffeine (instant coffee 65mg).[1710] A daily caffeine dose of 250mg or more is said to be harmful.[1342] Herbal teas are caffeine-free but to reduce caffeine intake in 'black' tea, consumers could buy low caffeine or decaffeinated tea. PG and Tetley make low caffeine brands whilst decaf teas include Lyons, Twinings, Luaka, Ridgways and Typhoo.

Herbal Tea Theoretically, you can make tea from any herbs. Many of the herbs that the companies on the Table use can be grown in the UK, but a surprising amount of herbs are imported from many countries such as Egypt and Turkey. The brands on the Table either gave no indication of country of origin or are labelled 'product of more than one country'. The import of herbs that can be grown in the UK is unnecessary. Herbal tea drinkers could grow their own herbs.

This solution would also avoid the overpackaging that herbal teas are also prone to. A 1990 Which? report said that, of all teabags, herbal teabags were particularly likely to be overpackaged. Many of them are tagged and individually wrapped. Milford and Pompadour teabags are made from unbleached paper but only the former is labelled as such. Pesticides may be used in the growing of herbs. Only Pompadour teas are organic but this is not indicated on the packets.

Best Buys

Black Tea: By far the Best Buys are the fair trade brands, Traidfair and WDM, which are available as loose tea or teabags, by mail order or from wholefood shops and Oxfam shops. Ahmad tea, King Cup, Nairobi, Old England, Vendona and Yorkshire Tea are the best non-fair trade buys. The organic 'black' tea Best Buy is Ridgways, whilst Luaka comes out best for decaffeinated tea, and Tetley for low caffeine. Luaka is only on sale in wholefood shops.
Herbal Tea: Pompadour, Celestial Seasonings, Milford and Symingtons are Best Buys but only Pompadour is organic.

(This report was first published in October 1990.)

112

Chapter 5

Household Products

CONSUMER CHOICE IN ACTION...

Cosmetics

Despite the move away from the 'made-up' look, 60% of women still use cosmetics.[1057] This report covers companies that make eye, face and lip make-up and nail varnish. The market is becoming increasingly dominated by a few multinationals such as Boots, Avon, Unilever and Procter & Gamble.

For reasons of space, the Table only shows the most well-known brands. A separate 'Brand List' shows these companies' other cosmetics brands. A 'Cruelty-Free' box lists a number of smaller, independent cosmetics companies, all of which have a company policy of no animal testing of products or ingredients.

What Price Vanity? The animal-testing issue has made a big impact on the cosmetics market in recent years. Not only are there now a large number of small, cruelty-free companies but a number of the major brands are now also promoting themselves as cruelty-free. Avon was the first to do so in 1989. In fact, the four best-selling brands - Boots, Avon, Max Factor and Rimmel - all now claim to be 'not tested on animals', as do the Revlon, Yardley and Estee Lauder brands.[1057]

This sea change in corporate policy is due largely to consumer pressure, directed in the UK by groups such as the British Union for the Abolition of Vivisection (BUAV) with its 'Choose Cruelty-Free' campaign. As long ago as 1986, 98% of Cosmopolitan readers were against the testing of cosmetics on animals and in a 1989 MORI poll conducted for BUAV, 85% of respondents were against it and would change brands. And, in 1990, Yardley said that its research had shown that the proportion of consumers which rated 'cruelty-free' as the most important criterion when choosing cosmetics had risen from 8% to 61% in a nine month period!

Although the number of animals used to test cosmetics has fallen significantly (12,090 in 1989 to 3,082 in 1991 in the UK), worldwide the figure is estimated to exceed 200,000 a year.[142] None of these tests is required by law. Cosmetics are required to be shown to be safe for human use, yet despite skin and eye irritancy tests and LD50 tests (such as forcefeeding rats the human equivalent of four and a half pounds of lipstick), 1 in 8 cosmetic users were said to suffer adverse reactions.[952] Tested animals are not treated, nor are antidotes sought, so these tests do not even help to prevent or treat human illness or injury. Critics maintain that animal test data is only used to defend the company against consumer lawsuits.[451]

As well as being wholly inappropriate the continued testing of cosmetics on animals is simply unnecessary. There are many cosmetics and ingredients already available whose safety has been demonstrated by years of use on humans.

The Cruelty-Free Debate

According to the RSPCA: "There is no natural or synthetic ingredient that can be guaranteed 'never' to have been tested on animals." Even so, there is still disagreement about what criteria merit the label 'cruelty-free'.

Most 'cruelty-free' companies are backed by BUAV in using the '5 year rolling rule'. It is the most widely recognised definition and almost 200 companies currently comply with this standard in the UK. To be approved by BUAV, companies must assure them that neither the finished product nor its ingredients have been tested on animals in the last five years and that present or future testing is against company policy. Critics say that this may mean that an ingredient can be animal tested (by another company), now or in the future, and five years after the test it can be labelled as 'cruelty-free'. A smaller number of cosmetics firms define cruelty-free using a 'fixed cut-off date' (FCD), whereby a company sets a date after which it will not use any new ingredients. Companies using this definition may be using ingredients tested on animals before their FCD but it ensures that no more animals are tested on for their sakes.

Companies in the 'Cruelty-Free' box marked with an asterisk use a fixed cut-off date.

Cosmetics Tests Illegal?

A campaign to ban the testing of cosmetics on animals in the European Community was started in 1990 by BUAV and other European animal rights groups. In February 1992 the European Parliament and Commission voted to ban cosmetics tests from January 1998. The import of products tested on animals outside the European Community would also have been banned. However at the first reading of the Cosmetics

Directive, the Council of Ministers, which has the final say, voted against it. The second and final reading of the Directive by the Council of Ministers was due to take place as this book was being published.

The Make-Up of Make-Up The use of slaughterhouse by-products such as animal fats is widespread in the cosmetics industry but we have not been able to find any evidence of their use for most of the companies. Companies listed in the 'Cruelty-Free' box do not use slaughterhouse by-products.

Alternatives Look in the mirror and see how beautiful you look not covered in coloured fat!

Best Buys

(This article was first published in September 1992.)

All the companies listed in the 'Cruelty-Free' box are the Best Buys. Second best are the Mavala and Tura brands. Tura formulates cosmetics for black skin.

Cruelty-Free

All the companies here are listed in the BUAV Approved Product Guide 1993-94 and the Vegan Society's Animal-Free Shopper.
* = use fixed cut-off date

Vegan	**Vegetarian**		
Cristina of London	Barry M	Colorsport	Miss Mary of
Pecksniffs	Beauty Without	Cosmetics To Go! *	Sweden
Stargazer	Cruelty *	Frenchie Cosmetics	Natural Beauty
Products	Body Shop	Laura Page *	Tuesdays Girl Ltd *
		Meadow Magic	Ultra Glow

Other Brands of Companies on the main Table

Benckiser
Margaret Astor
Boots
No 17, 2000
Estée Lauder
Clinique, Prescriptives
Glopec
Leichner
Litor Ltd
Chanel

LVMH/Guinness
Givenchy, RoC
MacAndrews & Forbes
Almay, Charles of the Ritz, Charlie, Germaine Monteil, Ultima II
Nestlé/L'Oréal
Biotherm, Helena Rubinstein, Vichy

Procter & Gamble
Clarion, Colorfast, Cover Girl, Mary Quant, Maxi, Outdoor Girl
Unilever
Cutex (nails), Elizabeth Arden, Sensiq
Wasserstein Perella
Cyclax, Lentheric, Maybelline

Brand Name	South Africa	Oppressive Regimes	Trade Union Relations	Wages & Conditions	Land Rights	Environment	Irresponsible Marketing	Nuclear Power	Armaments	Animal Testing	Factory Farming	Other Animal Rights	Political Donations	Boycott Call	Company Group
ASDA	■	■		◢				■	■	■					ASDA Group
Avon		■		◢									USA		Avon Products
Bourjois								■							Litor Ltd
BWC															Beauty Without Cruelty
Christian Dior	■	■		◢					■		■				Guinness/LVMH
Clarins		◢													Clarins
Co-op	■	■		◢				◢	■	■			LAB		Co-op Movement
Cosmetics to Go!															Constantine & Weir
Coty	■	■						■	■	■		◢	USA		Pfizer
Colourings															Body Shop
Estée Lauder	■										■				Estée Lauder
Gateway	■	■		◢				■	■	■					Isosceles
Guerlain	■	◢							■						Guerlain
Innoxa	■														Glopec (UK) Ltd
Kanebo		◢													Kanebo/Basler
Lancaster	■	◢													Benckiser
Lancome	■	■	◢	◢		■			■		■		■		Nestlé
L'Oreal	■	■	◢	◢		■			■		■		■		Nestlé
Marks & Spencer	■	■		◢				■	■	■	CON				Marks & Spencer plc
Mavala															Mavala
Max Factor	◢	■		◢				■		◢			■		Procter & Gamble
Morrisons	■	■						■	■	■					Wm Morrison
No 7	■	■		◢	■					■	CON	■			Boots
Revlon	◢	◢													MacAndrews & Forbes
Rimmel	■	■	◢		■	◢			■	■			■		Unilever
Safeway	■	■						■	■	■	CON				Argyll Group
Sainsbury's	■	■		◢				◢	■	■			■		J Sainsbury
Sally Hansen										■					Del Labs
Shiseido		◢								■					Shiseido
Tesco	■	■		◢				■	■	■			■		Tesco
Tuesday's Girl															Tuesday's Girl
Tura															Lornamead Ltd
Ultra Glow															Ultra Glow Cosmetics
Yardley		◢								■					Wasserstein Perella
Waitrose	■	■						■	■	■					John Lewis

Nappies

This report covers disposable and re-usable nappies. Over 80% of UK babies are now wrapped in disposable nappies. Pampers was the UK's fastest-growing supermarket brand in 1991/2, sales increasing by 83%. Over nine million are thrown away every day in the UK - about 100 per second.

Disposable nappies typically consist of 72% fluff pulp, 8% paper, 12% plastics and 6% absorbent gel. Fluff pulp is a wood-derived product and provides most of the absorbency function. Various plastics are used for linings and fastenings. Relatively recently, absorbency has been 'improved' by the addition of an 'absorbent gel'. Manufacturers have claimed that the toxicity of this gel is low, but contact with eyes can cause corneal damage and inhalation may cause lung damage.[1884]

A Load of Environmentally-Friendly Fluff Pulp

In 1989, Peaudouce surprised the world by announcing it would start using 'environmentally-friendly' non-chlorine bleached fluff pulp in its nappies. At the time, the issue of chlorine bleaching, and the associated dioxins, was only just gaining public awareness. WEN was about to launch a major campaign against chlorine-bleached paper products and nappies had not even been particularly singled out. Maybe Peaudouce knew the campaign was coming, or maybe, as cynics suggested, their declining market share, and a new parent company with plentiful supplies of the new pulp, might have prompted the move.[371] Anyway, most brands now sport an 'environmentally-friendly fluff pulp' logo. These claims are absurd because, chlorine or no chlorine, fluff pulp production still creates some of the most toxic effluents of any industry.[28] And it may even be the case that the non-chlorine process is more polluting in other ways.[362] In any case, these 'environmentally-friendly' logos distract consumers from all the other issues involved. It is hard to understand why the Advertising Standards Authority lets the companies get away with it.

Procter & Gamble's 'Pampers' is one of the few brands without one of these logos - the reason being that P&G uses a reduced-chlorine process. In place of the environmentally-friendly logo, P&G secured a sponsorship deal with the Worldwide Fund for Nature, allowing it to use the WWF logo instead. The logo also featured on Ariel Ultra, a product which, unbeknown to WWF, was tested on animals. In August 1992, WWF was discussing labelling changes with P&G.[1890]

Nappy Wars & the Environment

So far, the 'nappy wars' have centred around Life Cycle Analyses (LCA's) which are supposedly scientific cradle-to-grave assessments of a product's environmental consequences. The first LCAs, sponsored by Procter & Gamble and by the American Paper Institute, both concluded that there was 'no overall difference' between reusables and disposables in environmental terms. They took into account a vast number of factors, even the plastic in the bucket used to soak nappies, but did not manage to include the plastic wrapping on disposables.[27]

LCAs were then commissioned by the US's National Association of Diaper Services, and the UK's Women's Environmental Network. Both concluded that there was a difference, and favoured reusables. WEN complained to the Advertising Standards Authority about a P&G leaflet which stated its belief in 'no overall difference'. In 1992 the ASA upheld WEN's complaint.

LCAs are complicated processes, but two points need to be made here. Firstly, treating timber as a renewable resource is misleading since much timber is still being clear cut from old growth forests, even in Scandinavia and Canada, and even the best managed forests are not, according to critics, in any way sustainable.[28, 306] Secondly, how exactly does one compare an amount of toxic effluent in water with a degree of air pollution or an amount of landfill space?

Public Health

David Hammond, chair of the Disposable Nappies Association and environmental affairs manager at Procter and Gamble has stated: "There is nothing *on record* showing that nappies constitute a risk to public or environmental health."[1885] (Our emphasis.) However, Jeff Cooper of the London Waste Regulation Authority has noted potentially serious health risks, not just from bacteria, but also of contracting polio from babies which have been inoculated against the potentially crippling disease. He would like to see manufacture cease, but acknowledges it's 'probably too much to hope for'.[1885]

Disposable nappies have been classified as 'clinical waste', theoretically necessitating they be collected separately and incinerated rather than land-filled. However, at the end of 1992, the Institute of Waste Management looked likely to recommend the Department of the Environmnent exempt them from the clinical waste definition.

Solids should of course be rinsed off before 'disposal', but does this happen? Once in the land-fill site, noxious chemicals can leach into underground water supplies. Additionally the methane gas given off by decaying pulp is potentially explosive. Disposable nappies will sit in the land-fill site for years. Since they have been popular for only just over a decade, it is likely that every one of the billions thrown away so far... is still there!

The Alternative

Traditionally, babies have been wrapped in squares of cotton terry towelling. These are cheap and versatile. More modern alternatives are now on the market, again usually made from cotton, but shaped to fit, with velcro or press stud fastenings. Also available are knitted woollen outers which keep a baby's clothes dry, but are breathable and so help prevent nappy-rash - a common problem with plastic outers. They can be used with fitted nappies, ordinary terries, or with special cotton flannel. Advice on nappy washing routines, which needn't be half as much a chore as some people make out, is available in a WEN leaflet, 'Nappies and the Environment', and in Karen Christensen's book, Home Ecology. If washing really is a problem, then there are now many washing services. WEN will send you a list if you write off for one, as will the Nappy Advisory Service. The latter also provides an information pack (£75) if you wish to start such a business in your area, and can be contacted at 23 London Rd, Loughton, Milton Keynes MK5 8AB (0908 666968).

Best Buys

We have found no criticisms of the companies supplying reusable nappy products. These are a clear Best Buy and are listed below the Table.

Plain Terries are a Best Buy as well.

For disposables, we have found no criticisms of the companies selling the following brands: Chicks, Clown Around, Staydry, 10-Zero, Swaddlers Togs, Tendercare, Unichem and Yogi's. We cannot recommend Cosifits or Ultra Fitti, since the company which makes them is registered in the Virgin Isles, and we have a policy of not recommending companies from tax havens.

(This report was first published in October 1991.)

Brand Name	South Africa	Oppressive Regimes	Trade Union Relations	Wages & Conditions	Land Rights	Environment	Irresponsible Marketing	Nuclear Power	Armaments	Animal Testing	Factory Farming	Other Animal Rights	Political Donations	Boycott Call	Company Group
ASDA	■	■				◺			■	■	■				ASDA Group
Boots	■	■		◺	■				■		CON	■			Boots
Chicks															Dhamecha Foods
Clown Around															LPC Group
Co-op	■	■		◺			◺	■	■		LAB				Co-op Movement
Cosifits															Disposable Soft Goods
Gateway	■	■		◺					■	■	■				Isosceles
Huggies	■	■			■				■						Kimberly-Clark
Luvs	◺	■		◺					■		◺		■		Procter & Gamble
Marks & Spencer	■	■		◺					■	■	■	CON			Marks & Spencer plc
Morrisons	■	■							■	■	■				Wm Morrison
Pampers	◺	■		◺					■		◺		■		Procter & Gamble
Peaudouce			◺		◺										Svenska Cellulosa
Safeway	■	■							■	■	■	CON			Argyll Group
Sainsbury's	■	■		◺			◺	■	■				■		J Sainsbury
Staydry															Breger Gibson
Step by Step	◺	■		◺					■		◺		■		Procter & Gamble
Swaddlers Togs															Finaf
10-Zero															Dhamecha Foods
Tendercare															Breger Gibson
Tesco	■	■		◺					■	■	■		■		Tesco
Ultra Fitti															Disposable Soft Goods
Unichem															Unichem
Waitrose	■	■							■	■	■				John Lewis
Yogi's															LPC Group

Reusable Nappies (& Outers)

Bumkins	Green Catalogue
Coochies Baby Business	Harlequin Fluffies
Cottontails	Indisposables
Ducky Diapers	Kooshies
Earthwise	Mikey Diapers
The End Product (Kooshies)	Morningside
Firstborn	Trads
Ganmill (part of Vernon-Carus)	Unimix
Green Baby Products	Weepee

Sanitary Protection

The first disposable commercial sanitary towels were made in the 1890s but for decades they were regarded as an expensive luxury; in the 1950s many women still used homemade washable protection. In 1990 the UK market for disposable sanitary towels and tampons was worth £160 million and their use virtually universal.[1855]

It wasn't until 1985 that sanitary protection products were allowed to be advertised on UK television, and only then with the provisos that no unwrapped towels or tampons would be shown and no one said 'obnoxious' words such as 'wet' or 'dry'. These 'tasteful' adverts marketed the products as easy and imperceptible ways of coping with menstruation, exaggerating the socially prescribed norm of keeping this natural process shameful and hidden. They do not, of course, address the hidden health and environmental implications of the products.

Sanitary Towels

The basic constituent of external sanitary protection is wood pulp. Until the last couple of years, the pulp was bleached with chlorine gas. This process produces some highly dangerous chemicals as by-products, including dioxins, residues of which can also be found in paper products themselves. The US EPA has recently concluded that dioxins cause cancer in humans, and that there is no safe level of exposure.[1855]

In 1992, the UK Association of Sanitary Protection Manufacturers (ASPM) stated that none of its members now uses chlorine gas-bleached materials.[1864] One alternative, using no chlorine at any stage, is the CTMP (chemical thermal mechanical pulp) process. It is also a cheaper process, using hydrogen peroxide as a bleach, and is more environmentally acceptable because it utilises 90% of the tree whereas conventional pulping only uses 45%. However, CTMP has a high biological oxygen demand; it removes oxygen from rivers, destroying their ecological balance. Another alternative is the confusingly named 'oxygen bleaching', which uses chlorine dioxide. Thus chlorine pollution is reduced, not eliminated. It is not clear from product-labelling which manufacturers use which process.[1566, 1855]

According to the ASPM, tests have shown levels of dioxins in sanitary products to be extremely low, and there is no firm evidence that they are absorbed through skin contact.

However, according to WEN "it is agreed that any level poses a risk and is therefore undesirable",[1566] so the health-conscious may wish to use dioxin-free sanitary protection where possible.

Some manufacturers have started to use recycled pulp in towels, but this usually means using pre-consumer waste.

Tampons

Tampons are usually made from cotton and rayon. Rayon is used to increase absorbency and is produced from woodpulp by a process involving chlorine; hence dioxins are again produced and traces of them have been found in rayon-containing tampons. However, Natracare and Co-op tampons are chlorine-free, being either 100% cotton or a non-chlorine bleached cotton/rayon mixed type of tampon (made using a different technology).

There are, however, other problems involved with tampons, the most famous being Toxic Shock Syndrome. This rare but sometimes fatal disease is caused by Staph. Aureus bacteria. Its mode of onset is unclear but it appears to be associated with tampon usage, a higher risk being linked with higher-absorbency tampons. Tampon manufacturers agreed to use clear on-pack warnings of the risk of Toxic Shock Syndrome from March 1993. High absorbency tampons have also been connected with the drying and ulceration of the vaginal membrane.

Moreover, the cotton used in tampons is likely to contain pesticide residues. The UK's main suppliers of cotton are the USA, China and Brazil and these latter two may both use pesticides such as DDT and Aldrin which have been banned or severely restricted in many other countries. Very little organic cotton is available worldwide.

'Environment Friendly?'

Although manufacturers label their products as 'environment friendly', the absence of dioxins does not automatically make sanitary products 'friends of the earth'. There is also a severe disposal problem. Roughly 75% of blocked drains in public places are caused by sanitary products, a problem which the industry says is the water authorities' responsibility. The industry claims that its products are completely flushable but this only means that they clear the U-bend of a toilet. Once in the sewage system as many as half a billion towels and tampons pass into the sea almost completely untreated, adding to the increasing amounts of bacteria present in the sea. They also have an uncanny knack of appearing on our beaches. Furthermore, whilst much of the bulk of towels and tampons biodegrade over time, dioxins and plastic liners from sanitary towels do not, and persist in the environment, as do plastic applicators. Tambrands has recently reintroduced these, which would appear to be a retrograde step environmentally.

The Women's Environmental Network launched a campaign in March 1993 to reduce flushing of towels and tampons down the loo, and to encourage their disposal through household waste.

Reusable Alternatives

Women seem to be faced with little choice in the light of all this information. Of sanitary protection as we know it, a 'chlorine-free' towel seems the lesser of the evils at the moment, given all the problems associated with tampons. A better option would be towels made from 100% recycled, chlorine-free pulp or organic, chlorine-free cotton tampons. However, although disposable sanitary products are convenient and the most practical option in many situations, better still may be reusable alternatives. They do exist and are available now from the following places:

1) Natural sponges are available from, amongst others, the Body Shop.

2) A reusable rubber menstrual cap is available from the USA. Worn internally, it lasts for ten years. Write to The Keeper, Box 20023, Cincinnati, Ohio 45220, USA.

3) Over here, Vernon-Carus makes reusable sanitary towels with the brand name 'Ecofem'. They are available by mail order from Ganmill Ltd, 38/40 Market Street, Bridgwater, Somerset TA6 3EP.

Best Buys

We have discovered no criticisms of the companies owning the Confident, Natracare or Privat brands. Natracare towels and tampons and Privat towels are also chlorine-free and are thus Best Buys.

All of the reusable products are also Best Buys.

(This article was first published in July 1989)

Thanks to WEN for supplying much of the updated information for this article.[1855]

Brand Name	South Africa	Oppressive Regimes	Trade Union Relations	Wages & Conditions	Land Rights	Environment	Irresponsible Marketing	Nuclear Power	Armaments	Animal Testing	Factory Farming	Other Animal Rights	Political Donations	Boycott Call.	Company Group
Tampons															
Confident															Hygieia Healthcare Holdings Ltd
Dr Whites	■	◤			◤				■						Smith & Nephew
Lillets	■	◤			◤				■						Smith & Nephew
Natracare															Sanpoint
Simplicity	■	■				■			■						Kimberly Clark Co
Tampax	◤	◤													Tambrands inc
Towels															
Always	◤	■		◤					■	◤			■		Procter & Gamble
Bodyform	◤		◤	■	■	◤			■			USA	■		Scott/Svenska Cellulosa
Cameo						◤									Robinson & Sons
Carefree	■	■			■				■			USA			Johnson & Johnson
Dr Whites	■	◤			◤				■						Smith & Nephew
Ecosense	■	◤			◤				■						Smith & Nephew
Libra		◤	◤	■	■	◤			■			USA	■		Scott/Svenska Cellulosa
Lillia	■	◤			◤				■						Smith & Nephew
Natracare															Dambi
Pennywise		◤	◤	■	■	◤			■			USA	■		Scott/Svenska Cellulosa
Poise	■	◤			◤				■						Smith & Nephew
Privat															Kallo
Promise	■	■			■				■						Kimberly Clark Co
Simplicity	■	■			■				■						Kimberly Clark Co
Vespré	■	■						■	■			USA			Johnson & Johnson
Own Brands															
Asda	■	■		◤					■	■	■				Asda Group plc
Boots	■	■		◤	■				■			CON	■		Boots plc
Co-op	■	■		◤				◤	■	■		LAB			Co-op Movement
Gateway	■	■		◤					■	■	■				Isosceles plc
Marks & Spencer	■	■		◤					■	■	■	CON			Marks & Spencer
Morrisons	■	■							■	■	■				William Morrison
Safeway	■	■							■	■	■	CON			Argyll Group
Sainsbury	■	■		◤				◤	■	■			■		J Sainsbury plc
Tesco	■	■		◤					■	■	■		■		Tesco
Waitrose	■	■							■	■	■				John Lewis

Shampoo

There are an overwhelming number of brands of shampoo currently on the market, nearly all of which variously claim to give your hair body, bounce and shine or rid your scalp of scaliness. The big drug, cosmetic and toiletry companies dominate the market. Drug companies are especially likely to be criticised for irresponsible marketing and details of specific instances appear in the Companies Section. There are, however, at least as many other brands available from companies of which we have not discovered any criticisms. Most of these appear in the box titled 'Cruelty-Free'.

Anti-Dandruff? Whilst Vidal Sassoon's 'Wash & Go' is the overall best seller, of the top four best sellers two are of the anti-dandruff/ medicated variety. Whether or not as many people actually have dandruff as believe they do, it has been claimed that these shampoos may aggravate the problem.[949] From the producers' point of view, this is a fortunate side effect; millions of people hooked on dandruff shampoos!
More seriously, they may also contain toxic chemicals such as selenium sulphide which is sometimes used in batteries and is a carcinogen in animals.[170] If you do suffer from dandruff, Karen Christensen in her book 'Home Ecology'[949] suggests that thorough brushing and regular scalp massage (especially with bicarbonate of soda) is a far more effective treatment.

Animal Testing The Consumer Protection Act of 1984 states that cosmetics and toiletries must be safe for human use, but nowhere in the world is it legally required that they are tested on animals. Yet, each year in the UK, thousands of rabbits may still be subjected to the Draize eye-irritancy test whereby concentrated solutions are dripped into the eyes of conscious rabbits who are prevented from moving and blinking. There it is left for a minimum of 72 hours and the effects observed.[451]

As a test for human safety it has been suggested that these studies are inaccurate because a rabbit's eye is physiologically different to a human's. Rabbits' eyes do not, for example, have tear ducts. Toxicologists and industrial researchers have agreed that the tests do not reflect the degree of irritancy that might occur in a human after accidental exposure.

Furthermore, there are many ingredients with a well-established history of safe human use. There are also alternative tests that are both more accurate and do not involve suffering - cell cultures, computer models and human corneas from eye banks.

All the companies with brands listed under 'Cruelty-Free' have a policy of no animal testing of finished products or their ingredients.

See the Cosmetics report for more details about animal testing.

The Environment

Both Friends of the Earth and 'The Green Consumer Guide' have said that your local sewage works should be able to cope with shampoo wastes. Even so, the synthetic detergents, perfumes, colours and preservatives contained in many shampoos create an unnecessary burden on a sewage system that already has to cope with many other household wastes. Many of these chemicals break down slowly and often incompletely and create further pollution problems at the production end. (See the Washing-up Liquid report for more details.)

Some of them also irritate the skin and eyes and are suspected human carcinogens (e.g. selenium sulphide and formaldehyde, used as a preservative).[949, 170] So much for animal tests establishing safe use in humans! Even though most shampoos do not list their ingredients, brands that contain natural ingredients and no additives usually do.

Many people also use too much shampoo too often which is both unnecessary and counter-productive - stripping the hair of its natural oils only means that they are replaced quicker and in greater quantity.

(This article was first published in May 1989.)

Shampoo

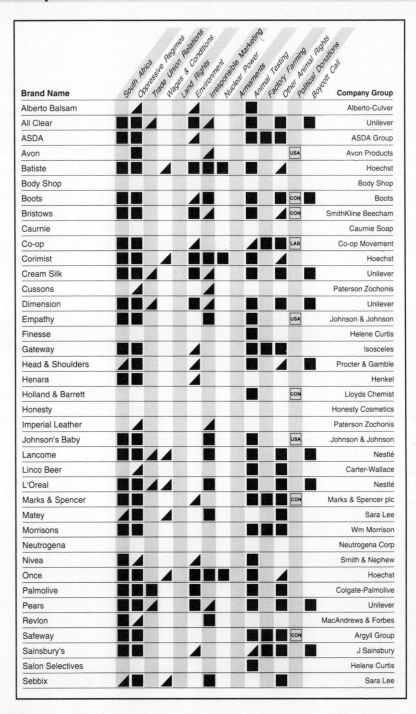

Brand Name	South Africa	Oppressive Regimes	Trade Union Relations	Wages & Conditions	Land Rights	Environment	Irresponsible Marketing	Nuclear Power	Armaments	Animal Testing	Factory Farming	Other Animal Rights	Political Donations	Boycott Call	Company Group
Alberto Balsam		◣		◣						■					Alberto-Culver
All Clear	■	■	◣	■	◣					■			■		Unilever
ASDA	■	■		◣				■	■	■					ASDA Group
Avon		■				◣							USA		Avon Products
Batiste	■	■	◣		■	■	■	■			◣				Hoechst
Body Shop															Body Shop
Boots	■	■		◣	■			■			CON	■			Boots
Bristows	■	■		■	■			■			◣	CON			SmithKline Beecham
Caurnie															Caurnie Soap
Co-op	■	■		◣	■				◣	■	LAB				Co-op Movement
Corimist	■	■	◣		■	■	■	■		■					Hoechst
Cream Silk	■	■	◣	■	◣			■		■			■		Unilever
Cussons		◣			◣										Paterson Zochonis
Dimension	■	■	◣	■	◣			■		■			■		Unilever
Empathy	■	■				■		■					USA		Johnson & Johnson
Finesse										■					Helene Curtis
Gateway	■	■		◣				■	■	■					Isosceles
Head & Shoulders	◣	■		◣				■			◣		■		Procter & Gamble
Henara	■	■		◣											Henkel
Holland & Barrett								■			CON				Lloyds Chemist
Honesty															Honesty Cosmetics
Imperial Leather		◣			◣										Paterson Zochonis
Johnson's Baby	■	■				■		■					USA		Johnson & Johnson
Lancome	■	■	◣					■		■			■		Nestlé
Linco Beer		◣													Carter-Wallace
L'Oreal	■	■	◣			■		■					■		Nestlé
Marks & Spencer	■	■			◣			■	■	■	CON				Marks & Spencer plc
Matey	◣	■	◣		■					■					Sara Lee
Morrisons	■	■						■	■	■					Wm Morrison
Neutrogena															Neutrogena Corp
Nivea	■	◣		◣				■							Smith & Nephew
Once	■	■	◣		■	■	■	■			◣				Hoechst
Palmolive	■	■	■	■				■		■					Colgate-Palmolive
Pears	■	◣		■	◣			■		■			■		Unilever
Revlon	■	◣				■									MacAndrews & Forbes
Safeway	■	■							■	■	■	CON			Argyll Group
Sainsbury's	■	■			◣				◣	■			■		J Sainsbury
Salon Selectives										■					Helene Curtis
Sebbix	◣	■	◣			■		■							Sara Lee

Brand Name	South Africa	Oppressive Regimes	Trade Union Relations	Wages & Conditions	Land Rights	Environment	Irresponsible Marketing	Nuclear Power	Armaments	Animal Testing	Factory Farming	Other Animal Rights	Political Donations	Boycott Call	Company Group
Seborin	■	■		◢	■	■	■		■	◢					Hoechst
Silkience	■	■		◢											Henkel
Silvikrin	■	■			■	◢			■		◢	CON			SmithKline Beecham
Simple	■	◢			◢				■						Smith & Nephew
Sunsilk	■	■	◢		■	◢			■		■		■		Unilever
Supersoft	■	■		◢	■	■	■		■		◢				Hoechst
Tesco	■	■			◢				■	■	■		■		Tesco
Tiki															G R Lane
Timotei	■	■	◢		■	◢			■		■		■		Unilever
Vidal Sassoon	◢	■			◢				■		◢		■		Procter & Gamble
VO5	◢				◢				■						Alberto-Culver
Vosene	■	■			■	◢			■		◢	CON			SmithKline Beecham
Waitrose	■	■			◢				■	■	■				John Lewis
Weleda															Weleda AG
Wella Balsam	■	◢													Wella AG

Cruelty-Free

All the companies below are listed in the BUAV's Approved Product Guide 1993/94 and the Vegan Society's Animal-Free Shopper. We have not discovered any criticisms of any of these companies.

Vegetarian

Barry M
Beauty Without Cruelty
Blackmores
Body Shop
Camilla Hepper
Creightons
Constantine & Weir
 (Cosmetics To Go!)

G R Lane (Tiki)
Martha Hill
Meadow Magic
Montagne Jeunesse
Natural Beauty Products
Tuesdays Girl
Weleda

Vegan

Austrian Moor
Caurnie Soap Co
East of Eden
Faith Products
Honesty Cosmetics
Pecksniffs
Pure Plant
Stargazer

Best Buys

All the brands listed in the 'Cruelty-Free' box are Best Buys for shampoo. Next best is Neutrogena followed by Finesse and Salon Selectives.
Recipes for making your own shampoo can be found in e.g. Camilla Hepper's 'Herbal Cosmetics'.[946]

Soap

Sunlight was the first brand of soap to appear in this country. Introduced in 1884 it was, and still is, a Lever Brothers (Unilever) product. Soap in its generic form has been around for at least 2,300 years but did not come into common use until the nineteenth century. In 1989 98.7% of households in the UK used toilet soap.

Ingredients & Properties

Soap is usually made by reacting animal or vegetable fats or oils with potassium or sodium hydroxide. It works by lifting dirt off the skin and suspending it in the water. At the same time it reduces water's surface tension making its cleaning power more effective.

Because of the simplicity of the product, manufacturers are constantly striving to make soap more interesting and desirable to the consumer. This involves including additives such as perfumes, colouring, emollients (bath oil, moisturiser, lanolin, vitamin E), deodorants and glycerine. Also modern soap may contain detergent which is more effective in hard water. This is particularly true of liquid 'soaps' which are basically detergent, not soap.[242]

Animal Ingredients

Some constituents of soap are derived from animals. Apart from the obvious animal fat or oil base, there is lanolin, from sheep's wool, and glycerine. Glycerine is a by-product in the conversion of animal or vegetable oils and fats into soap. Although soap's ingredients are rarely listed, those products without animal derivatives are usually labelled as such. The brands in this report which are vegetarian and vegan appear in the 'Cruelty-Free' box.

Environment

In its unadulterated state, soap is probably the most innocuous cleaning product humanity has ever come up with. However, many of today's manufacturers insist on adding ingredients to enhance their products and persuade consumers that they cannot survive without soap that matches the hue of their toilet.

Not only are products with added smell, smoothness and protection against perspiration no more effective, they may contain chemicals that are harmful to us as well as the environment. The bactericide hexachlorophane has been known to be added to soaps. This was also found in a baby powder in France in 1972, at ten times the recommended level. It was blamed for the deaths of thirty six babies as well as the suffering of many more.[106]

Where packaging is concerned many brands of soap are simply wrapped in a paper sheath, but Imperial Leather now has both plastic and cardboard packaging and liquid soaps come in plastic pump dispensers.

According to Karen Christensen, left over bits of soap can be kept and made into a soft jelly by adding boiling water. This can then be used as an alternative washing up liquid.[949]

Best Buys

We have not discovered any criticisms of the companies in the 'Cruelty-Free' box so all their brands are therefore Best Buys. We have also discovered no criticisms of Neutrogena but it does not appear in BUAV's 'Approved Product Guide' nor 'Animal-Free Shopper'.

(This article was first published in December 1990.)

Soap

Brand Name	South Africa	Oppressive Regimes	Trade Union Relations	Wages & Conditions	Land Rights	Environment	Irresponsible Marketing	Nuclear Power	Armaments	Animal Testing	Factory Farming	Other Animal Rights	Political Donations	Boycott Call	Company Group
Albion	■	◣		◣				■							Smith & Nephew
ASDA	■	■		◤			■	■	■						ASDA Group
Austrian Moor															Austrian Moor Products
Badedas	■	■			■	◤		■		◤	CON				SmithKline Beecham
Barry M															Barry M Cosmetics
Blackmores															Blackmores Ltd
Body Shop															Body Shop Int'l
Boots	■	■			◤	■		■		◦	CON		■		Boots
BWC															Beauty Without Cruelty plc
Camay	◤	■		◣				■		◤			■		Procter & Gamble
Camilla Hepper															Camilla Hepper
Caurnie															Caurnie Soap Company
Cidal	■	◣						■							Smith & Nephew
Clearasil	◤	■		◣				■		◤			■		Procter & Gamble
Cleopatra	■	■	■		■			■		■					Colgate-Palmolive
Co-op	■	■		◣			◤	■		◤	■	LAB			Co-op Movement
Cosmetics to Go!															Constantine & Weir
Creightons			◤												Creightons Naturally plc
Cussons		◣			◣										Paterson Zochonis
Dettol	■	■						■		■	BUI/CPS				Reckitt & Colman
Dove	■	◣		■	◣			■		■			■		Unilever
East of Eden															East of Eden International
Fairy	◤	■		◣				■		◤			■		Procter & Gamble
Faith Products															Faith Products
Fenjal	■	■			■	◣		■			CON				SmithKline Beecham
Fresh	■	■	■		■			■		■					Colgate-Palmolive
Gateway	■	■		◣				■	■	■					Isosceles
Holland & Barrett								■		CON					Lloyds Chemist
Honesty															Honesty Cosmetics Ltd
Imperial Leather		◣			◣										Paterson Zochonis
Johnson's Baby	■	■				■		■		USA					Johnson & Johnson
Kays															Kays (Ramsbottom) Ltd
Knights Castile	■	■	◣		■	◣		■		■			■		Unilever
Lifebuoy	■	■	◣		■	◣		■		■			■		Unilever
Lux	■	■	◣		■	◣		■		■			■		Unilever
Marks & Spencer	■	■		◣			■	■	■		CON				Marks & Spencer plc
Martha Hill															Martha Hill Ltd
Montagne Jeunesse															Montagne Jeunesse
Morrisons	■	■						■	■	■					Wm Morrison

Brand Name	South Africa	Oppressive Regimes	Trade Union Relations	Wages & Conditions	Land Rights	Environment	Irresponsible Marketing	Nuclear Power	Armaments	Animal Testing	Factory Farming	Other Animal Rights	Political Donations	Boycott Call	Company Group
My Fair Lady		◣			◣										Paterson Zochonis
Natural Beauty Products															Natural Beauty Products
Neutrogena															Neutrogena Corp
Nivea	■	◣		◣				■							Smith & Nephew
Palmolive	■	■	■	■				■	■						Colgate-Palmolive
Pearl		◣			◣										Paterson Zochonis
Pears	■	■	◣	■	◣			■	■					■	Unilever
Pure & Simple	■	■		■	◣			■			CON				SmithKline Beecham
Radox Moments	◣	■		◣	■				■						Sara Lee Corp
Safeway	■	■							■	■	CON				Argyll Group
Sainsbury's	■	■		◣					◣	■			■		J Sainsbury
Shield	■	■	◣	■	◣			■	■				■		Unilever
Silvikrin Supersoap	■	■		■	◣			■			CON				SmithKline Beecham
Simple	■	◣		◣	◣								■		Smith & Nephew
Sunlight	■	■	◣	■	◣			■	■				■		Unilever
Tesco	■	■		◣					■	■			■		Tesco
Tuesdays Girl															Tuesdays Girl Ltd
Waitrose	■	■							■	■	■				John Lewis
Weleda															Weleda (UK) Ltd
Wright's Coal Tar	■	◣								◣					London International Group
Zest	◣	■		◣				■		◣			■		Procter & Gamble

Cruelty-Free

The companies listed below appear in the BUAV 'Approved Product Guide 1993/94' and/or the Vegan Society's 'Animal-Free Shopper' so all their products are therefore not tested on animals. They also appear on the Table.

Vegan

Austrian Moor
East of Eden International
Faith Products
Honesty Cosmetics Ltd
Caurnie Soap Company

Vegetarian

Barry M Cosmetics
Blackmores
The Body Shop
Beauty Without Cruelty plc
Camilla Hepper
Creightons Naturally plc

Constantine & Weir
  (Cosmetics to Go!)
Kays (Ramsbottom) Ltd
Martha Hill Ltd
Montagne Jeunesse
Natural Beauty Products
Tuesdays Girl Ltd
Weleda (UK) Ltd

Tissue Paper Products

This report covers companies making kitchen towels, tissues and toilet paper.

The UK tissue paper market is dominated by some of the world's leading pulp and paper companies which, by and large, are involved in all the stages of paper production from the growing of the trees to the sale of toilet rolls. Other smaller companies appear on the Tables but they are supplied (probably by one of the main pulp & paper companies) with reels or cut sheets of tissue paper which they convert into consumer products. AM Paper Converters, Jeyes, Newcel Paper Converters, Peter Grant Papers, London Paper Products (Dhamecha Foods) and Kent Paper Products are all 'converters'.

Virgin Paper The UK's main supplies of wood come from fast-growing conifer and eucalyptus plantations in Canada, Sweden, Finland, USA, Portugal, Norway, Spain and Brazil.[1566] Native, mixed forests and their wildlife habitats are often destroyed to be replaced with these tightly spaced plantations of a single species of tree (monoculture) which are often non-native. There has been concern about the loss of animal and plant species due to this type of forestry, especially in Sweden.[1506] Eucalyptus monocultures are thirsty and greedy, and strip the soil of water and nutrients whilst returning little in the way of humus.[621] A new phenomenon is the destruction of tropical forests for the establishment of these plantations.[1136]

The most polluting aspect of the paper industry is the breaking down of the wood or the pulping. There are several pulping processes which all release carbon dioxide and sulphur into the air and discharge polluting effluent. Processes which use chlorine bleaching also produce highly toxic dioxins and other organochlorines. (For more information on this subject, see the Sanitary Protection report.) Consumers can discourage the use of this process by choosing tissue paper products labelled as 'unbleached' or 'unrebleached'.

Recycled Paper Recycled paper requires no plantations and uses half the amount of energy and a third of the water in its production. It is thus cheaper to produce, helps the UK balance of payments (because we import most of our virgin paper), and it cuts down on the amount of waste requiring disposal.

Although pulping of waste paper does not require the use of chlorine, many recycled products may contain material that has been chlorine-bleached in its previous life, and may have been rebleached with chlorine to make them whiter.

Recycled Con?

According to a 1990 Friends of the Earth study,[1140] products labelled as 'recycled' may not be as environmentally undamaging as we are led to believe. The waste paper that they are made from is usually high-grade waste that may be 'pre-consumer waste', such as mill and printers' off-cuts. Using this type of waste does not encourage recycling. Like using virgin paper, using high-grade waste for tissue products is both unnecessary and inappropriate. It is claimed that only the use of low-grade waste such as newspapers, magazines and packaging will encourage recycling.[1140]

Friends of the Earth urges producers to provide information about the type of waste used in their recycled products. They also urge consumers to choose products labelled as made from low-grade or post-consumer waste.[368]

The Alternatives

Recycled tissue products are obviously better than those made from virgin timber but they are still disposable items which will not be recycled. Reusable alternatives make far better economic and environmental sense.

In place of kitchen towels we could have reusable cotton dishcloths or towels and, for draining fatty, fried food, Karen Christensen in Home Ecology suggests using brown paper bags, envelopes or open cardboard egg cartons.

In place of tissues, everyone has handkerchiefs that used to be unwanted Christmas presents.

Toilet paper, however, does not seem to have an acceptable reusable alternative. Theoretically, any used paper such as newspapers can be used as toilet paper. On the continent, bidets are very popular and, of course, 90% of the world's population do without 'toilet paper'.

Best Buys

Best Buys for all three products are the recycled brands. We have not discovered any criticisms of the companies that own the Fluffy, Suma and Traidcraft brands. Look out especially for those labelled as made from low-grade or post-consumer waste and labelled as unbleached or unrebleached.

(This article was first published in April 1990.)

135

Brand Name	South Africa	Oppressive Regimes	Trade Union Relations	Wages & Conditions	Land Rights	Environment	Irresponsible Marketing	Nuclear Power	Armaments	Animal Testing	Factory Farming	Other Animal Rights	Political Donations	Boycott Call	Company Group
Kitchen Towels															
Babysoft				■											Fort Howard
Ballet	■	■		■				■							Kimberly-Clark
Checkpoint				■											Fort Howard
Dixcel Thick & Fast			◢	■				■							James River
Duette															AM Paper Converters
Fiesta			◢	■	■	◢		■					USA ■		Scott Paper Co
Fjord											■				Hazlewood Foods
Just				■											Fort Howard
Luxi											■				Hazlewood Foods
Scottowels			◢	■	■	◢		■					USA ■		Scott Paper Co
Studio				■											Fort Howard
Recycled kitchen towels															
Dixcel Family Choice			◢	■				■							James River
Kleenex Maxi Dri	■	■		■				■							Kimberly-Clark
Nouvelle				■											Fort Howard
Suma															Suma
Traidcraft															Traidcraft
Tissues															
Andrex			◢	■	■	◢		■					USA ■		Scott Paper Co
Checkpoint				■											Fort Howard
Dandy				■											Fort Howard
Dixcel			◢	■				■							James River
Fjord											■				Hazlewood Foods
Handy Andies			◢	■	■	◢		■					USA ■		Scott Paper Co
Just				■											Fort Howard
Kleenex	■	■		■											Kimberly-Clark
Ladylove															Kent Paper Products
Luxi											■				Hazlewood Foods
Scotties/Scottissues			◢	■	■	◢		■					USA ■		Scott Paper Co
Studio				■											Fort Howard
Three Dolphins															Dhamecha Foods
Whispers															Kent Paper Products
Recycled tissues															
Dixcel Family Value			◢		■			■							James River
Suma															Suma

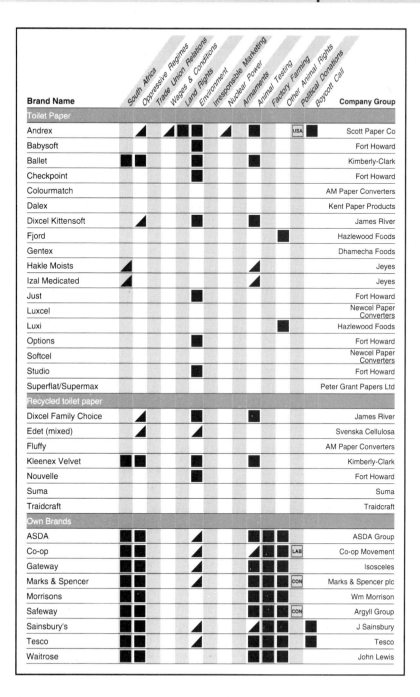

Brand Name	South Africa	Oppressive Regimes	Trade Union Relations	Wages & Conditions	Land Rights	Environment	Irresponsible Marketing	Nuclear Power	Armaments	Animal Testing	Factory Farming	Other Animal Rights	Political Donations	Boycott Call	Company Group
Toilet Paper															
Andrex	◣		◣	■	■		◣		■				USA	■	Scott Paper Co
Babysoft				■											Fort Howard
Ballet	■	■		■						■					Kimberly-Clark
Checkpoint				■											Fort Howard
Colourmatch															AM Paper Converters
Dalex															Kent Paper Products
Dixcel Kittensoft	◣					■				■					James River
Fjord											■				Hazlewood Foods
Gentex															Dhamecha Foods
Hakle Moists	◣						◣								Jeyes
Izal Medicated	◣						◣								Jeyes
Just				■											Fort Howard
Luxcel															Newcel Paper Converters
Luxi											■				Hazlewood Foods
Options				■											Fort Howard
Softcel															Newcel Paper Converters
Studio				■											Fort Howard
Superflat/Supermax															Peter Grant Papers Ltd
Recycled toilet paper															
Dixcel Family Choice	◣					■	·								James River
Edet (mixed)	◣					◣									Svenska Cellulosa
Fluffy															AM Paper Converters
Kleenex Velvet	■	■				■				■					Kimberly-Clark
Nouvelle						■									Fort Howard
Suma															Suma
Traidcraft															Traidcraft
Own Brands															
ASDA	■	■				◣				■	■	■			ASDA Group
Co-op	■	■				◣				◣	·		LAB		Co-op Movement
Gateway	■	■				◣				■	■	■			Isosceles
Marks & Spencer	■	■				◣				■	■	■	CON		Marks & Spencer plc
Morrisons	■	■								■	■	■			Wm Morrison
Safeway	■	■								■	■	■	CON		Argyll Group
Sainsbury's	■	■				◣				◣	■	■	■		J Sainsbury
Tesco	■	■				◣				◣	■	■	■		Tesco
Waitrose	■									■	■	■			John Lewis

Toothpaste

Ingredients Although only active ingredients are required to be listed, toothpastes may contain additives such as saccharin, titanium dioxide, fluoride and artificial flavours and colourings. Saccharin is an animal carcinogen.[617] Titanium dioxide is used to make toothpaste white, and whilst it is non-toxic in use, its manufacture results in the production of acid effluents.[620] Greenpeace has been campaigning against its production. Fluoride is a controversial issue. Received wisdom maintains that a certain amount is needed for healthy teeth, but too much has been linked with mottling of the teeth (dental fluorosis) and even cancer.[617] Fluoride is now already present in many people's water supply.

Herbal varieties of toothpaste are less likely to contain these additives (though Kingfisher contains fluoride), and many of them list their ingredients.

Alternatives Regular cleansing and a diet which minimises the consumption of acid-producing foods (such as sugar and alcohol), are essential for dental health. Regular cleansing does not, however, need to involve a toothpaste. Water, a little salt or baking soda with the addition of a few drops of peppermint oil are all adequate alternatives.[949]

Best Buys Best Buys for toothpaste are the cruelty-free companies for which we have not discovered any criticisms: Kingfisher, Tom's of Maine and Weleda and all those listed in the Cruelty-Free Box.

Clinomyn and Dentinox also do well on the Table and so they are second best. The Sarakan, Sensodyne, Amm-I-Dent, Revive and Topol brands would be best in the absence of any of these.

Cruelty-Free

The following cruelty-free companies are listed in the BUAV's 'Approved Product Guide 1992/3' and the Vegan Society's 'Animal-Free Shopper'. We have not discovered any criticisms for any of these companies.

Vegetarian	*Vegan*
Blackmores, Camilla Hepper, Constantine & Weir (Cosmetics to Go!), Creightons, Montagne Jeunnesse, Tom's of Maine, Weleda	Austrian Moor, East of Eden, Honesty, Kingfisher, Maxim Pharmaceuticals

Brand Name	South Africa	Oppressive Regimes	Trade Union Relations	Wages & Conditions	Land Rights	Environment	Irresponsible Marketing	Nuclear Power	Armaments	Animal Testing	Factory Farming	Other Animal Rights	Political Donations	Boycott Call	Company Group
Amm-I-Dent	■														Block Drug Co
Aquafresh	■	■		■	◤		■			◤			CON		SmithKline Beecham
ASDA	■	■		◤			■	■							ASDA Group
Boots	■	■		◤	■		■						CON	■	The Boots Co
Clinomyn															C B Fleet
Colgate	■	■	■	■			■			■					Colgate-Palmolive
Co-op	■	■		◤			◤	■		·			LAB		Co-op Movement
Crest	◤	■		◤			■			■				■	Procter & Gamble
Denivit	■	■		◤											Henkel
Dentinox															DDD Ltd
Eucryl	■	◤					◤								London International Group
Euthymol	■	■				■				■	■				Warner-Lambert
Gateway	■	■		◤						■	■				Isosceles
Gordon Moore	◤	■	◤			■				■					Sara Lee Corp
Kingfisher															Kingfisher Natural Toothpaste
Macleans	■	■		■	◤		■			◤			CON		SmithKline Beecham
Marks & Spencer	■	■		◤						■	■		CON		Marks & Spencer plc
Mentadent	■	■	◤	■	◤		■			·				■	Unilever
Morrisons	■	■								■	■				Wm Morrison
Oral-B	■	■		◤			■							■	Gillette
Pearl Drops	◤									■	■				Carter-Wallace
Phillips		■		■	■			■							Eastman Kodak
Punch & Judy	■	■				■				◤				■	Roche Holdings
Revive		■													Block Drug Co
Safeway	■	■								■	■	■	CON		Argyll Group
Sainsbury's	■	■		◤			◤			■				■	J Sainsbury
Sarakan										■					Arrowmed Ltd
Sensodyne		■													Block Drug Co
Signal	■	■	◤	■	◤					■	■			■	Unilever
SR	■	■	◤	■	◤					■	■			■	Unilever
Tesco	■	■		◤						·	■	■		■	Tesco
Tom's of Maine															Tom's of Maine
Topol										■					Dep Corp
Ultrabrite	■	■	■		■					■			■		Colgate-Palmolive
Waitrose	■	■								■	■	■			John Lewis
Weleda															Weleda AG
Wisdom	■	◤		◤											Addis BV

Washing Powder

This report assesses the records of manufacturers of powders
and the increasingly popular laundry liquids. The UK market
has traditionally been dominated by two giants, Unilever and
Procter & Gamble, accounting between them for 76% of the
UK market in 1990. It was only in 1989 that the environmental
debate surrounding detergents suddenly took off. Since then we
have witnessed a range of 'initiatives' from the major players
and the emergence of 'green' brands.

History From the launch of Unilever's Persil in 1909 to about 1950 the
main detergents were ordinary soap powders. These were
environmentally benign but less effective in very hard water.
By the 50s it had become possible to make petroleum based or
'soapless' detergents. Coupled with phosphates (acting mainly
as a water softener), these new detergents soon swept the
market. However, they decomposed so slowly that piles of
foam many feet thick could often be seen at sewage outlets, in
rivers and even out of taps.

The solution by the mid 60s was to make a petroleum-based
detergent that was more biodegradable (or soft). However it
was now that the phosphates were to be implicated in a series
of environmental disasters. Some of the first evidence
appeared in the US's Great Lakes (particularly Lake Erie) in
the 60s and 70s. Phosphates were acting as nutrients for algae
which could multiply so fast that they would use up all the
available oxygen, thus destroying all other life in the lake.

With the use of phosphates becoming severely restricted across
Europe, companies began to look for alternative softeners.
NTA was one of the first but was soon discovered to have
environmental consequences of its own - suspending poisonous
heavy metals in water. Phosphate use has now been greatly
reduced.

The recently introduced laundry liquids are all phosphate free
for chemical rather than environmental reasons. However,
they may contain three or four times more petroleum-based
detergent per wash.

**The
Environmental
Debate** The main problem with the debate is that very little
information comes from independent sources. The detergent
giants argued that phosphates were not an issue in the UK
because our fast flowing rivers tended not to be vulnerable to

Brand Name	South Africa	Oppressive Regimes	Trade Union Relations	Wages & Conditions	Land Rights	Environment	Irresponsible Marketing	Nuclear Power	Armaments	Animal Testing	Factory Farming	Other Animal Rights	Political Donations	Boycott Call	Company Group
ACDO															Astley Dye & Chemical
Albrite	◤	■			■		■	■	◤						Tenneco
Ariel	◤	■			◤			■		◤			■		Procter & Gamble
Ark															Ark Consumer Products
ASDA	■	■			◤			■	■	■					ASDA Group
Bio-D															Bio-D
Bold	◤	■			◤			■		◤			■		Procter & Gamble
Brightwhite	■	■			◤										Henkel
Clearspring															Faith Products
Co-op	■	■			◤			◤	■	LAB					Co-op Movement
Daz	◤	■			◤			■		◤					Procter & Gamble
Down to Earth	■	■	◤		◤			■		BUI/CPS					Reckitt & Coleman
Dreft	◤	■			◤			■		◤					Procter & Gamble
Ecover					◤										Ecover/Group 4
Fairy	◤	■			◤			■		◤			■		Procter & Gamble
Faith															Faith Products
Formula 7	■	■	◤	■	◤	■		■	■	◤	■		■		British Petroleum
Gateway	■	■			◤			■	■	■					Isosceles
Greenforce	■	■	◤	■	◤	■		■	■	◤	■		■		British Petroleum
Marks & Spencer	■	■			◤			■	■	CON					Marks & Spencer
Morrisons	■	■						■	■	■					Wm Morrison
Persil	■	■	◤		■	◤		■		■			■		Unilever
Q-Matic	■	■	◤	■	◤			■	■	◤			■		British Petroleum
Radion	■	■	◤		■	◤		■		■			■		Unilever
Safeway	■	■						■	■	CON					Argyll Group
Sainsbury's	■	■			◤			◤	■				■		J Sainsbury
Softmatic	■	■	◤	■	◤			■	■	◤	■		■		British Petroleum
Surcare	■	■	◤	■	◤			■	■	◤	■		■		British Petroleum
Surf	■	■	◤		◤			■		■			■		Unilever
Tesco	■	■			◤			■	■	◤					Tesco
Tide	◤	■			◤			■		◤			■		Procter & Gamble
Trend	■	■	◤	■	◤			■	■	◤			■		British Petroleum
Waitrose	■	■						■	■	■					John Lewis
Wisk	■	■	◤		■	◤		■		■			■		Unilever

algae growth. They have also argued that their products have been largely biodegradable since the 70s. These points, even if conceded, barely address the other question marks hanging over the industry. If petroleum is a limited resource wouldn't it be better to use vegetable-oil based detergents? What about all the other ingredients - the enzymes, the optical brighteners, the bleaches and the perfumes? What effect do they have? The mainstream industry has not really begun to answer these types of question publicly - and their behaviour looks very much like a rearguard action.

In a letter to supermarkets, the Chairman of the Soap and Detergent Industry Association (none other than John O'Keefe - the then managing director of P&G) sought the supermarkets' support to 'vet' the information on packets of alternative powders like Ecover. "Our concern is on the potential for confused and misleading information being communicated to consumers who are your customers."[685] At the most fundamental level, a 'green' or environmentally responsible consumer must have good quality information on which to base decisions. The newer 'green' powders have at least attempted to list their ingredients on the packet. Labelling from the majors has been very poor.

It is important to remember that manufacturers have an interest in making you use more than is actually necessary. Ecover has recommended quantities significantly lower than those on other products.

For more information on the debate about the environmental impact of detergents, see the Washing Up Liquid report.

For further information on ideas such as making your own washing powders see for example Home Ecology by Karen Christensen (Arlington Books 1989).

Ecover Ecover's products appear to have been formulated entirely from ingredients <u>known</u> to be environmentally benign, and it has produced extensive information on the reasoning behind its formulation decisions. However, it has fallen out with some UK environmentalists since Group 4 Securitas, which now owns 50% of the company, became involved in the removal of protestors from the Twyford Down anti-road demonstration.

Best Buys

(This article was first published in July 1989.)

We have found no criticisms of the companies owning the following brands: ACDO, Ark, Bio-D and Clearspring. These are therefore Best Buys. All are available in either liquid or powder form.

Washing-up Liquid

Washing-up liquids are a relatively new invention. Before the Second World War people washed their pots and pans with soap and water. Further back in the mists of time people would have used ash, straw or even sand.

The 'surfactants' that comprise the main ingredient of modern washing-up liquid separate dirt containing fats and oils from dirty dishes and cutlery and keep it suspended in the washing water. Surfactants are formed from either petroleum or vegetable oils (or, less commonly, animal fats).

Biodegradability

Surfactants in their unadulterated form have been found to have a high toxicity to aquatic organisms.[1504] It has been argued that even at low concentrations some surfactants will increase the penetration of other harmful chemicals through the protective layers of plants and animals.[1377] Recent research has shown that a concentration of just 1ppm (parts per million) of some surfactants can have a lethal effect on frogspawn.[102] Full biodegradability is thus of considerable importance so that surfactants being discharged from, say, sewage works would have no impact upon the aquatic environment.

Since the 1960s, surfactants have, by law, had to comply with certain levels of biodegradation. The OECD has set a minimum standard test whereby 80% of the surfactant has to have degraded in a period up to 19 days.[1504]

Petroleum itself is a very impure substance. Although it can be almost completely purified for goods such as baby products and cosmetics, this is not common practice for at least half the world's production of surfactant. The remaining impurities, and the complex structure of the petroleum molecules, can mean petroleum-based surfactants take longer to biodegrade, and in certain cases can lead to the creation of toxic substances during biodegradation.[102]

Vegetable-based surfactants, on the other hand, tend to be derived from nearly pure raw materials. Many of them have linear structures with an even number of carbon molecules, which enables them to biodegrade easily. For example, some coconut oil surfactants can degrade completely within five days in the OECD test.[319]

Washing-up Liquid

Renewability The renewability of vegetable oil as a resource, as opposed to the non-renewability of petroleum, is often seen as giving vegetable-based surfactants the environmental edge over petroleum-based ones.[319]

Production There is, however, another school of thought which argues that the cultivation, processing and manufacture of vegetable-based surfactants may give rise to environmental problems which might weigh against them in a comparison with oil derivatives. A recent study sponsored by Procter & Gamble attempted to undertake a Life Cycle Analysis (LCA) of different kinds of surfactant in the USA. From its findings, it concluded that there was no basis on which to maintain the superiority of one type of surfactant over the other.[1090]

The methodology for LCAs is still very much in its infancy and so we must be cautious as to how much weight we give these findings. For example, an unpublished study by the German detergent manufacturer, Henkel, is said to have come down in favour of vegetable-based surfactants in a cradle-to-grave environmental analysis of the issue.[381]

The debate on which type of surfactant should be used in washing-up liquids is confused by the fact that the chief proponents for each side of the argument tend to be the manufacturers using them. We at ECRA do not have the technical expertise to assess the conflicting claims of either side. Until an independent study appears which assesses the full environmental implications of each sort of surfactant, consumers will have to rely on their own judgement or intuition on the issue.

Brands that use vegetable-based surfactants include Amway, Ark, Bio-D, Caurnie, Clear Spring, Down-to-Earth, Ecover, Greencare (Sainsbury's), Honesty and Little Green Shop. Those washing-up liquids containing vegetable-based surfactants will usually indicate so on the bottle. It is probably safe to assume that if the content is not referred to, the product contains petroleum-based surfactants.

Other Ingredients Aside from surfactants, the other main ingredients of washing-up liquids include fragrances, colouring and preservatives. Unless it is specifically stated otherwise, these may be derived from a petrochemical source and may therefore have problems with biodegradability.[319] Contrary to what advertisers would like you to believe washing-up liquid does not contain phosphates and so labelling products as 'phosphate-free' is completely meaningless.[1708]

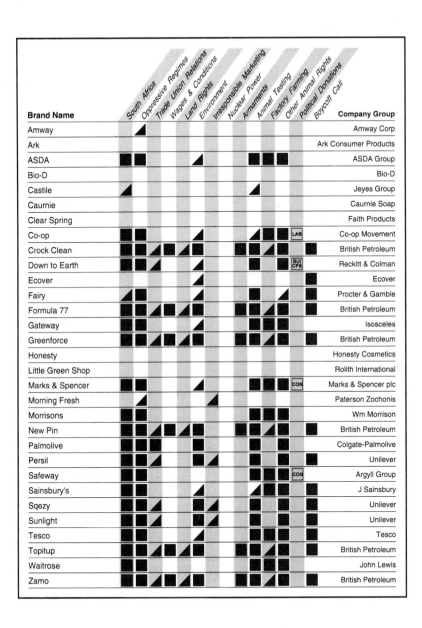

Brand Name	South Africa	Oppressive Regimes	Trade Union Relations	Wages & Conditions	Land Rights	Environment	Irresponsible Marketing	Nuclear Power	Armaments	Animal Testing	Factory Farming	Other Animal Rights	Political Donations	Boycott Call	Company Group
Amway	◣														Amway Corp
Ark															Ark Consumer Products
ASDA	■	■		◣			■	■	■						ASDA Group
Bio-D															Bio-D
Castile	◣							◣							Jeyes Group
Caurnie															Caurnie Soap
Clear Spring															Faith Products
Co-op	■	■		◣			◣	■	■				LAB		Co-op Movement
Crock Clean	■	■	◣	■	◣		■	■	◣				■		British Petroleum
Down to Earth	■	■	◣	◣			■						BUI/CPS		Reckitt & Colman
Ecover				◣									■		Ecover
Fairy	◣	■					■		◣				■		Procter & Gamble
Formula 77	■	■	◣	■	◣		■	■	◣				■		British Petroleum
Gateway	■	■		◣			■	■							Isosceles
Greenforce	■	■	◣	■	◣		■	■	◣				■		British Petroleum
Honesty															Honesty Cosmetics
Little Green Shop															Rolith International
Marks & Spencer	■	■		◣			■	■	■			CON			Marks & Spencer plc
Morning Fresh	◣			◣											Paterson Zochonis
Morrisons	■	■					■	■	■						Wm Morrison
New Pin	■	■	◣	■	◣		■	■	◣				■		British Petroleum
Palmolive	■	■	■	■			■	■							Colgate-Palmolive
Persil	■	■	◣	■	◣		■	■					■		Unilever
Safeway	■	■					■	■	CON						Argyll Group
Sainsbury's	■	■		◣			◣	■	■				■		J Sainsbury
Sqezy	■	■	◣	■	◣		■	■							Unilever
Sunlight	■	■	◣	■	◣		■	■							Unilever
Tesco	■	■		◣			■	■	■				■		Tesco
Topitup	■	■	◣	■	◣		■	■	◣				■		British Petroleum
Waitrose	■	■					■	■	■				■		John Lewis
Zamo	■	■	◣	■	◣		■	■	◣				■		British Petroleum

Washing-up Liquid

Healthy Washing-Up

The question of whether rinsing plates of the soap suds is really necessary, has been the subject of considerable research. One study has found that at the levels of surfactant that would be ingested by this method, there is no risk to human health. Another study suggests that surfactants in small quantities can be easily disposed of by the human body, via the liver and urine.[1504] However, the swallowing of neat washing-up liquid can cause severe damage to the upper digestive tract, which has suggested to some that even trace amounts left on plates may damage the delicate digestive tracts of very young children.

Which? suggests that rinsing might be a good idea, for gastronomic reasons, to remove any residual detergent or perfumes.[1708]

Alternatives

At its most simple, one could revert to using soap, or even ends of soap for doing the washing-up. It has been suggested by Karen Christensen, in 'Home Ecology',[949] that the soap pieces could be put in a wire shaker or a tea ball for ease of distribution. (This method would seem to be more appropriate to soft water areas.) Sodium bicarbonate or salt with a scrubbing brush are useful for stubborn stains. Rinsing or soaking things in water, immediately after use, is a good basic technique. For those preferring to use more 'conventional' methods of washing up, then the environmental concerns surrounding it would suggest that amounts used should be kept to the minimum.

Best Buys

The Ark, Bio-D, Caurnie, Clear Spring, Honesty and Little Green Shop brands are the Best Buys.

(This article was first published in September 1992.)

146

Companies Section

Companies
A to Z

STOP THE DUMPING!
WE ARE TO RE LABEL
THE BARRELS AS
LIFE SAVING DRUGS
AND SELL THEM TO
THE THIRD WORLD

DAVID HOLLAND

Below is a list of the companies that we have found criticisms of. These appear in alphabetical order with details of each mark that they receive on the Tables.
This is followed by the names and addresses of companies of which we have not discovered any criticisms.

Acatos & Hutcheson plc

Orchard Place, London E14 0JH

OAR: Pura Foods manufactures lard products.[1814]

Addis BV

NL-1102 BR Amsterdam Zuidoost, Koekenrode 8, Netherlands

SA: Listed as owning 25% of a company (Addis Brushes (Pty) Ltd.) in South Africa.[21] (See also refs: 13, 17)

OR: Addis owns a subsidiary in Sri Lanka.[21]

ENV: In 1990, Addis was fined £2,800 with £1,300 costs for marking domestic fire extinguishers containing halon-1211 "Non CFC propellant, ozone friendly". According to 'C for Chemicals', halon is a powerful ozone depleter and greenhouse gas. Most halons contain bromine which is an even more powerful ozone destroyer than the chlorine in CFCs.[373]

Alberto-Culver Co

2525 Armitage Avenue, Melrose Park, Il 60160, USA

OR: Alberto-Culver has subsidiaries operating in Guatemala, Honduras and Mexico.[21]

ENV: In a settlement in 1991 with ten US State Attornies General, it was agreed that Alberto-Culver must stop claiming that its hairsprays are 'ozone friendly' and 'environmentally safe' and must pay $50,000 to the respective states. The agreement settled charges brought by the Attornies General that although the aerosols do not contain ozone-depleting CFCs, they do contain volatile organic compounds (such as hydrocarbons) which can contribute to urban ozone or smog.[1832]
(See also refs: 3)

AT: Alberto-Culver does not carry out in-house animal testing, but testing for the company is conducted through outside laboratories.[3]
(See also refs: 1750, 1113, 10)

Allied Lyons plc

24 Portland Place, London W1N 4BB

SA: Allied Lyons has licensing, distribution or franchise agreements in South Africa.[1750] (See also refs: 1811)

OR: Allied Lyons is involved in Brazil, China, India,[1810] Indonesia,[3] Kenya, Sri Lanka and Uganda.[21]

ENV: Allied Lyons exceeded water pollution discharge consents more than 35 times in the year to March 1991, and has been convicted for a number of these offences.[20]

AT: In April 1992, Allied Lyons was listed as a subscriber to BIBRA through the Brewers' Society.[1]

OAR: Allied Lyons owns Lyons Seafoods and Becker Meat Products.[21]

PD: Allied Lyons gave £80,000 to the Conservative Party in 1991/2.[1811]

BC: Allied Lyons appears on the Mid-Somerset Earth First! boycott list of companies which make health foods and which are involved in unethical practices.[1168]

Altana Industrie Aktien und Anlagen

D-6380 Bad Homburg vdH, Seedammweg 55, Germany

SA: Altana has operations in South Africa...

OR: ...and in Brazil and Mexico.[21]

IM: Milupa is one of the major violators of the WHO Baby Milk Marketing Code. It was found to be totally or substantially violating several sections concerning labelling, promotion in healthcare facilities, promotion to healthcare workers, giving free samples and the marketing of soft foods.[14]

Milupa has also been criticised for its marketing of heavily sugared baby herbal drinks. In December 1990, a Frankfurt court ordered the company to pay compensation to parents for causing severe dental caries in two children. The company was accused of negligence and providing insufficient warnings on packaging about the sugar content of its products. About 100,000 children are said to have suffered severe tooth damage from these drinks marketed by Milupa and other producers.[1847]

OAR: Some of Milupa's baby foods contain meat.[1790]

American Home Products

685 Third Avenue, New York, NY 10017, USA

SA: AHP has a licensing, distribution or franchising agreement in South Africa.[1750]

OR: The company operates in Brazil, Colombia, Egypt, India, Iran, Mexico, Peru, the Philippines and Turkey.[21]

IM: Wyeth is one of the major violators of the WHO baby milk marketing code. It is listed as totally or substantially violating the Code's requirements of no promotion in healthcare facilities, no promotion to health workers and no free samples or supplies.[14]

Companies

Wyeth also manufactures the benzodiazepine tranquilliser, Ativan. It is one of the companies which has been criticised for not warning doctors of the drug's possible addictiveness and therefore of the need to prescribe it for short periods only.[235]

AT: The company tests its products on animals and continues to use acute toxicity tests such as the Draize test.[15]

PD: In 1987/88, AHP gave $41,300 to US political campaigns.[15]

BC: AHP is the subject of boycott calls in the US and Australia for its irresponsible marketing of baby milk.[88, 1848]

Amway Corp

7575 East Fulton Road, Ada, Michigan 49301, USA

OR: Amway owns a company in Guatemala.[21]

Anheuser-Busch Cos Inc

One Busch Place, St Louis, Mo 63118, USA

OR: Anheuser-Busch has a subsidiary in Brazil.[21]

BC: In February 1992, a boycott of Budweiser beer was called by the British Whale and Dolphin Conservation Society because orca (killer) whales are kept in Anheuser-Busch's Sea World marine parks in the USA.[1866] In December 1990, a separate boycott of Anheuser-Busch was called by the US group The Dolphin Project, for its alleged inhumane treatment of dolphins in the Sea World parks.[190]
(See also refs: 1761)

Archer-Daniels-Midland

4666 Faries Parkway, Box 1470, Decatur, IL 62525, USA

OR: A-D-M operates in Brazil.[21]

ENV: According to the CEP publication 'Shopping for a Better World', A-D-M has "a poor public record of significant violations, major accidents and/or history of lobbying against sound environmental policies".[1446]

IM: Granose has been accused of violating the WHO Code on the marketing of soft foods. It promotes and labels its foods for babies at an earlier age than is nutritionally necessary.[2]

BC: Archer-Daniels-Midland appears on the Mid-Somerset Earth First! boycott list of companies which make health foods and which are involved in unethical practices.[1168]

Argyll Group

Argyll House, Millington Road, Hayes, Middlesex UB3 4AY

SA: Argyll sells own-label fresh and tinned fruit that is sourced from South Africa...

OR: ...and Brazil, China, Honduras, India, Israel, Kenya, Mexico, Peru and Turkey.[320]

AT: Safeway cannot guarantee that the ingredients of its own-brand toiletries are not tested on animals by its suppliers.[1097]
(See also refs: 3)

FF: Safeway stocks meat and eggs that are not labelled as free range or with other animal welfare symbols.[320]

OAR: Safeway stocks meat products.[320]

PD: In the year to 31/3/91, Argyll gave £30,000 to the Conservative Party.[1076]

Armitage Brothers

Armitage House, Colwick Industrial Estate, Nottingham NG4 2BA

OAR: Although the company's Wafcol dog food is vegetarian, Rathburns produces leather leads.[1849]

Arrowmed Ltd

Pyramid House, 59 Winchester Road, Four Marks, Alton, Hants GU34 5HP

OAR: According to BUAV, some Arrowmed products contain slaughterhouse by-products.[136]

ASDA Group

ASDA House, Southbank, Great Wilson Street, Leeds LS11 5AD

SA: ASDA stocks South African produce.[3, 320]

OR: ASDA stocks products sourced from oppressive regimes, including: Brazil, China, Colombia, Honduras, India, Israel, Kenya, Lebanon, Mexico, the Philippines and Uruguay.[320]

ENV: Sells furniture made from tropical hardwood in some 30 of its 180 Allied Maples stores, but the company is reviewing its position on this.[3]

AT: Ingredients used in ASDA own brands may have been tested on animals, and it stocks branded cosmetics, toiletries and household products that do not say that they are not animal tested.[3 320]

FF: ASDA stocks factory-farmed meat and eggs.[320]

OAR: ASDA supplies meat produce in its stores.[320]

Avon Products

9 West 57th Street, New York, NY 10019, USA

OR: Avon owns companies in Brazil, Colombia, China, El Salvador, Guatemala, Honduras, Mexico, Peru and the Philippines.[21, 3]

IM: Avon Banishing Cream - a brand of skin lightener containing hydroquinone on sale in Malaysia - has been criticised by the Consumers' Association of Penang. Prolonged use of hydroquinone, combined with exposure to the sun, can result in patchy pigmentation and lumpiness of the skin, both of which are irreversible. A London dermatologist has said that there is no evidence to suggest that hydroquinone is safe even at low levels.[1835]

PD: In 1987/88, Avon gave $64,486 in federal donations.[15]

F W Baker

The Abattoir, Crick, Northampton NN6 7TZ

OAR: The company's dog food contains meat.[1790]

Basler Handels-Gesellschaft

Petersgraben 35, CH-4003 Basel, Switzerland

OR: Basler owns an associate company in China.[21]

Bass plc

66 Chiltern Street, London W1N 1PR

SA: Bass owns Holiday Inns which has twenty two hotels in South Africa.[3]

OR: The company has operations in Brazil, China, Indonesia, Mexico, Peru and the Philippines.[21]

LR: Holiday Inns is one of the companies vying for space on the Goa coastline, where the government is taking land from local people to sell to hoteliers. Swimming pools at new developments have already put pressure on fresh water supplies and the destruction of dunes has left villages vulnerable to cyclones.[1742]

ENV: Bass Brewers was listed on 31/12/91 as a member of the BRF.[1743]

Bass exceeded its discharge consent at least once between 1/4/88 and 31/3/91 according to the NRA and/or the RPBS.[20]
(See also LR above.)

AT: Bass subscribed to BIBRA in 1992 through the Brewers Society.[1]

W A Baxter & Sons Ltd

Northern Preserve Works, Fochabers, Morayshire IV32 7LD

OAR: Baxter manufactures products containing meat and game.[668]

PD: It gave £5,600 to the Conservative Party in 1989 and £5,000 in 1990.[1076]

Benckiser Holding

D-67000 Ludwigshafen 1, Benckiserplatz 1, Postfach 21 01 67, Germany

SA: Benckiser was listed in 1988 as owning a company in South Africa[6]...

OR: ...and currently owns one in Turkey.[21]

Edward Billington & Son Ltd

Cunard Building, Liverpool L3 1EL

OAR: Edward Billington has meat packing and animal feeds businesses.[21]

Block Drug Co Inc

257 Cornelison Avenue, Jersey City, NJ 07302, USA

OR: The Block Drug Co owns companies in Brazil, Colombia, Mexico and the Philippines.[21]

Booker

Portland House, Stag Place, London SW1E 5AY

OR: Booker owns companies in Brazil, Colombia. India and Mexico.[21]

ENV: Middlebrook Mushrooms exceeded its discharge consents for pesticides DDT, Aldrin, Dieldrin, Endrin and Gamma Lindane a total of seventeen times in 1990-91. All these pesticides are on the government's 'Red List' of substances presenting the greatest hazard to the environment due to their toxicity.[20]

FF: Booker owns Arbor Acres Farm, the world's largest chicken breeding business with operations in twenty six countries.[823] Booker's subsidiaries in the Third World are mainly involved in poultry production or breeding.[1447] Booker said in 1991 "...we are proud of our part in providing low cost protein to feed people in poor countries."[1854]

OAR: Fitch Lovell is a leading manufacturer of meat products,[3] and also breeds fish.[1447]

PD: Fitch Lovell gave £5,000 to the BUI in the financial year to 30/4/89.[1087]

BC: Booker is on the Mid-Somerset Earth First! boycott list of companies which make health foods and which are involved in unethical practices.[1168]

Boots plc

1 Thane Road West, Nottingham NG2 3AA

SA: Boots owns three companies in South Africa[21]...

OR: ...and companies in India, Kenya, the Philippines and Uganda.[21]

ENV: According to the NRA, Boots exceeded its river discharge consent at least once in the year to March 1991.[20] It jointly owns Do-It-All with WH Smith. Do-It-All timber is currently the subject of a boycott call by Friends of the Earth for its sale of tropical hardwood.[305]

Companies

IM: Boots owns the Farley baby milk company which was listed in 1991 as one of the six worst violators of the World Health Organisation's marketing code. It promotes its baby milk in hospitals and to health workers in the Third World, and gives out free samples.[14]

In April 1993, Boots revealed that its heart drug, Manoplax, can lead to significantly higher mortality. Boots said that clinical trials showed that patients with severe congestive heart failure taking 100mg of Manoplax had a "significantly increased risk of death compared with those not receiving the drug". Manoplax has been on sale in the UK since September 1992 and in the USA since March 1993.[1856] (See also refs: 2, 3, 89)

AT: Boots tests its drugs on animals but says its own-brand cosmetics and toiletries are not animal-tested.[3]

OAR: Farley makes baby food containing meat.[694]

PD: Boots owns the Ward White group which gave £7,500 to the Conservative Party in 1988.[1087]

BC: Boots is targeted by two groups for its use of animal testing, ALIU and London Boots Action. Do-It-All timber is also targeted by Friends of the Earth (see under ENV above).

British Petroleum Company

Britannic House, Moor Lane, London EC2Y 9BU

SA: BP has interests in South Africa, including a 50% share in the country's largest oil refinery.[478]

OR: It owns subsidiaries in Bahrain, Brazil, Egypt, Haiti, India, Indonesia, Iran, Kenya, Liberia, Mali, Mauritania, Niger, Papua New Guinea and Turkey.[21]

TU: In July 1988 the Piper Alpha disaster led to a series of strikes on North Sea oil rigs. Workers wanted union recognition and improved safety rights. BP did not agree and started to recruit non-union labour.[1072]

W&C: In 1990, two explosions in ten days at BP's Grangemouth refinery cost the lives of three workers and the company £750,000 for breaches of the Health and Safety at Work Act.[1088,1785] In 1989 a number of workers at two BP-owned plants in Brazil were said to be suffering from pulmonary silicosis, as a result of inhaling dust containing silica at the plants.[4]
(See also refs: 711, 1072, 1797, 1798, 1799, 1800)

LR: BP has been criticised a number of times in the past for its mineral operations on tribal peoples' lands.[402,627,1795] The company has now pulled out of minerals. It does however continue to search for oil and, along with other companies, it has been criticised for operations in the Amazon, where a number of Indian Reserves have been affected.[312] For example, in association with Brascan, BP had 112 companies seeking concessions in 1987 in Brazil alone.[312] The company is no longer prospecting for oil in Brazil, but continues to do so in other Amazonian countries.[312]

ENV: In February 1991, a 300,000 gallon spill from a BP-chartered oil tanker spread for twenty square miles and severely disrupted the environment of nearby Huntington beach in California.[1130] The State of California then drafted new legislation to improve tanker safety and to elicit a $500m spill response fund to be paid for by the oil companies.[86] This was part of the far-reaching 'Big Green' environmental proposals defeated in late 1990 by a 3:2 majority. BP spent $171,000 to help oppose the bill.[1320]

BP has also been exploring for oil in Ecuadorean rainforest.[1308]

BP operations also feature in the Greenpeace Filthy 50 list[1748] and in Friends of the Earth's Secret Polluters list.[1770]
(See also refs: 20, 298, 312, 383, 398, 402, 404, 418, 761, 814, 900, 1123, 1128, 1261, 1620, 1746, 1787, 1788, 1789, 1796, 1797, 1801, 1870, 1871, 1872)

ARMS: Between 1985-9 BP received contracts from the Ministry of Defence for more than £100 million and is the supplier of strategic and non-civilian products used in weapons systems.[1171]
(See also refs: 3)

AT: BP has animal testing undertaken by sub-contractors.[3] In April 1992, two subsidiaries of BP were listed as being members of BIBRA.[1]

FF: Through its subsidiary BP Nutrition, the company is involved in breeding animals,[3] including poultry layers.[1378]

OAR: BP Nutrition owns petfood businesses which supply meat-based products.[115]

BC: BP appears on the Mid-Somerset Earth First! boycott list of companies which make health foods and which are involved in unethical practices.[1168]

Britvic Soft Drinks

Britvic Soft Drinks is owned 50% by Bass, 20% by Allied Lyons, 20% by Whitbread and 10% by Pepsico Inc. On the Table Bass' record, as the largest shareholder, appears in black. The records of Allied Lyons and Whitbread, as minority shareholders, appear in lighter-shaded squares. Pepsico's record appears in black on the Table, where it is the licensor of a brand, and in lighter squares where it is not. See the individual entries for the records of these four companies.

BSN

7 rue de Tehran, F75008 Paris, France

OR: BSN has subsidiaries in Brazil and Mexico, and associates in China and India.[21] Through its subsidiary, Gallia, BSN also has links with Niger.[2]

IM: BSN owns Nutripharm and Jacquemaire, both of which have been criticised for their irresponsible marketing of baby milks in the Third World. These criticisms include the companies' use of promotion in healthcare facilities, providing free samples and the inappropriate marketing of soft foods.[14]
(See also refs: 2)

OAR: BSN produces meat products, including Lea & Perrins which contains anchovies,[1790] and jointly owns Galbani, an Italian company which produces salted meats.[472]

BC: BSN appears on the Mid-Somerset Earth First! boycott list of companies which make health foods and which are involved in unethical practices.[1168]

Companies

H P Bulmer plc

The Cider Mills, Plough Lane, Hereford HR4 0LE

OR: Bulmer owns companies in Mexico and Brazil.[21]

ENV: Bulmer was listed in December 1991 as being a member of the BRF.[1743]

Cadbury-Schweppes plc

1-4 Connaught Place, London W2 2EX

SA: Cadbury-Schweppes has a number of subsidiaries in South Africa,[21] and in 1989 had 2,745 employees there. It bought its South African subsidiary Bromor Food in October 1986, the very month that the UK government announced the voluntary ban on new investment in South Africa.[13]

OR: Cadbury has subsidiaries in Brazil, Egypt, India, Indonesia and Kenya.[21]

W&C: Cadbury-Schweppes appears on a 1992 TUC list of companies which pay under the EC recommended level of wages in South Africa.[1755]

ENV: A plant belonging to PT Trebor Indonesia was cited by the Indonesian authorities in 1991 as the biggest polluter of the Ciliwung river in Jakarta,[287] the pollution from which has been said to have affected the local people since the 1970s.[1754] The company failed to meet a two year deadline, set by the Indonesian government, to clean up its act which then had to be extended a further six months to December 1991. By March 1992, the company had still failed to install the necessary screening equipment[1754] and admitted that it would not have the equipment up and running by the end of 1992.[1753]

The company has also been involved in water pollution incidents in the UK. According to the registers of the National Rivers Authority and/or the River Purification Boards of Scotland, in the year to 31/3/91 the company exceeded its discharge consent three or more times.[20]

AT: In April 1992 Cadbury-Schweppes was listed as subscribing to BIBRA.[1]

Carlsberg A/S

Vesterfoelledvej 100, DK-1799 Kobenhavn V, Denmark

AT: In April 1992, Carlsberg Brewery was listed as a subscriber to BIBRA, through its membership of the Brewers' Society.[1]

Carter-Wallace

1345 Avenue of the Americas, New York, NY 10105, USA

OR: Carter-Wallace has a subsidiary in Mexico.[21]

AT: According to the CEP, Carter-Wallace tests its products on animals.[1750] (See also refs: 10)

OAR: Carter-Wallace is involved in the manufacture of leather goods.[21]

156

Clarins SA

4 rue Berteaux Dumas, F-92200 Neuilly-sur-Seine, France

OR: Clarins owns two companies in Mexico.[21]

The Coca-Cola Co

1 Coca-Cola Plaza, Northwest Atlanta, GA 30313, USA

SA: Although the company sold its South African operations in 1986, products bearing its trademark are still on sale in South Africa and accounted for 69% of the total soft drinks market there in 1988.[15]

OR: Coca-Cola has subsidiaries in Brazil, Colombia, Papua New Guinea and the Philippines.[21]

ENV: In 1985 Coca-Cola bought 200,000 acres of tropical rainforest in Belize to plant orange groves. After protests from worldwide environmental groups, Coca-Cola sold most of the land but retained 50,000 acres, including 25,000 suitable for orange plantations.[15, 146]

In 1991, Doosan Electro-Materials Co, a South Korean company which manufactures some Coca-Cola products, was involved in what has been described as the country's 'worst environmental scandal'. Doosan admitted leaking phenol into a river which supplied drinking water to 10 million people. According to the International Herald Tribune, Singapore, consumer groups there boycotted products produced by Doosan, including Coca-Cola.[230]

IM: Coca-Cola sells its diet-Coke brand, containing saccharin, in Malaysia where the law requires that such drinks should say "requires the supervision of a physician" on the label. The Consumers' Association of Penang claims that while such warnings do appear on diet Coke cans, they are printed too small to be seen.[1762]

AT: In 1992, Coca-Cola was involved in testing the toxicity of the colorant Caramel on rats.[1876] It was also listed in April 1992 as subscribing to BIBRA.[1]

OAR: Coca-Cola owns shrimp ponds in Ecuador.[1757]

PD: The company gave $129,340 to Democrat candidates and $86,350 to Republican candidates for political campaigns in 1987-8.[15]

BC: Coca-Cola is currently the target of a boycott called by the US Coke Disinvestment Campaign, because of the company's failure to fully divest from South Africa.[1848] The US-based Irish National Caucus has also called for a boycott of Coca-Cola for its endorsement of 'discrimination in sports' by advertising at a stadium in Belfast owned by a team which reportedly discriminates against Catholic players.[1848]

Colgate-Palmolive

300 Park Avenue, New York, NY 10022, USA

SA: Owns a subsidiary in South Africa, and in 1990 had a 27% share of the South African detergents market.[21, 19]
(See also refs: 3, 15)

Companies

OR: Colgate-Palmolive has subsidiaries in: Angola, Brazil, Colombia, Egypt, Guatemala, India, Indonesia, Kenya, Mexico, Morocco, Papua New Guinea, Peru, the Philippines, Senegal, Sri Lanka and Turkey.[21]

TU: Colgate has been criticised for anti-union practices against SINTRACOLPA, a union at one of its plants in Colombia. Included in the accusations are that the company offered higher remuneration and benefits to non-union members and then, in April and May 1990, suspended union leaders who had protested against these discriminatory measures.[18]
(See also refs: 15)

ENV: In March 1992 thousands of protestors took to the streets of Mexico City to protest against the polluting practices and excessive water consumption of the company's local factory. Demands for relocation of the plant to outside the city have been made by local officials amongst others and have so far been ignored. Talks with local citizens were called off in November 1991.[1228]
(See also refs: 885)

AT: Colgate-Palmolive has animal testing undertaken for it by outside contractors.[3] BUAV recently uncovered details of an experiment carried out for the company by Columbia University in which guinea pigs were locked into small plastic tubes and a strong solution of surfactant was applied for four hours a day for three days, causing cracked and bleeding skin on the animals.[139]
(See also refs: 10, 15)

OAR: Colgate owns a company which makes meat-based pet food.[575]
(See also refs: 1772)

Co-operative Movement

CWS: P O Box 53, New Century House, Manchester M60 4ES

CRS: 29 Dantzic Street, Manchester M60 4ES

The two largest Co-operative societies are Co-operative Retail Services (CRS) which operates about 800 Co-op stores and the Co-operative Wholesale Society (CWS) which operates approximately 400 stores. The CWS, in addition, is the manufacturing and wholesaling arm for the Co-op Movement as a whole. It is also the producer and/or wholesaler of the Co-op own-brands. CWS holds 10% of the shares of CRS, while CRS owns about 30% of the CWS. The CWS is, in fact, entirely owned by the various retail co-operative societies.

Because of the close links between the societies, we are combining their records to give a record for the Co-operative Movement as a whole. Because of the independence of many of the societies not every criticism may apply to them all.

SA: CWS and CRS have resumed trading links with South Africa.[75, 196]

OR: The Co-op stocks produce from oppressive regimes, including: Brazil, China, India and Turkey. CWS is also listed as a retailer of Jaffa Israeli fruit in the Fresh Produce Journal.[320 1816]

ENV: Associated Co-operative Creameries Ltd, a subsidiary of CWS, has been fined £1,500 on three separate occasions, in cases brought by the NRA for water pollution incidents on 24/4/90, 18/2/91 and 27/3/91. The company was also made to pay additional costs, damages and compensation.[11]

CWS has a limited use for tropical hardwoods, but states this area is under review.[3]

AT: The Co-op own-brand cosmetics, toiletries and household products fulfil BUAV's non-animal testing criteria but it continues to stock branded items not included in the BUAV guide.[3][253]

FF: The Co-op stocks factory-farmed meat and eggs.[320]

OAR: The Co-op is Britain's largest farmer and has a large dairy farming business and milk distribution system.[828] It stocks meat products in its stores.[320]

PD: Both CWS and CRS regularly make political donations to the Co-operative Party, which has close links with the Labour Party.[3] The CWS South East Retail Group gave £25,000 to the Labour Party in 1989.[257]

Adolph Coors Co

1819 Denver West Drive, Building 26, Suite 400, Golden, Colorado 80401, USA

OR: Coors has a subsidiary in Brazil.[21]

ENV: In May 1992, Coors spilt 150,000 gallons of beer into Clear Creek, Denver, causing the death of 17,000 fish.[1882]

In November 1989, Coors was fined $650,000 for dumping contaminated water in Denver Creek from its plant in Colarado, USA. Coors was listed as one of Multinational Monitor's Ten Worst Companies of 1990 for this and other reasons. According to Multinational Monitor, it is controlled by an "anti-environment, anti-women, anti-gay, anti-minority...right-wing family."[1205]
(See also refs: 1209)

IM: In December 1990, a coalition of public interest and environment groups in the USA awarded Coors an award for one of the year's "most misleading, unfair or irresponsible" advertising campaigns. It had run a campaign of drinks advertising using the slogan "The Search for Halloween Headquarters", which was deemed likely to attract children.[1205]

CPC International

PO Box 8000, International Plaza, Eaglewood Cliffs, NJ 07632 USA

OR: The company operates in Brazil, Colombia, Guatemala, Honduras, Morocco and the Philippines.[21]

AT: In 1988, CPC awarded research contracts worth $15,000 to US company Biosearch for experiments in which rats and mice were drowned in Mazola cooking oil to test the validity of a single consumer's complaint.[1109]
(See also refs: 1115)

OAR: CPC's food interests include Bovril and Knorr soups, which contain meat products.[1790]

Croda International

Cowick Hall, Snaith, Goole, Humberside DN14 9AA

SA: Croda has operations in South Africa[21]...

OR: ...and Brazil and Mexico.[21]

Companies

ENV: Three Croda subsidiaries were fined a total of £5,500 between 1989 and 1990 for several pollution incidents. These included spillages of tarry and phenolic wastes from a bitumen works.[380]

Croda Chemicals' plant in Goole is included on Greenpeace's 'Filthy 50' list as one of the companies with the largest consents for discharging toxic chemicals, such as mercury, cadmium, lead and lindane. It was also found to be polluting illegally on seventeen chemicals in thirteen samples taken since 1991.[1748]
(See also refs: 11)

AT: In April 1992, several Croda subsidiaries were listed as subscribers to BIBRA.[1]

OAR: Croda manufactures animal and marine fats and oils.[21]

Helene Curtis Industries

325 North Wells Street, Chicago, Il 60610-4972, USA

AT: Helene Curtis Industries was listed by PETA in 1991 as testing its products on animals.[10]

Dalgety

100 George Street, London W1H 5RH

SA: Dalgety has largely withdrawn from South Africa but still supplies some products there.[3]

OR: The company has subsidiaries in Brazil and Mexico and an associate in China.[21]

ENV: Dalgety Agriculture Ltd was prosecuted on 23/11/89 in a case brought by NRA for a water pollution offence in the South West region on 9/8/89. The company was fined £1,000 plus £290 costs.[11]

AT: In April 1992, Dalgety and Spillers Premier Products were listed as subscribers to BIBRA.[1]

FF: Dalgety's interests include sheep, goat and beef cattle farming, and it owns the Pig Improvement Company.[21]

OAR: It has meat-based pet food and animal feeds businesses.[21]

Del Labs Inc

565 Broad Hollow Road, Farmingdale, NY 1735, USA

AT: Del Labs and Sally Hansen are both listed as testing their products on animals.[10]

Denes Veterinary Herbal Products

2 Osmond Road, Hove, E Sussex BN3 1TE

OAR: The company's pet food contains animal derivatives.[1849]

Dep Corp

2101 Via Arada, Rancho Dominguez, CA 90220 6189, USA

OAR: According to BUAV, some Dep products contain slaughterhouse by-products.[136]

Dole Food Co

31355 Oak Crest Drive, Westlake Village, Ca 91361, USA

OR: Dole owns companies in Colombia, Honduras and the Philippines.[21]

W&C: In June 1992, a Standard Fruit worker in Honduras died of cancer believed to have been caused by his exposure to DBCP, a pesticide banned in the USA. A lawsuit against the company was filed in the USA by Honduran workers in 1992.[1236] In a similar case in the USA in 1991, Costa Rican workers sued the company for continuing to use DBCP there until 1979, although it knew in 1977 that the pesticide caused sterility in workers. The Costa Rican government banned its import and use in 1979 by which time between 1000 and 3000 Standard Fruit plantation workers had been made sterile from working with the chemical. As a result of the ban, Standard Fruit exported remaining stocks of DBCP to Honduras.[1758]

The Stop the Philippines Bananas Pesticide Campaign, instigated in 1985 by Japanese consumer groups, criticised Dole subsidiary Stanfilco for supplying pesticides not registered for use in Japan (some of which WHO classify as 'extremely hazardous') to independent banana growers in the Philippines. A Filipino union leader who took part in the campaign, Oscar Bantayan, was murdered in 1988 and his death was attributed to government-backed paramilitary groups.[614]
(See also refs: 1750, 1795)

ENV: In a report in the November 1992 Ecologist, the banana industry in Costa Rica, (Dole, Chiquita and Del Monte), was described as the main agent of deforestation there. Forest is either felled and burned to clear land for plantations or local farmers are pushed off their land to make way for the plantations and move into the rainforest where they clear more land to farm.[1858]

In March 1992, Standard Fruit was found guilty by the International Water Tribune of contaminating the River Estrella in Costa Rica with pesticides.[1757]

According to the CEP, Dole has a poor public record of significant violations, major accidents and/or a history of lobbying against sound environmental policies.[1750]
(See also ref: 418)

OAR: Dole farms prawns in the Philippines.[1545]

BC: Dole pineapples and bananas are currently the subject of a boycott in the USA initiated in 1989 by the Fresh Fruit/Veg Workers union for the company's dumping of banned pesticides in developing countries, discrimination against women and unfair labour practices in the USA.[1848, 1758] Dole's Colombian bananas are also included in the boycott called in response to the suppression of human rights in the banana industry there.

Companies

Eastman Kodak

343 State Street, Rochester, NY 14650, USA

OR: Kodak owns companies in Brazil, Egypt, Iran, Kenya, Mexico, Peru and Uganda.[21]

ENV: In 1988, a pipeline at a Kodak plant in the USA broke and spilled 30,000 gallons of methylene chloride near a school and residential area. Methylene chloride is a possible carcinogen. Tests conducted in 1989 showed that 11 other chemicals were present in the groundwater around the plant in amounts exceeding state guidelines. In 1987 it was named as the largest single emitter of methylene chloride in the USA for which it was fined $2 million in 1990.[15] According to 1989 US EPA data, Kodak was the ninth worst toxic chemical polluter in the USA and one of the leading releasers of 'known or suspected carcinogens'.[1775] The Workington plant of a Kodak subsidiary, Ectona Fibres, is number one on Friends of the Earth's 1992 list of the top 100 'Secret Polluters'. The plant is allowed to discharge up to 682kg of toxic metals every day into the sewers.[1770]

IM: In 1989, its drug company, Sterling Winthrop, was criticised for its marketing of the painkiller, dipyrone, for minor applications in the Philippines, Indonesia and many other Third World countries. Dipyrone is banned or restricted in many countries and should only be prescribed for severe pain because it can cause the potentially fatal disease, agranulocytosis (lack of white blood cells).[279]

ARMS: In 1991, a Kodak US subsidiary received about $85 million in contracts for explosives and ammunition.[1774]
(See also refs: 15, 1750)

AT: Kodak tests its industrial chemicals and drugs on animals.[15]
(See also refs: 1, 10, 1750)

OAR: Kodak owns a company producing gelatine.[21]

Ecover/Group 4 Securitas (International)

NL-2508 CP Den Haag, Prinsevinkenpark 2, Postbus 85911, Netherlands
In October 1992, Group 4 Securitas bought a 50% shareholding in Ecover.

ENV: Group 4 has been criticised for its role in the violent removal of protestors attempting to prevent work on the M3 extension through Twyford Down.[1863]

BC: Ecover appears on the Mid-Somerset Earth First! boycott list of companies which make health foods and which are involved in unethical practices.[1891]

ESS-Food

Axelborg, Axeltorv 3, DK-1609, Kobenhavn V, Denmark

OAR: ESS-Food has a subsidiary called Danish Bacon.[21]

James Finlay plc

Finlay House, 10-14 West Nile Street, Glasgow G1 2PP

OR: James Finlay has subsidiaries in Kenya and Sri Lanka.[21] John Swire & Sons Ltd, which owns 29% of James Finlay, additionally has subsidiaries in China and Papua New Guinea.[21]

TU: In 1988 it was alleged that at James Finlay's tea estate in Rasidpur, Bangladesh: "Union activists are routinely intimidated, beaten up, transferred or dismissed on false pretexts".[1776]

W&C: A BBC 2 programme in 1989 highlighted the fact that the conditions on the company's Bangladeshi tea plantations were continuing to breach the Plantation Labour Rules, despite the publicity this issue has attracted.[183]

        Amongst Bangladesh's 1977 Tea Plantation Rules is the stipulation that companies have a legal duty to replace 100-year old 'kutcha' mud huts with 'pukka' housing (ie waterproof houses with a proper roof and floor). However, a 1988 inspection of James Finlay's Rasidpur estate in Bangladesh found very few of these in existence. Latrines had also not been built, a contravention of the Labour Rules.[1776] At the same time, well water supplied as 'drinking water' at Rasidpur was criticised as causing skin disease and infection amongst workers. According to Dr Eklasur Rahman, pharmacist on the estate, the estate management had not taken any action to purify the water.[1776]

PD: In 1990 James Finlay made a donation to the Conservative Party of £2,500.[1076] In the same year, John Swire & Sons made a donation to the Conservative Party of £26,000.[1076]

Albert Fisher Group plc

Fisher House, 61 Thames Street, Windsor, Berkshire SL4 1QW

OAR: Albert Fisher owns the Danoxa brand of corned beef,[1857] and seafood businesses.[1805]

Fort Howard Corp (USA)

1919 South Broadway, Greenbay, WI 54305, USA

ENV: Fort Sterling's plant in Bury is number 19 in Friends of the Earth's top 100 list of 'Secret Polluters' - companies with permits to discharge toxic metals into the sewers. Its discharges are the waste waters derived from paper tissue manufacture.[1770]

        Projected expansion at Fort Sterling Ltd's mill in Stubbins, Ramsbottom, East Lancashire was the subject of local opposition in 1990. Local residents were demanding the mill cleaned up its act. The mill emits hydrogen sulphide gas into the atmosphere which is highly poisonous and has a very offensive smell. The mill claims to have invested in equipment to eliminate odour but residents say they haven't noticed any significant change. The locals were also fearful that expansion of the mill would increase heavy goods traffic through the village by 40%.[1840] (See also refs: 28,1841)

Companies

Fosters Brewing Group Ltd

GPO Box 128, 1 Garden Street, South Yarra, Victoria 3141, Australia

Fosters is 38% owned by Broken Hill Proprietary Co (Australia), so the records of Fosters and Broken Hill have been combined on the table.

SA: Broken Hill has operations in South Africa.[21]
(See also refs: 6)

OR: In May 1993, Fosters signed an agreement to start brewing in China.[1889] Broken Hill has operations in Brazil, Indonesia, Liberia, Mexico, Morocco, Papua New Guinea and the Philippines.[21] It also has operations in Burma, but was reported in March 1993 to be pulling out.[1818]

W&C: In 1987, health workers identified the "Angurugu Syndrome", manganese poisoning affecting considerable numbers of people of the Angurugu community who work at BHP's Groote Eylandt manganese mine, Australia. In 1992, the workers there were stepping up their fight to reduce the dust hazards from mining.[1817]

LR: In 1989, BHP acquired land and mining rights to an iron sand deposit at Waikato Heads, New Zealand. This is the site of important Maori burial grounds, and local traditional landholders have vociferously opposed the licence, saying that the sacred sites are not adequately protected.[1817]

ENV: In early 1990, Greenpeace divers blocked off a waste outlet at Broken Hill's Port Kembla plant, Australia, claiming that huge amounts of cyanide, zinc, ammonia, chromium and phenols were being dumped into a creek leading into a harbour. Broken Hill later admitted that it had been illegally discharging cyanide into the waters.[1817]

In the late 1980's, at Ok Tedi mine, Papua New Guinea (20% owned by BHP), highly toxic mining waste was dumped directly into the Fly River. Half the fish were killed even 50km downstream[1817], and the food supply of 20,000 villagers was contaminated.[1878] The decision not to construct a dam to contain the waste is cited as "one of the most fateful and dangerous ever made in the history of mining in the Pacific region." Moreover, by 1988, the Ok Tedi mountain had been lowered by 150 metres and more than 200km of roads had been built through the rainforest.[1817]

BHP is one of the companies which has carried out oil exploration in Burma since 1989. Environmental impacts of exploration include pollution, erosion and deforestation of virgin tropical forest for roads etc which also give access to the military regime.[1877]
(See also refs: 1200)

IM: Elders and other Australian drinks manufacturers were taken to court in 1989 by three Aborigines, accusing them of encouraging heavy drinking amongst the country's indigenous people.[1789]

NP: Through its BHP-Utah subsidiary, Broken Hill has interests in uranium.[1817]

AT: In April 1992, Courage was listed as a subscriber to BIBRA, through its membership of the Brewers' Society.[1]

OAR: Fosters owns companies called Elders Meat Investments, Western Livestock, Elders Meat, Tama Meat Packaging and Australia Meat Holdings.[21]

164

Elders was criticised in 1989 for exporting live sheep from Australasia to Europe and the Middle East. Some of their boatloads were said to contain up to 100,000 sheep on a three week journey, cramped in spaces little bigger than themselves, and standing in their own excreta.[42]

(See also refs: 1880)

General Mills Inc

Number One General Mills Boulevard, Minneapolis, Mn.55440, USA

OR: The company has operations in Guatemala.[21]

OAR: General Mills owns a chain of seafood restaurants called Red Lobster.[15]

Gilbertson & Page

PO Box 321, Welwyn Garden City, Herts AL7 1LF

OAR: The company's Gilpa dried cat and dog foods contain poultry derivatives.[1849] Although not covered by our definitions, readers may be concerned that the company produces Dog & Country, a field sports magazine.

Gillette Co

Prudential Tower Building, Boston, MA 02199, USA

SA: Gillette owns a South African company[21]...

OR: ...and companies in Brazil, Colombia, Egypt, India, Mexico, Peru and the Philippines.[21]

ENV: In 1989, the company was accused by Greenpeace and the National Toxics Campaign of polluting Boston Harbour with 1,705 lbs of toxic chemicals per year.[3]

AT: In the USA, Gillette has been on PETA's boycott list since 1986 for its continued use of animal testing.[10]

(See also refs: 1750)

BC: See AT above.

Glopec UK Ltd

Beauty House, Hawthorne Road, Eastbourne BN23 6QA

SA: Glopec owns five companies in South Africa.[21]

Companies

Gold Crown Group Ltd

82 Wood Street, Liverpool L1 4LU

> *Gold Crown Foods is 8.75% owned by Barclays and therefore receives its record in lighter shading. We have discovered no criticisms of Gold Crown itself.*

SA: Barclays owned the largest bank in South Africa until 1986 when it sold it largely because of the UK boycott of Barclays by students. However, it still has substantial loans outstanding to South Africa.[1822]

Barclays was listed in 1992 as owning Barclays National Investments in South Africa.[21]

OR: Barclays owns companies in Brazil, Colombia, Egypt, Israel, Kenya, Liberia, the Philippines and Uganda.[21]

ENV: Barclays was one of the Big 4 banks targeted by the 'In Whose Interest?' campaign (FoE, Third World First, WDM) for being heavily involved in Third World debt. The debt crisis has made a significant contribution to the increase in tropical deforestation. In the countries worst hit by the crisis, the rate at which their rainforests are being destroyed has increased by two and a half times, while their level of debt has doubled. The campaign wants the banks to cancel or reduce the debts.[1827] In 1991, Barclays had outstanding loans of £715 million to the Third World.[1825]

ARMS: Barclays was listed by EIRIS in February 1993 as being involved in the military sale or production of civilian, non-civilian and strategic goods or services for military users, including those used in weapons systems.[1824]

BC: On the 12th September 1991, the World Development Movement launched a boycott of credit cards from the Big 4 banks in a bid to pressurise them into cancelling Third World debt.[1828]

Grand Metropolitan

20 St James Square, London SW1Y 4RR

SA: Grand Metropolitan has 31 subsidiaries in South Africa.[21]

OR: It also operates in Brazil, Kenya, Mexico, the Philippines, Sri Lanka and Uganda.[21, 802]

TU: In February 1991, a Green Giant food processing plant was relocated from Watsonville, California to Irapuato in Mexico which resulted in a drop in the weekly wage per person from $300 to $20. Californian ex-employees, calling themselves Committee of Displaced Workers, called a boycott of Grand Met in April 1991 demanding their own reinstatement and "justice, fair wages and union rights for Irapuato employees". The Committee claims that the wages are not enough to feed the Mexican workers' children, and workers involved in trying to unionise at the new plant have been sacked. The Committee also claims that the relocation saves Grand Met over $6 million in reduced wages alone.[190]

W&C: See TU above.

ENV: According to EIRIS, in the financial year 1991/2, Grand Met exceeded its UK pollution discharge consents more than 35 times.[20]

The vast amounts of water used at the Irapuato plant has resulted in a drop in the water table leaving local wells without potable water. Water used at the plant is then dumped, without adequate treatment, into the river which irrigates the crops of local farmers.[190]

Grand Met was listed in December 1991 as being a member of the BRF.[1743]

AT: In April 1992, Grand Met was listed as subscribing to BIBRA.[1] .

OAR: Burger King beefburgers are a major part of the company's operations.[21]

BC: See TU above. Grand Met is also on the Mid-Somerset Earth First! boycott list of companies which make health food and which are involved in unethical practices.[1168]

Greencore plc

St Stephens Green House, Earlsfort Terrace, Dublin 2, Ireland

OAR: Greencore owns a company called Armer Salmon (UK) Ltd.[21]

Guerlain SA

68 Avenue des Champs-Elysées, F-75008, Paris 8, France

SA: Guerlain was listed in 1988 as owning a company in South Africa[6]...

OR: ...and it has operations in Mexico.[21]

AT: Guerlain still tests its cosmetics on animals.[10]

Guinness

International House, 7 High Street, London W5 5DB

SA: Guinness owns three companies operating in South Africa.[21]

OR: It also owns companies in Brazil, India, Liberia and Mexico.[21]

ENV: In 1991, Guinness exceeded its river discharge consents more than 35 times.[20]

AT: Guinness belongs to the Brewers' Society which subscribed to BIBRA in April 1992.[1]

OAR: Guinness brewing by-products are used to make animal feed,[3] and it also owns a company called Westbury Meats.[21]

Hall & Woodhouse Ltd

The Brewery, Blandford Forum, Dorset DT11 9LS

AT: In April 1992, the company was listed as subscribing to BIBRA, through the Brewers' Society.[1]

Companies

Harrisons & Crosfield

20 St Dunstan's Hill, London EC3R 8LQ

SA: The company owns a subsidiary in South Africa.[21]

OR: It also operates in India, Indonesia, Mexico and Papua New Guinea.[21] Additionally, it has marketing agents for its Linatex rubber products (used in heavy mining) in Iran and Egypt.[1883]

W&C: According to the Ethical Investor, Summer 1991, the company has been prosecuted for health and safety violations.[1537]

ENV: Harcros Pigments was prosecuted on 3/1/92 at Towcester, in a case brought by the NRA for a water pollution offence in the Anglian region in 1990 at Deanshanger. The company was fined £500, with £200 costs.[12]

In the Northumbrian region, Durham Chemicals exceeded its discharge consent for mercury twice in the year to 31/3/90 and seven times in the previous twelve months. Due to its high toxicity, mercury is on the government's Red List of substances presenting the greatest potential hazard to the aquatic environment.[20]

The company owns timber supply companies which supply tropical hardwoods.[1537]

AT: The company tests products on animals[1537] and Harcros Chemicals was listed in April 1992 as subscribing to BIBRA.[1]

FF: In its 1992 annual report, the company claims to be the UK's largest producer of pigs.[1887]

OAR: Following the acquisition of animal feed businesses from Unilever in 1992, the newly named BOCM-Paul became the UK's biggest animal-feed producer, with interests in pig, cattle, sheep, poultry and fish feed.[1886, 1888] The company's pet foods contain meat.[1790]

PD: In 1990, the company donated £4,050 to the Conservative Party.[1075]

Hazlewood Foods

Empire Works, Rowditch, Derby DE1 1NB

OAR: The company owns various subsidiaries involved in the production of meat and fish products.[21]

Health & Diet Company

Europa Park, Stoneclough Road, Radcliffe, Manchester

SA: Health & Diet sells Rooibosch herbal tea which is grown in South Africa. The Managing Director claimed in 1990 to be "an ardent campaigner against apartheid" but said that sanctions would only result in unemployment and starvation for South African workers.[1820]

IM: In a 1992 Food Commission survey of diabetic foods, Health & Diet cereal bars were labelled 'diabetic' but they were not lower in fat/sugar content than regular equivalents, as is legally required for such labelling.[1777]

Heineken Holdings NV

NL-1000 AA Amsterdam, 2e Weteringplantsoen 5, Netherlands

> **OR:** Heineken has operations in Angola, Brazil, China, Haiti, Indonesia, Jordan, Lebanon and Papua New Guinea.[21]

H J Heinz

600 Grant St, 60th Floor, Pittsburgh, Pa 15219 USA

> **OR:** The company has operations in China,[21] Egypt[513] and Mexico.[3]
>
> **IM:** Heinz has been criticised for violating the WHO Code of Marketing of Breastmilk Substitutes for advertising its soft foods for babies before nutritionally necessary.[2] (See also refs: 585)
>
> **AT:** In April 1992 Heinz was listed as a subscriber to BIBRA.[1]
>
> **OAR:** Heinz makes products containing meat and fish.[21]

Henkel

D-4000 Dusseldorf 1, Henkelstr. 67, Postfach 11 00, Germany

> **SA:** Henkel has an associate in South Africa[21]...
>
> **OR:** ...and operations in Brazil, Colombia, El Salvador, Guatemala, Honduras, India, Indonesia, Kenya, Mexico, Morocco, the Philippines and Turkey.[21]
>
> **ENV:** On 6/9/91, Henkel was prosecuted at Bexley in a case brought by the NRA for a pollution offence at Erith (Thames region). The company was fined £5,000 with £220 costs.[12]

Hero AG

Niederlenzer Kirchweg 3, CH-5600 Switzerland

> **OAR:** Hero owns meat packing plants and manufactures sausages and other meat products.[21]

Hillsdown Holdings

Hillsdown House, 32 Hampstead High St, London NW3 1QD

> **SA:** Poupart Ltd is a distributor of South African fruit.[1809]
>
> **OR:** Hillsdown has subsidiaries in Haiti,[3] Mexico and Turkey.[21]
>
> **ENV:** Farm Kitchen Foods was prosecuted on 4/12/91 at Stowmarket, in a case brought by the NRA, for two incidents of illegally discharging trade effluent into a tributary of the River Sapiston earlier that year. The company was fined £4,000 with £854 costs.[12]
>
> In 1990, in another case brought by the NRA, Buxted Poultry Ltd was fined £800 with £400 costs for an agricultural pollution incident in 1989.[11]

Companies

IM: In 1990, slaughterhouse company FMC Torrington had its export licence suspended after EEC Inspectors found 'numerous hygiene faults, including serious contamination of carcases. Water supplies used to douse meat and clean knives contained unacceptable levels of bacteria normally associated with faecal contamination'.[1339]

FF: Hillsdown now owns Europe's biggest slaughterhouse, with the capacity for killing one million birds per week. It is also the largest breeder of animals and the UK's leading producer of beef, lamb, pork and bacon. The company also owns DayLay, the battery egg producer.[947]

In 1989, the company was fined £800 after inspectors found that 1298 chickens had died due to rough treatment while being transferred.[43]

The company is also said to be pushing hard to encourage intensive poultry production across Africa and Asia.[1306]

OAR: Hillsdown is also involved in meat processing, and has divisions for fresh meat, eggs and poultry. It is now responsible for almost one in four chickens sold in Britain.[554]

PD: Anglo United gave £20,000 to the Conservative Party in 1991.[1076] In 1992, Hillsdown spent £2,600 to improve Minister of Agriculture John Gummer's grounds at his home in Suffolk, prior to his hosting a lunch and mini-agricultural show for EC farm ministers.[1873] Officials in the House insisted that ministerial guidelines on accepting gifts had not been breached.[1874]

BC: Hillsdown appears on the Mid-Somerset Earth First! boycott list of companies which make health foods and which are involved in unethical practices.[9]

Hoechst AG

D-6230 Frankfurt 80, Postfach 80 03 20, Germany

SA: Hoechst is listed as owning 18 South African companies.[21]

OR: Hoechst owns companies in Afghanistan, Angola, Brazil, China, Colombia, Egypt, El Salvador, Guatemala, India, Indonesia, Iran, Kenya, Mali, Mexico, Morocco, Peru, the Philippines, Sri Lanka, Turkey and Uganda.[21]

W&C: In 1987, Roussel Labs paid two workers in South Africa less than the EC recommended minimum rate.[1082]

ENV: According to 1989 US EPA data, Hoechst Celanese was one of the leading releasers in the USA of known or suspected carcinogens.[1775]

Hoechst has been targeted by German Greenpeace for several years because it continues to produce CFCs. Hoechst relented and agreed to phase out their use by 1994 but it will replace them with hydrocarbons which also destroy the ozone layer.[1228]

Residents in Pampa, Texas brought a lawsuit against Hoechst Celanese in 1990, alleging that toxic emissions from its plant caused near epidemic levels of leukaemia and Downs Syndrome.[1228]

Harlow Chemical Co (50% owned by Hoechst) was prosecuted by the NRA for an industrial water pollution offence in the Thames region on 2/3/90. It was fined £1,750 with £175 costs.[11]

(See also refs: 1226, 1837, 408, 1551)

IM: Hoechst-Roussel was on a list produced in 1990 by the US Generic Pharmaceutical Industry of companies accused of fraudulent and deceptive practices. Its Neo Melubrina (dipyrone) painkiller was sold over-the-counter in Mexico despite the fact that dipyrone is banned or severely restricted in developed countries because of the risk of the potentially fatal side effects, agranulocytosis (lack of white blood cells) and shock.[1836] Hoechst is the largest manufacturer of dipyrone and introduced it in 1922.[279]

Hoechst has also been criticised for recommending dipyrone for trivial pains. It recommended it for: influenza in March 1988 in Thailand; pains, fever and spasms in Africa in March 1989; muscular rheumatism in the Philippines in April 1988; pain and fever in India in February 1988; fever, lumbago, sciatica, influenza and cold in Brazil in 1988.[279]

Hoechst markets the organotin molluscide Brestan in the Philippines, to control the over-proliferated Golden Apple Snail. It can be a serious health hazard, with reports of finger and toenails peeling off, headaches, nausea, shortness of breath, burns and blindness. Despite its banning in the Philippines in mid-1990 by the Food & Pesticides Authority, it was reported in February 1991 that 20 women had been found dead in fields recently sprayed with Brestan.[1818]

In 1991, the US FDA fined Hoechst $202,000 for failing to disclose that its anti-depressant drug, Nomifensine, had caused several deaths in Europe.[1228]
(See also refs: 396, 1836, 1839, 230)

NP: Uhde supplies reprocessing, radwaste treatment, architects and engineers to the nuclear industry. SIGRI supplies graphite, insulation and sealing materials to the nuclear industry.[1737]

AT: Hoechst was reported in 1990 to be testing CFC substitutes on animals.[1107]

In April 1992, Hoechst UK Ltd and Roussel Laboratories were listed as subscribers to BIBRA.[1]

OAR: Hoechst makes vaccines for sheep and lambs.[1838]

Huhtamaki Oy

Etelaranta 8, SF-00130 Helsinki, Finland

OR: Huhtamaki Oy has an associate company in China.[21]

Isosceles plc

Stockley House, 130 Wilton Road, London SW1V 1LU

SA: Gateway stocks produce from South Africa...

OR: ...and from Brazil, China, Honduras, India, the Philippines and Turkey.[320]

ENV: In 1990, Gateway was fined £1,200 with £846 damages by the National Rivers Authority for river pollution in the Anglian region.[11]

AT: Gateway finished products are not tested on animals, but it cannot guarantee this for the ingredients.[1098]
(See also refs: 3)

FF: Gateway stores stock non free range eggs and meat...

OAR: ...and other meat and dairy products.[320]

Companies

Jeyes Group Plc

Brunel Way, Thetford, Norfolk IP24 1HA

SA: Although it has withdrawn direct links with South Africa, Jeyes claims to operate either by "exporting direct or ..on a licence basis" in areas including "S. Africa".[1022]

AT: The company does not at present conduct animal tests for its products, but retains the right to do so in certain circumstances.[197]

JLI Group plc

PO Box 54, JLI House, Guildford Street, Chertsey, Surrey KT16 9ND

OAR: JLI products include tinned meat and fish.[7, 21]

Johnson & Johnson

One Johnson & Johnson Plaza, New Brunswick, NJ 08933, USA

SA: Johnson & Johnson owns four companies in South Africa.[21] In 1988, Johnson & Johnson employed nearly 1,400 workers there where it is one of the top ten US investors.[15]
(See also refs: 1750)

OR: Johnson & Johnson also owns companies in Angola, Brazil, China, Colombia, Egypt, Guatemala, India, Indonesia, Kenya, Mexico, Morocco, Peru, the Philippines and Turkey.[21]

IM: Janssen Pharmaceutica is the manufacturer of Hismanal, a widely prescribed antihistamine which is also available over-the-counter in Malaysia. A report in The Lancet 29/8/92, stated that Hismanal may have adverse reactions such as heart problems when the recommended dose is exceeded or when it interacts with other drugs. Since July 1992, Janssen has been required to warn US doctors of its potential dangers, but Malaysian doctors have not been informed. In the USA, 13 deaths and 95 heart problems associated with the drug have been reported to the FDA.[1795]

McNeil was on a 1990 list submitted to the US Congress by the US Generic Pharmaceutical Industry of companies accused of fraudulent and deceptive practices. It was accused of suppression of acute renal injury data associated with the use of Suprol (withdrawn in 1987), failure to disclose reports of severe/fatal renal damage with Flexin, Paraflex and Triurate, and dismissal of researchers for refusing to withhold fatal allergic reaction data on its analgesic Zomax (withdrawn 1983).[1836]

In 1990, Johnson & Johnson were criticised for their marketing of Imodium anti-diarrhoeal drops to children in Pakistan.[1502] According to J&J, the drops were given to 19 infants. "There were side effects as a result of serious overdosing in these cases and six of these children died." J&J withdrew the drops from the Pakistan market in March 1990 and undertook to withdraw them in other Third World countries.[1845]
(See also refs: 387, 570, 1636)

AT: Johnson & Johnson was listed by PETA in 1991 as testing its products on animals.[10] Johnson & Johnson tests its healthcare products on animals. It was the fifth largest user of animals in tests in 1988 and the ninth largest user of animals in painful tests without anaesthetic.[15]
(See also refs: 1750)

PD: Johnson & Johnson gave $75,950 in political donations in the USA in 1987/88.[15]

Kanebo Ltd

5-90 Tomobuchi-cho 1-chome, Miyakojima-ku, Osaka 534, Japan

OR: Kanebo Ltd owns companies in Brazil, China and Indonesia.[21]

Kellogg Company

One Kellogg Square, P O Box 3599, Battle Creek, Mi.49016-3599, USA

SA: Kellogg is the subject of a boycott called by the US group, Educators Against Apartheid, for its continued presence in South Africa.[1761]

In reply to criticism of Kellogg's continued presence in South Africa, the Chair defended the company's decision to stay. He claimed it remained there to fight apartheid, and that the company's pay levels were one of the highest in the country.[1094]
(See also refs:15, 21)

OR: The company has operations in Brazil, Colombia, Guatemala and Mexico.[21]

W&C: In a 1991 publication, Educators Against Apartheid alleged that white workers "receive higher wages", that "some black workers are paid wages below subsistence level", and that "most black workers must live in Kwa Thema, a black township. Black and white workers may not join the same labor union."[15]

IM: In a survey by the Food Commission Kellogg's Frosties were found to contain 41% sugar. The Commission criticised sweet breakfast cereals which it said could be argued to be 'physically harmful' as sugar is a proven cause of dental decay.[575]

AT: In April 1992, the Kellogg Company of Great Britain was listed as subscribing to BIBRA.[1]
(See also refs: 15)

PD: The company made a donation of £20,000 to the Conservative Party and £10,000 to the CPS in 1990.[1076] It made donations to both Democratic and Republican candidates in US elections of 1987-88 totalling more than $90,000.[3]
(See also refs: 577)

BC: Kellogg is the subject of a boycott called by the US group, Educators Against Apartheid, for its continued presence in South Africa.[1761]

Kennel Nutrition

Dellamires Lane, Ripon, N Yorks HG4 1TT

OAR: Its dried dog food contains animal derivatives, though the company is working on a vegetarian option.[1849]

Companies

Kimberly-Clark Corp

PO Box 619100, Dallas, Texas 75261-9100, USA

SA: Kimberly-Clark has $8.3 million of assets in South Africa and has not signed the Statement of Principles pledging companies to provide equal opportunities there.[1750]
(See also refs: 3, 19, 21)

OR: Kimberly-Clark has operations in Brazil, Colombia, El Salvador, Honduras, Indonesia, Mexico and the Philippines.[21]
(See also refs: 3)

ENV: Kimberly-Clark was prosecuted in September 1991 by the NRA for a major water pollution offence. Paper mill effluent containing 100 times the normal concentration of ammonia was discharged into the Tyne, killing 100 mature salmon and forcing the closure of a nearby water intake. It was fined £5,000 plus over £7,000 costs and compensation.[382]

Kimberly-Clark is one of the USA's largest makers of disposable nappies, and in 1991 successfully lobbied against a one cent tax on such products, despite their contribution to environmental waste. For this and other reasons it is listed as one of the CEP's 13 X-rated companies.[1750]

Kimberly-Clark jointly owns a paper mill in Aylesford, Kent, with Svenska Cellulosa. The mill is placed 8th out of 56 on a WEN list of UK paper mills most frequently breaking discharge consent requirements between 1990 and 1992. The consent for biological oxygen demand was broken in 44% of tests taken in the period.[1844]
(See also refs: 12, 28, 144, 628)

AT: In May 1991, Kimberly-Clark was listed by PETA as testing its products on animals.[10] By 1992, it had given CEP no indication of a serious effort to reduce testing or find alternatives.[1750]

It contracted Biosearch Laboratories, Philadelphia, to test its tampons in 1987/88. It made liquid from the tampons and applied the resulting dried powder to the vaginas of rabbits for five days, then killed and necropsied them.[1109]

Koninklijke Wessanen

NL - 1180 AK, Amstelveen, Laan van Kronenberg 14, Postbus 410, Netherlands

OAR: The company is involved in the manufacture of animal feedstuffs.[21]

Estée Lauder Inc

71 Grosvenor Street, London W1X 0BH

SA: Estee Lauder was listed in 1988 as owning two companies in South Africa.[6]

OAR: Estee Lauder uses squalene in some of its cosmetics, an oil taken from the livers of basking sharks.[620]

Laxgate Ltd

Group House, King Street, Middlewich, Cheshire CW10 9LY

OAR: Laxgate produces sausages and other meat products.[21]

Sara Lee Corp

Three First National Plaza, Chicago, Il 60602, USA

SA: Sara Lee has a trademark agreement with one of its former subsidiaries in South Africa.[19]
(See also refs: 15, 1750)

OR: It also operates in India, Israel,[15] Indonesia, Kenya, Mexico, Morocco and the Philippines.[21]

W&C: In 1989, the US Occupational Safety and Health Agency censured Sara Lee for four wilful violations of occupational safety regulations in one New London plant in the USA. According to the Bakery, Confectionery & Tobacco Workers International Union, Sara Lee "continues to tolerate serious incidences of crippling cumulative trauma injuries."[15]

IM: Sara Lee owns Douwe Egberts, which manufactures and markets tobacco products.[21]

OAR: Sara Lee owns a tanning subsidiary, Coach Leatherware, and is involved in the manufacture of sausages and other meat products.[21]

John Lewis Partnership

171 Victoria Street, London SW1E 5NN

SA: Waitrose stocks products from South Africa...

OR: ...and from the following oppressive regimes: Brazil, Honduras, Kenya and Mexico.[320]

AT: Waitrose and John Lewis own-brand products do not comply with BUAV's criteria for non-animal-testing.[3] They also stock branded products that do not appear on BUAV's cruelty-free list.[320]

FF: Waitrose stocks meat and eggs that are not labelled free-range.[320] In a survey of seven major food retailers, Compassion in World Farming found that Waitrose was the only one to admit selling Dutch veal that had been reared in the cruel crate system.[46]

OAR: Waitrose stocks meat.[320]

Litor Ltd

Chanel (USA), 9 West 57th Street, New York, NY 10019, USA

AT: Chanel was listed by PETA in 1991 as a company that tests its products on animals.[10]

Companies

Lloyds Chemists

Manor Rd, Mancetter, Atherstone, Warwickshire CV9 1QY

AT: As a retailer, Lloyds Chemists receives a mark on the Table for selling animal-tested products.

PD: In 1992, the company gave £30,000 to the Conservative Party.[1823]

London International Group plc

35 New Bridge Street, London EC4V 6BJ

SA: The London International Group owns W Woodward and LRC Industries in South Africa.[21]
(See also refs: 13)

OR: The London International Group owns a company in India.[21]

AT: In April 1992 London International Group plc and LRC Products were listed as subscribing to BIBRA.[1]

LVMH

30 Avenue Hoche, F75008 Paris, France

OR: LVMH owns companies in Brazil, Kuwait, Mexico and Turkey.[21]

AT: Givenchy and RoC continue to use animal testing, though Christian Dior claims to have ceased.[3]

OAR: LVMH produces Louis Vuitton leather luggage.[21]

MacAndrews & Forbes Holdings Inc

36 East 63rd Street, New York, NY 10021, USA

SA: MacAndrews & Forbes owns a company in South Africa.[21]
(See also refs: 1750)

OR: It also owns companies in Brazil and Israel[21]...

IM: ...and manufactures cigars.[21]

Mackle Petfoods

40 Corrigan Hill Rd, Moy, Dungannon, Co Tyrone, N Ireland BT71 6SL

OAR: The company's pet foods contain meat.[1790]

Marks & Spencer plc

Michael House, Baker Street, London W1A 1DN

SA: M&S stocks South African fresh fruit and wine...

OR: ...and produce from Brazil, Colombia, Israel, Kenya, Peru and the Philippines.[320][1157]

ENV: M&S stocks products made from tropical hardwoods such as mahogany.[1258]

AT: M&S was listed in 1992 as subscribing to BIBRA.[1] Although it says that none of its cosmetics or toiletries have been tested on animals for ten years, this only refers to the finished products and not the ingredients.[3][1105]

FF: M&S sells non-free-range eggs and meat.[320] Its veal is produced in Holland from calves reared in the group-housed system. Compassion in World Farming has criticised this system whereby small groups of calves are kept on slatted floors after an initial period in veal crates.

OAR: M&S sells meat and dairy products.[46]

PD: In the year to 31/3/92, M&S gave £50,000 to the Conservative Party and £10,000 to the Liberal Democrats.[1157]

W & H Marriage & Sons

Chelmer Mills, New Street, Chelmsford, Essex CM1 1PN

OAR: Marriages manufactures animal feeds.[5]

Mars Inc

6885 Elm Street, McLean, Va 22101, USA

IM: In 1991 health watchdog Action and Information on Sugars (AIS) and the Health Education Authority jointly made a complaint to the Independent Television Committee (ITC) regarding Mars' promotion of Milky Way as "the sweet you can eat between meals without ruining your appetite". ITC guidelines state that confectionery adverts must not encourage children to eat between meals. Although the case was not upheld Mars was warned that it must clarify this position in its adverts.[576,578]

AT: In April 1992 Mars was listed as subscribing to BIBRA.1

OAR: Mars produces meat-based petfoods, through its Pedigree subsidiary.[21]

Martin Mathew & Co Ltd

1 Chase Side Place, Horseshoe Lane, Enfield, Middlesex EN2 6QA

OAR: Martin Mathew products include tinned tuna and ham.[1790]

McCain Foods Ltd

Main Road, Florenceville, NB EOJ 1KO, Canada

ENV: McCain Foods (GB) Ltd was prosecuted on 5/7/91 in a case brought by the NRA for an industrial water pollution offence in the Anglian region on 23/1/91. The company was fined £2000 plus £300 costs.[11]

PD: McCain Foods (GB) Ltd donated £3,500 to the Conservative Party in 1990.[1076] (See also refs: 577)

Companies

McCormick & Co Inc

11350 McCormick Road, Hunt Valley, Md 21031, USA

    OR: McCormick operates in Brazil, China, El Salvador, India, Mexico and Morocco.[21]

MD Foods

Skanderborgvej 277, DK-8260, Viby J, Denmark

    OR: An MD Foods associate, MD Foods International, has dairy production facilities in Bahrain and Brazil.[1805]

Milk Marketing Board of England & Wales

Giggs Hill Green, Thames Ditton, Surrey KT7 0EL

    ENV: Dairy Crest, the subsidiary which manufactures MMB's consumer brands, was fined a total of £7,800 for pollution offences in five prosecutions brought by the NRA in the 24 months to September 1991.[384]
(See also ref: 377)

    OAR: In 1989 the MMB was reported to have been connected with the secret testing of BST (bovine somatotropin) on about a thousand cattle in Britain in the preceding four years. BST is a genetically-engineered growth hormone which increases milk yields by an average of 20%. Milk from BST-tested cattle was mixed with all other milk and sold unlabelled to the consumer. However, it was not clear how much this decision was imposed on the MMB by MAFF.[1815]

Mitsubishi Group

6-3 Marunouchi 2-chome, Chiyoda-ku, Tokyo 100, Japan

    Mitsubishi is a member of the Mitsubishi zaibatsu and for the purposes of this report the record of all the member companies have been combined on the Table.

    SA: Both the Mitsubishi Corp and Mitsubishi Electric Corp were listed in 1988 as having agents in South Africa.[6]

    OR: The Mitsubishi Group has subsidiaries in Bahrain, Brazil, China, Colombia, India, Indonesia, Iran, Liberia, Mexico, Morocco, Peru and the Philippines.[21]

    LR: In 1992 Survival International criticised the operations of a Mitsubishi subsidiary, Alberta Pacific in Canada. Survival argues the company's clear-cutting of large areas of north-east and north-central Alberta is affecting a large number of Cree and Dene people, some of whom are living in unceded territory subject to land claims.[1766]

    ENV: The Mitsubishi Corporation is involved in importing large quantities of tropical rainforest timber into Japan. A Mitsubishi Group subsidiary has, for the last 15 years, been clear-cutting huge areas of tropical rainforest in Sarawak to supply the Japanese market. Its logging activities there continue 24 hours a day, with the aid of floodlights.[1768] Mitsubishi has further logging interests in nine other countries.[633] Another subsidiary is preparing to open a mine in the last large area of Ecuadorean coastal rainforest. The area is home of the Awa Indian nation as well as the

Cotacachi-Cayapas Ecological Reserve, identified as Ecuador's highest area of priority for biodiversity conservation by the US Agency for International Development.[1768]
(See also refs: 1236, 1767)

NP: Mitsubishi Heavy Industries is listed as providing services for the nuclear industry, including: construction services, reactor cores, fuel handling equipment, plutonium supply, radioactive waste incinerators, reprocessing and water treatment.[22]

ARMS: Mitsubishi Heavy Industries is also a manufacturer of armaments, including: aircraft, guided weapons and missiles, and armoured, tracked and fighting vehicles.[981]

OAR: Princes produces tinned ham and corned beef.[1857]

BC: The Rainforest Action Network is calling a boycott of Mitsubishi for its import of tropical timber to Japan.[1769]

Molkerei Alois Müller

Zollerstrasse 7, D-8935 Aretsried, Germany

ENV: In 1989 Müller's original plant in Aretsried, Bavaria discharged 6,000 litres of cream into a local river causing widespread pollution.[1879]

The Molson Cos Ltd

Scotia Plaza, 40 King Street West, 3600, Toronto, Ont. M5H 3Z5, Canada

OR: Molson Cos Ltd has subsidiaries in Brazil, Guatemala, Indonesia, Kenya, Mexico, Morocco and the Philippines.[21]

AT: Diversey Wyandotte Corp is listed in 1991 by PETA as testing its products on animals.[10]

Philip Morris Cos Inc

120 Park Avenue, New York, NY 10017, USA

SA: Philip Morris licenses South African companies to manufacture Kraft General Foods products and Chesterfield cigarettes in South Africa.[5]

OR: Philip Morris owns companies in Brazil, China, Colombia, India, Mexico and the Philippines.[21]

IM: In 1989, tobacco accounted for 72% of the company's profits.[3] In 1988 Philip Morris was one of three companies judged by a US court to be partly responsible for the death of a woman who died from lung cancer.[15] Its Marlboro brand (the world's best selling brand) was estimated to have killed 75,000 Americans in the same year.[1204]

AT: Kraft General Foods was criticised by BUAV for tests on cats in the development of a stomach-friendly coffee.[141]

OAR: Philip Morris produces meat and dairy products and owns a US company, Oscar Mayer, which slaughters pigs.[1192]

PD: In 1990, Philip Morris gave a total of $124,650 to Republican and Democrat politicians.[1210]

BC: Philip Morris is the subject of a boycott call in the USA by Stop Teenage Addiction to Tobacco for the company's use of aggressive advertising to sell cigarettes to teenagers.[191]

Wm Morrison Supermarkets

Hilmore House, Thornton Road, Bradford BD8 9AX

SA: According to our survey, Morrisons stocks South African fresh fruit...

OR: ...and produce from Brazil, Israel, Kenya, Mexico and Turkey.[320]

AT: It also sells some toiletries labelled as not tested on animals but not all cosmetics, toiletries and household products are thus labelled.[320] Morrisons does not comply with BUAV's criteria.[136]

FF: Non-free-range meat and eggs are sold under the Morrisons brand...[320]

OAR: ...as are other meat products.[320] Morrisons also owns a fresh meat processor.

Napier Brown Holdings Ltd

International House, 1 St Katharines Way, London E1 9UN

OR: Napier Brown has a subsidiary in Turkey.[21]

OAR: Napier Brown is an associate of Whitworths Holdings which manufactures animal feeds.[21]

Nestlé SA

Avenue Nestlé, CH Vevey, Switzerland

Nestlé owns 49% of the cosmetics company, L'Oréal, so their records have been combined on the Table.

SA: Nestlé has subsidiaries in South Africa...[21]

OR: ...and Brazil, China, Colombia, Egypt, El Salvador, Guatemala, Honduras, India, Indonesia, Kenya, Lebanon, Mexico, Papua New Guinea, the Philippines, Senegal, Sri Lanka and Turkey. L'Oréal adds Peru and Morocco to the list.[21]

TU: In 1989 workers at a Nestlé chocolate plant in Cacapava, Brazil went on strike. The workers complained of poor working conditions, including discrimination against women, lack of protective clothing and inadequate safety conditions. Within two months of the beginning of the strike the company had sacked forty of its workers, including most of the strike organisers.[1544]

In 1988, the sacking of 15 workers at a Nestlé-owned plant in Colombia resulted in a sympathy strike by the rest of the workforce demanding their reinstatement. It was quelled by the presence of tanks and the company's threat to call in the army.[3]

W&C: See TU above.

IM: Nestlé continues to be the main target of the boycott against companies which promote the bottle feeding of infant formula. Nestlé encourages bottle feeding primarily by either giving free samples of babymilk to hospitals, or neglecting to collect payments.[1764] It has been criticised for misinforming mothers and health-workers in promotional literature. Nestlé implies that malnourished mothers, and mothers of twins and premature babies are unable to breastfeed, despite health organisations' claims that there is no evidence to support this. Evidence of direct advertising to mothers has been found in over twenty countries such as South Africa and Thailand.[1764] Instructions and health-warnings on packaging are often either absent, not prominently displayed or in an inappropriate language. All these actions directly contravene the Code.[1764]

Even in the UK, bottle-fed babies are up to ten times more likely to develop gastro-intestinal infections, but in the Third World, where clean water may be absent, mothers may be illiterate and independent health care and advice may be lacking, bottle feeding can be more dangerous.[1764] This can lead to a situation where babies are left vulnerable to dysentery, malnutrition and death, and Nestlé is able to retain its estimated $4 billion market share in the baby-milk industry.[1764] For more information see the Coffee Report, 'The Nestlé Boycott'.
(See also refs: 2, 14, 86, 87, 88, 89)

AT: L'Oréal is currently the subject of a boycott for its continued use of animal testing.[1765] Nestlé itself was criticised by BUAV for testing its coffee's carcinogenicity on mice.[1113]

OAR: Nestlé manufactures products containing meat.[1345]

BC: Nestlé is currently the subject of a worldwide boycott for its irresponsible marketing of baby milk,[1764] and L'Oréal is being boycotted for its animal testing.[1765]

New Zealand Dairy Board

P.O. Box 417, 25 The Terrace, Wellington, New Zealand

OR: The New Zealand Dairy Board has subsidiaries in Bahrain, China, Egypt, Guatemala, Mexico, Papua New Guinea, Peru and the Philippines.[21]

OAR: Animal husbandry subsidiaries include: The South Island Breeding Centre, Exotic Sheep Production Ltd, the Livestock Improvement Corp Ltd and cattle semen import and export businesses.[21]

Northern Foods

Beverley House, St Stephen's Square, Hull HU1 3XG

FF: Subsidiary Mayhew Chicken is involved in chicken rearing in 'controlled environment housing'.[3]

OAR: Northern Foods' meat product brands include Pork Farms and Hollands Pies.[3]

O Kavli

Sandbrekkevegen 91, Postboks 338, N-5051 Nestun, Norway

OAR: Some of its Primula cheese spreads contain ham, bacon or sea-foods.[1790]

Companies

Oronte SA

This Panamanian company can be contacted via its UK subsidiary: Bunge & Co Ltd, Bunge House, PO Box 540, 15-25 Artillery Lane, London E1 7HA

SA: Bunge & Co Ltd is listed as owning a subsidiary in South Africa.[21]
(See also refs: 13)

ENV: A Beoco Ltd plant in Bootle is number 64 on Friends of the Earth's top 100 list of Secret Polluters - companies with permits to discharge toxic metals into the sewers. Its discharges include waste waters from the production and refining of edible oil.[1770]

Paterson Zochonis

Bridgewater House, 60 Whitworth Street, Manchester M1 6LU

OR: The company operates in Indonesia,[3] Kenya and Senegal.[21]

IM: Paterson Zochonis was criticised in 1988 for the marketing of a skin-lightening cream called 'Venus de Milo', containing hydroquinone, in Nigeria. There are numerous health risks associated with hydroquinone, even - a King's College Hospital doctor argues - at levels of 2% which is used in Venus de Milo, such as very bad skin damage or even possible cancer.[1723]

In May 1993, a Which? article discussed the health risks of creams containing hydroquinone, and stated that many dermatologists considered even 2% hydroquinone dangerous. Venus de Milo was one of the creams featured in this article.[1865]

Pepsico Inc

Anderson Hill Road, Purchase, N.Y. 10577, USA

SA: Pepsico sold its South African bottling plants in 1985 but continues a sales and licensing agreement with a South African company. It also continues to franchise 185 Kentucky Fried Chicken outlets there.[19]

OR: Pepsico has subsidiaries in Burma,[1831] Mexico, the Philippines and Turkey.[21] It also has a joint venture in India and bottling plants in China.[3]

ENV: In 1990 part of a Pepsi Cola bottling plant near Mexico city was one of 15 plants temporarily closed, after discharging untreated water into a ravine and draining system, resulting in damage to 14 co-operative farms.[15]

In early 1987 the company was ordered by the Philippines' National Pollution Control Commission to close 11 of its 12 plants in the country for violations of anti-pollution laws. Untreated or inadequately treated wastewater discharged from the factories had led to the pollution of rivers and creeks in 1986.[1288]

IM: Pepsi sells its diet-Pepsi brand, containing saccharin, in Malaysia where the law requires that such drinks should say "requires the supervision of a physician" on the label. The Consumers Association of Penang claims that while such warnings do appear on diet-Pepsi cans, they are printed too small to be seen.[1762]

AT: Pepsico has in-house animal-testing facilities, where it conducts nutritional studies on laboratory rats. It also sponsors experiments to test the safety of certain ingredients.[15]

182

OAR: Kentucky Fried Chicken is the world's largest quick-service chicken restaurant with outlets in 58 countries.[3]

PD: In 1987/8 the company donated to political campaigns in the USA, giving $58,800 to Democrat candidates and $130,141 to Republican candidates.[15]

BC: Pepsico is the subject of a boycott called by the Ottawa Public Interest Group (OPIRG) because of its investments in Burma. OPIRG maintain that Pepsi's recent business presence in Burma legitimises the country's military regime.[1831]

Pernod-Ricard SA

142 Boulevard Haussman, F-75008 Paris, France

SA: Pernod-Ricard has operations in South Africa[21]...

OR: ...and Brazil and Mexico.[21]

Pfizer Inc

235 East 42nd Street, New York, NY 10017, USA

SA: Pfizer owns two companies in South Africa[21]...

OR: ...and companies in Angola, Brazil, China, Colombia, Egypt, India, Indonesia, Kenya, Mexico, Morocco, Peru, the Philippines, Turkey and Uganda.[21]

ENV: In 1992, Greenpeace listed a Pfizer plant as one of the 10 worst polluters in the South East of England. The plant breached its discharge consent four times since the beginning of 1991 and also discharged ten chemicals for which it did not have a permit, including organochlorines.[1881]

Pfizer was the target of a Greenpeace campaign in 1988 for dumping industrial waste in Eire,[1551] and a US group listed Pfizer as one of the top fifteen corporate contributors to global pollution, based on 1987 figures.[634]

IM: In 1990, the US Generic Pharmaceutical Industry listed Pfizer as one of the companies accused of fraudulent and deceptive practices for its failure to report severe side effects of its Feldene drug before it obtained US approval.[1836]

Shiley Inc marketed a heart valve between 1979 and 1986, 394 of which had ruptured causing 252 deaths by 1990, according to Pfizer.[1750] Shiley allegedly knew of the valve's faults but continued to market it whilst trying to right them. 82,000 of the valves are implanted worldwide.[735] The US magazine Multinational Monitor listed Pfizer as one of the ten worst companies of 1988 following this saga.[1203] Pfizer has still not directly contacted the valve recipients. In January 1991, a suit was filed against the company in the USA on behalf of 55,000 valve recipients.[1750]

AT: Pfizer tests cosmetics and drugs on animals, using 18,398 in 1988.[15]
(See also ref: 10)

OAR: The company produces antibiotics for the dairy industry.[1131]

PD: In 1987-88, Pfizer gave $198,737, 51% of which went to the Democrats, the rest to the Republicans.[15]

Companies

Pimhill

Lea Hall, Harmer Hill, Shrewsbury, Shropshire SY4 3DY

OAR: Pimhill manufactures animal feeds.[1849]

Portfolio Foods Ltd

Pasadena Close, Hayes, Middlesex UB3 3NQ

OAR: Red Mill Snack Foods produces the Mr Porky pork crackling and scratchings snack.[1850]

Procter & Gamble

1, Procter & Gamble Plaza, Cincinatti, Ohio 45202, USA

SA: Procter & Gamble has a licensing agreement in South Africa which it will retain until 1995.[97]

OR: P&G operates in the following regimes: Brazil, China, Colombia, Egypt, India, Indonesia, Kenya, Lebanon, Mexico, Morocco, Peru, the Philippines and Turkey.[21]

ENV: At the end of 1991 the company was criticised for continuing to pollute the Fenholloway River with up to 50 million gallons of waste water each day from its cellulose plant in Florida. Fish in the river were being contaminated with dioxin, and water in wells in the vicinity was allegedly unsafe to drink. All this pollution is within legal limits but state officials are said to be reviewing P&G's permit at the plant.[1206]
(See also refs: 1691, 1786)

AT: In July 1991, BUAV revealed that P&G had conducted tests on about 300 guinea pigs to determine irritancy and allergic sensitivity to sunscreen ingredients. Human data was already available.[139]

In 1992, using US government records, 'In Defense of Animals' reported that P&G had increased its use of dogs, hamsters and ferrets between 1986 and 1989. Total animal use is estimated at about 50,000 per year. See Boycott Call below.

OAR: P&G owns a manufacturer of animal feed ingredients.[1195]

BC: P&G is the subject of an ongoing boycott by the US group 'In Defense of Animals' for its continued use of animals in testing.[1783]

Quadriga Holdings

Mayflower House, 45 Neal Street, London WC2H 9PJ

OR: The company has operations in Israel[21] and Turkey.[1862]

OAR: Gerber Foods produces canned fish.[1055]

The Quaker Oats Co

Quaker Tower, 321 North Clark Street, Chicago, Il 60610, USA

OR: Quaker owns companies in Colombia, El Salvador, Guatemala, Honduras, Mexico and Peru.[21]

IM: In April 1990, the Food Commission criticised the marketing of Quaker's Sugar Puffs. There was eight adverts for them in four hours of Saturday morning childrens's TV. Sugar Puffs are 65% sugar.[575]

In response to the survey a Quaker spokesperson said "It is wrong to suggest to mothers that pre-sweetened breakfast cereals are harming their children's health. The popularity of Sugar Puffs helps mums ensure their children do actually eat a breakfast".[660]

OAR: Quaker makes meat-based pet food, such as Felix and Chunky, and Sutherlands meat spreads.[1790]

PD: Quaker gave $33,000 to American political campaigns in 1987/88.[15]
(See also refs: 3)

Reckitt & Colman

1 Burlington Lane, Chiswick, London W4 2RW

SA: Reckitt & Colman has six subsidiaries in South Africa.[21]

OR: The company also has operations in Colombia, Egypt, India, Kenya, Mexico, Papua New Guinea, Peru, Sri Lanka and Uganda.[21]

TU: In June 1990, 135 striking members of the chemical workers' union, CWIU, were arrested and charged with trespass at a Reckitt & Colman plant in South Africa.[18]

ENV: In the year to March 1991, Reckitt & Colman exceeded its discharge consent at least once according to the NRA and/or the RPBS.[12] Reckitt & Colman was listed in December 1991 as being a member of the BRF.[1743]

AT: Reckitt & Colman tests its pharmaceutical products on animals. According to the company, its Household and Toiletries Division no longer undertakes animal testing, nor does it use contract research houses to carry out testing on its behalf.[1094]
(See also refs: 3, 10, 137, 1113)

OAR: Some of Robinson's baby foods contain meat.[1790]

PD: In 1990, Reckitt & Colman gave £30,000 to the BUI and £2,500 to the CPS.[1076]

James River Corp

Tredegar Street, Richmond, Va 23217, USA

OR: James River has subsidiaries in Brazil, Mexico and Turkey.[21]

ENV: According to a 1990 report, the discharges from British Tissues' Bridgend Paper Mill in Mid-Glamorgan into the River Llynfi turned the trout and salmon river from a good class 2 to a fair class 3 - only just able to support fish life. In 1987, a spill from the mill of the chemical kymene resulted in the death of 20,000 trout, 7000 sewin and 100 salmon. The company was fined £10,000 and ordered to pay £200,000 damages to restock the river over seven years.[825]

Companies

James River's mill in Marathon, Ontario was described in the late 1980s by Canadian Greenpeace as 'one of the worst in the country' for its poor environmental record. The mill is said to produce 14,000 tonnes of toxic organochlorines every year as by-products of its pulping and bleaching processes. It discharges toxic effluents and suspended solids directly into Lake Superior. In 1988 tests revealed that the mill's effluent was lethally toxic to fish.[28]
(See also refs: 284, 360, 1446)

AT: According to the ratings chart in CEP's 1992 'Shopping for a Better World', James River tests on animals.[1750]

Roberts & Co (Dunchurch)

London Rd, Dunchurch, Rugby, Warks CV22 9JB

OAR: The company's cat and dog foods contain meat.[1849]

Robinson and Sons Ltd

Wheat Bridge, Chesterfield, Derbyshire S40 1YE

AT: In April 1992, Robinson Healthcare was listed as subscribing to BIBRA.[1]

Roche Holdings AG

Grenzacherstr. 124, CH-4002 Basel, Switzerland

SA: Roche owns two companies in South Africa, Givaudan and Roche Products.[21]

OR: Roche owns companies in Brazil, Colombia, Egypt, Guatemala, India, Indonesia, Mexico, Morocco, Peru, the Philippines and Turkey.[21]

IM: According to the medical publication SCRIP, Roche is one of a number of companies being sued in the UK by patients claiming damages for injuries caused by benzodiazepine drugs, such as Roche's Valium. Lawyers claim that the companies failed to warn doctors of the risk of dependency. 3,000 claims had been made by 1991.[235]

Roche was listed by Multinational Monitor magazine as one of the ten worst companies of 1991 for its marketing of its Versed sedative. According to internal company documents released in 1991, Roche ignored early warnings from its research division that its Versed sedative could cause deadly side effects if it was sold in a highly concentrated form. However, Versed was marketed in this form for two years and was linked to about 80 deaths and many more near fatalities. The company allegedly hoped that Versed would replace Valium when its patent expired, but Versed is 4-6 times as potent. Roche now sells Versed in a less concentrated form.[1240, 1206]

A survey of Swiss drug sales in the Third World in 1988/9, showed Roche as selling the most non-essential and inappropriate drugs of all the Swiss drug companies. 85% of all the drugs it sold in the Third World were found to be non-essential and 51% were inappropriate.[608]
(See also refs: 1646, 1782, 1304)

AT: Givaudan was listed in May 1991 as testing its products on animals.[10]
(See also refs: 1643, 1, 1781)

OAR: Roche makes the colorants carophyll and canthaxanthin which are used in poultry feeds to alter egg yolk pigmentation.[49]

BC: Roche appears on the Mid-Somerset Earth First! boycott list of companies which make health foods and which are involved in unethical practices.

Royal Foods Ltd/Anglo American Corporation

45 Main Street, Marshalltown, Johannesburg, South Africa

Royal Foods acquired Del Monte Foods International in October 1992 with the backing of Anglo American. We have therefore combined their records on the Table.

SA: Despite Anglo American's public image as a leading campaigner against apartheid, it controls 43.5% of capital on the Johannesburg Stock Exchange, contributing to South Africa's wealth and therefore the power of the white minority.[1004]

OR: Del Monte Foods International operates in Brazil, Indonesia, Kenya, the Philippines and Turkey.[431, 1094]

W&C: according to the US magazine, Multinational Monitor, the company 'has an anti-labour history that involves the use of the repressive services of the apartheid apparatus, as well as its own security personnel, to control and exploit workers.' Black miners earn as little as one fifth the salary of white workers.[1237]

In 1990, two of the mines controlled by Anglo American, Freegold and Vaal Reefs, were the targets of industrial action over pay and racist conditions.[752] The company owns a gold mine at Welkom, which was the scene of racial violence. A demonstration by black workers was said to have arisen due to segregation in its mines, although the company claims this is 'coincidental' arising from differences in seniority between black and white workers.[1812] The demonstration was broken up by mine security which opened fire on the crowd with rubber bullets and tear gas.[1813]
(See also refs: 1004)

LR: Anglo is one of the companies with concessions for mining operations in northern Roraima, Brazil which is Yanomani territory. The Yanomani have been campaigning for ten years for the creation of a park in the region but government policy and the absence of legal protection have opened the door to invasions by mining companies.[312]
(See also refs: 1207)

ENV: The company controls 12.7% of the area involved in the Grand Carajas project in Brazil which has been criticised for ecological damage and land-rights infringements.[1207]

NP: According to 'The Gulliver File', Anglo American produces 43% of South Africa's uranium.[1817]

J Sainsbury plc

Stamford House, Stamford Street, London SE11 9LL

SA: Sainsbury's stocks South African produce.[320] 3

Companies

OR: Own-branded and branded products were found at Sainsbury's from the following oppressive regimes: Brazil, China, Colombia, Honduras, India, Israel, Kenya, Mexico, Peru and Turkey.[320]

ENV: Timber products from Sainsbury's Homebase stores are currently the subject of a boycott called by Friends of the Earth in a bid to force the DIY retailers to only stock wood of non-rainforest origin, or at least from proven 'sustainably managed sources'.[1132 305] See also Boycott Call.

AT: Sainsbury's own-branded cosmetics and toiletries have been formally approved as meeting BUAV's 'no testing' criteria.[3 1112] However this policy does not apply to own-brand cleaning products or food ingredients or to its branded products so it still receives a half-mark for animal testing.[320]

FF: Breckland's Farms is involved in pig farming, with the majority of pigs being reared indoors. Moreover, the store stocks chickens and turkeys which have been reared intensively in "large open deep-litter sheds".[1094] The company also stocks non-free-range eggs and meat and farmed salmon.[320]

OAR: Sainsbury's controls every stage in the production of meat for its stores from the animal feed through to the slaughterhouse, through a series of ties with other companies.[309] Haverhill Meat Products is involved in the processing of bacon and pork products.[1419] It sells meat products in its stores.[320]

BC: It is the subject of a boycott call by Manchester Earth First! for plans to build a superstore on the Bruntwood Hay Meadow in Cheadle, Stockport. See also Environment.

Sandoz AG

Lichtstrasse 35, CH-4002 Basel, Switzerland

SA: Sandoz owns one company, Sandoz Products (Pty) Ltd in South Africa.[21]

OR: It also owns companies in Brazil, China, Colombia, Egypt, Indonesia, Mexico, the Philippines and Turkey.[21]

ENV: In November 1990 the authorities in Rotterdam, where the Rhine reaches the sea, required Sandoz to reduce its regular emissions of toxic wastes to the river by more than half, but two tonnes each of copper and chrome will still be discharged by Sandoz annually.[1875]

IM: In a 1990/91 survey, Wander's baby food marketing failed to comply fully with any of the WHO Code requirements.[14] In the Philippines during 1988, Sandoz's dipyrone painkiller was indicated for pain and fever, and it was recommended for toothache in Colombia in 1988. Dipyrone is banned or severely restricted in many countries because of the risk of the potentially fatal side effects, agranulocytosis and shock.[279]

In 1990, Sandoz was fined by the US EPA for exporting pesticides without telling the importing country that they were not registered for use in the USA.[645]

AT: In 1990 the company claimed to have cut its use of live animals in experiments by 50% - but it is still apparently reliant on them.[1643] In 1992, when the Swiss held a referendum on banning animal testing, Sandoz threatened that it would have to move its headquarters out of Switzerland if the ban became law.[768]

Companies

Scottish & Newcastle plc

Abbey Brewery, Holyrood Road, Edinburgh EH8 8YS

AT: In April 1992, Scottish & Newcastle was listed as subscribing to BIBRA, through its membership of the Brewers' Society.[1]

PD: Between 1979 and 1991, Scottish & Newcastle Breweries donated a total of £298,000 to the Conservative Party.[1868] It was on the Financial Times list of donors to the Conservative Party as donating £50,000 in 1991.[712]
(See also refs: 3)

Scott Paper Co

Scott Plaza 1, Philadelphia, Pa 19113, USA

OR: Scott Paper has subsidiaries in Mexico, Honduras[21] and Brazil.[3]

W&C: In September 1987, the OSHA issued two citations alleging that Scott wilfully violated safety rules by underreporting injuries at its factory in Winslow, Maine USA. In December 1987 the OSHA issued four more citations citing 121 safety violations, including electrical hazards, faulty scaffolding and an unguarded floor opening. A settlement was reached with Scott paying fines of $475,000 but this did not constitute an admission of guilt.[15]
(See also refs: 28)

LR: According to a 1992 Survival International report, Scott Paper in the US is buying pulp from Millar Western, a company which is clear-cutting in Saskachewan on lands currently being blockaded by Elders of the Meadow Lake tribal area. It is also alleged that Scott Paper UK is involved in the purchase of pulp from native land in British Colombia.[1766]

ENV: In 1988 and 1989 Scott Paper came under criticism for water pollution at its Abercrombie Point kraft pulp mill and chloralkali plant. The local environmental group, CAP, alleged that Scott exceeded the preventional guidelines for the dumping of industrial effluent into Boat Harbour (a natural lagoon used as a treatment facility and operated by the provincial government). It was alleged that effluent from the mill contained organochlorines including dioxins which can enter the waterways from the treatment lagoon. Mercury from the chloralkali operation was also released into the environment.[28]

In 1989 Scott Paper withdrew from a major logging, pulp and paper project planned for the Merauke area in Irian Jaya (W Papua) in Indonesia. This would have involved the clear-felling of 800,000 hectares of tropical forest and replacement by eucalyptus plantations. The plan was widely criticised by environmentalists (including Survival International and the Women's Environmental Network) for being disastrous both for the environment and local Auyu forest people whose traditional lands would be devastated.[1846]

In 1991 the Pennsylvania Department of Environmental Resources was in litigation with Scott Paper over the treatment of water prior to discharge at the company's Chester Mill raw water processing plant. Scott's Mobile, Alabama plant was cited in 1989 as a 'high risk' air polluter by the US EPA due to its releases of chloroform.[3]

See also Boycott Call.
(See also refs: 15, 28, 113, 372, 373, 381, 763, 1750, 1758, 1842, 1843)

NP: Durafab was listed in the 1991 World Nuclear Industry Handbook as serving the nuclear industry, supplying protective clothing.[22]

AT: According to CEP's 1992 'Shopping for a Better World', Scott Paper tests on animals but has reduced by 40% or more the numbers used over the previous 5 years and/or has given $250,000 or more annually to fund alternative research.[1750] (See also refs: 10)

PD: In 1987/8 Scott Paper's Political Action Committee gave $79,780 to US state and federal political candidates.[3] (See also refs: 15)

BC: The Scott Boycott Committee began a boycott of Scott Paper in 1989 because of the company's allegedly irresponsible timber management in Nova Scotia. The Committee accuses Scott of continuing to clear-cut many acres - a tree-harvesting method which can lead to severe soil erosion. Moreover, they argue the monoculture softwood plantations planted in the clear-cut areas can be susceptible to insect outbreaks. The group also criticises the company's use of dangerous insecticides and herbicides such as Roundup, and its violations of spraying guidelines.[3]

Shiseido Co Ltd

5-5 Ginza 7-chome, Chuo-ku, Tokyo 104, Japan

OR: Shiseido owns companies in China, Indonesia and the Philippines.[21]

AT: Shiseido tests its cosmetics on animals.[10]

Simpson Ready Foods Ltd

Stretford Road, Urmston, Manchester M31 1WH

OAR: Simpson's products include the Goblin brand of tinned meats and meat puddings.[1790]

Smith & Nephew PLC

2, Temple place, Victoria Embankment, London WC2R 3BP

SA: Smith & Nephew has operations in South Africa.[21] (See also refs: 3, 13)

OR: Smith & Nephew has operations in India, Indonesia and Mexico.[21] (See also refs: 3)

ENV: Smith & Nephew has a 33% interest in the Swedish company Cedderoth, which is involved in the manufacture of CFCs.[3]

AT: Smith & Nephew does not test cosmetics or toiletries on animals; however, it is required to use animal testing for new drugs.[3] In April 1992, Smith & Nephew Research Ltd was listed as a subscriber to BIBRA.[1]

SmithKline Beecham plc

Beecham House, Great West Road, Brentford, Middlesex TW8 9BD

SA: SmithKline Beecham has fourteen subsidiaries in South Africa[21]...

OR: ...and has operations in Brazil, China, Colombia, El Salvador, Guatemala, Honduras, India, Indonesia, Mexico and the Philippines.[21]

ENV: In the year to March 1991, SmithKline Beecham exceeded its discharge consent more than thirty five times according to the NRA and/or the RPB.[20]

The company's plant at Irvine in Scotland was listed at No.2 in Greenpeace's 1992 'Filthy 50' list of plants licensed by the NRA or RPB to discharge toxic waste into the rivers and sea. It was found to have breached its consent 19 times since the beginning of 1991. It was also found to have discharged cadmium, nickel and lead for which it had no consent.[1748]
(See also refs: 308)

IM: In 1991 SKB settled out of court with parents of children who claimed their teeth had been damaged by Baby Ribena. The parents alleged that the labelling of the product was open to misunderstanding.[498] In March 1992 more parents were planning legal action against the company for the same reason. The labelling on the packaging of Baby Ribena was changed in 1985 to include warnings about tooth decay and a spokesperson for the company said there were no further plans to change the packaging or the sugar content.[967]

AT: The company has its own animal testing facilities and it has been accused of unnecessary cruelty in housing its animals. In 1990, an undercover National Anti-Vivisection Society worker reported baby mice having their toes removed, beagles kept in metal pens with concrete floors and no bedding, and dogs being transported packed two to a crate. An SKB spokesperson said all the animal facilities had been approved by the Home Office Inspectorate.[1677, 749]
(See also refs: 1, 3, 822)

OAR: SmithKline Animal Health produces antibiotics for laying hens and other farm animals.[455]

PD: In 1990 the company gave £30,000 to the Conservative Party and £5,000 to the CPS.[1076]

SPL Ltd

Drury Lane, Chadderton, Oldham OL9 7PH

OAR: SPL products include canned sild and herring.[1790]

Svenska Cellulosa

Skepparplatsen 1, S-85188 Sundsvall, Sweden

OR: The company has associates in Colombia and Mexico.[21]

ENV: SCA jointly owns a paper mill in Aylesford, Kent, with Kimberly Clark. The mill is placed 8th out of 56 on a WEN list of UK paper mills most frequently breaking discharge consent requirements between 1990 and 1992. The consent for biological oxygen demand was broken in 44% of tests taken in the period.[1844]

Companies

SCA Packaging was prosecuted on 21/5/91, in a case brought by the NRA, for a water pollution offence in the Welsh region on 2/11/90. The company was fined £1,500 with £463 costs.

Tambrands Inc

1 Marcus Avenue, Lake Success, New York 11042, USA

SA: Tambrands is maintaining a trademark licence in South Africa with a former subsidiary.[19]

OR: Tambrands has operations in Brazil, China and Mexico.[21]
(See also refs: 3)

ENV: Although it does not receive a mark in this column, Tambrands was criticised in 1989 by WEN for running an advertising campaign emphasising its "environmental awareness". Like most brands, whilst its tampons have always been biodegradable, they contain residues of dioxins in rayon and pesticides in cotton from which they are manufactured.[1689]

The 'environment friendly' stickers being used on Tampax boxes were thus not deemed justifiable by WEN.
(See also refs: 1851)

Tate & Lyle

Sugar Quay, Lower Thames St, London EC3R 6DQ

SA: Tate & Lyle owns the Pure Cane Molasses Co (Durban).[21]

OR: It also operates in Brazil, Kenya, Mexico, Somalia and Sudan.[21]

TU: According to Changing Corporate Values, the company has no recognition agreements with trade unions representing its black workers in South Africa.[3]

W&C: Union officials at its US subsidiary, A E Staley, claim that it "has fared increasingly badly in terms of safety standards and environmental issues since Tate took over" five years ago.[1853] Although the company claims to have spent $10m on safety since 1990, that did not prevent OSHA fining it $1.6m in 1991.[1853] Nor is it any consolation to James Beals, a maintenance worker who died after he was overcome by toxic fumes whilst repairing a processing tank.[1853]

ENV: The company was listed on 31/12/91 as being a member of the BRF.[1743]
See also W&C above.

IM: The health lobby, Action and Information on Sugars (AIS), formally complained to the IBA in June 1990 about a TV advertising campaign jointly funded by Wittington and Tate & Lyle which implied that sugar was natural and safe. AIS claims that sugar is highly refined and chemically treated. In December 1989, a government study by the Committee on the Medical Aspects of Food Policy condemned sugar as "the most important factor in the cause of dental caries" and recommended a reduction in its consumption.[674, 662]

The Food Commission has also criticised The Sugar Bureau (jointly funded by Wittington and Tate & Lyle) for sending biased promotional material about sugar to schools.[580]

ARMS: Richards (Shipbuilders) is contracted to supply small vessels to the MoD.[3]

AT: The company says it will carry out animal experiments when required to do so by regulatory authorities.[3] In April 1992, Speciality Sweeteners was listed as a subscriber to BIBRA.[1]

OAR: The company owns animal feed businesses.[1852]

PD: In 1991 the company gave £25,000 to the Conservative Party.[712]
(See also refs: 1080)

Tenneco

Tenneco Building, PO Box 2511, 1010 Milam, Houston, Tx 77252, USA

SA: In 1990, Tenneco was listed as maintaining licensing/distribution agreements in South Africa.[19]

OR: Tenneco operates in the following regimes: Brazil, India, Indonesia, Mexico, the Philippines and Turkey.
(See also refs: 51, 385)

ENV: Albright & Wilson's Marchon plant in Whitehaven is number 12 on Greenpeace's 'Filthy 50' list of plants licensed by the NRA or Scottish RPBs to discharge toxic waste into the marine environment.[1748]

According to ENDS magazine, in mid 1992 the Marchon plant was the UK's single largest source of heavy metal emissions.[1771] In 1991 the company was fined £2,000 with £10,000 costs for breaching discharge consent at the Marchon plant after a private prosecution by Greenpeace.[381] Greenpeace had attempted to block the plant's discharges. The company was claiming £250,000 from Greenpeace in lost production and damages.[1793] In late 1991 the parties settled out of court, following reassurances from the company. In 1992 though, Greenpeace threatened but then dropped plans to take the NRA to court to further pressurise A&W.[1794]

Albright & Wilson's plant in Oldbury is number 15 on Friends of the Earth's 1992 Top 100 list of Secret Polluters - companies with permits to discharge toxic metals into the sewers. It discharges effluent from the manufacture of inorganic and organic phosphorous derivatives, including cadmium, mercury and lead.[1770]
(See also refs: 12, 362, 371, 378, 1315)

NP: Newport News provides construction, decommissioning, inspection and maintenance services for the nuclear industry.[1737]

ARMS: According to Kinder Lydenberg Domini (a US ethical investment company) Tenneco receives over 2% of its total revenue from weapons-related contracts. It ranks in the Top 50 US Defense Department prime contractors, or has over $10m in nuclear weapons-related prime contracts.[1774]

Tenneco is the only company with the capacity to build Nimitz class aircraft carriers.[1803]
(See also refs: 114, 1791, 1792)

AT: In April 1992, Albright & Wilson was listed as subscribing to BIBRA.[1]

Companies

Tesco plc

Tesco House, Delamere Road, Cheshunt, Waltham Cross, Hertfordshire EN8 9SL

SA: Tesco's policy is to source only fresh fruit and vegetables from South Africa, not other own-brand goods like wine or tinned produce.[1099]

OR: It does, however, source a wide range of own-brand goods from Brazil, China, Colombia, Honduras, India, Israel, Kenya, Mexico, the Philippines and Turkey.[320]

ENV: Tesco's building of superstores, especially on green field sites, has attracted opposition in places such as Cirencester, Trowbridge, Bournemouth, Bristol and Bath. The schemes are opposed for the increase in traffic in the area, and damage to the environment caused by the building of the stores and new road schemes to facilitate this traffic.[629]

AT: Tesco cosmetics, toiletries and household products have never been tested on animals but the ingredients may have been.[3, 1105]

FF: Tesco sells non-free-range meat and eggs...

OAR: ...and meat products.[320]

BC: Friends of Golden Hill, Bristol are calling for a boycott of Tesco stores for its building of new stores on green field sites.

Thorntons plc

Thornton Park, Somercotes, Derby, Derbyshire DE55 4XJ

IM: The Food Commission undertook a survey of diabetic foods, comparing calories and fat content with standard and low-sugar alternatives. To be labelled 'diabetic', foods must by law be lower in fat and/or calories than equivalent regular foods. Thorntons chocolate was labelled 'diabetic' but failed to fulfil the above requirement.[1777]

Tomkins plc

East Putney House, 84 Upper Richmond Road, London SW15 5ST

SA: Tomkins has subsidiaries and associates in South Africa.[21]

ENV: RHM Foods Ltd was fined £1,000 in January 1992 for contravening its consents for discharging trade effluent into Greatham Creek, Hartlepool.[12] Ledbury Preserves was found to exceed its discharge consent once on biological oxygen demand and twice on suspended solids in the year to 31/3/91.[20]

In 1991 RHM was listed as a member of the BRF.[1743]
(See also refs: 11)

ARMS: Tomkins owns the US small arms, ammunitions, leg irons and handcuff manufacturer, Smith & Wesson.[21, 1094, 1474]

OAR: RHM manufactures animal feeds and products containing animal by-products.[1763]

PD: Tomkins gave £40,000 to the Conservative Party in 1990[1076] and RHM gave them £20,000 in 1991.[712]

BC: RHM appears on the Mid-Somerset Earth First! boycott list of companies which make health foods and which are involved in unethical practices.[9]

194

Unigate

Unigate House, Western Avenue, London W3 0SH

W&C: Unigate's Malton bacon factory was fined £5,000 in January 1993, for an ammonia leak in May 1992 that left three workers hospitalised - this was the second leak in a few weeks and appropriate detection equipment was not properly installed.[1779, 1780]

ENV: Unigate subsidiary, St Ivel, has been prosecuted a number of times for water pollution offences in the period from September 1989 to August 1991.[384]

IM: Unigate associate company Nutricia is listed as a frequent violator of WHO/ UNICEF Code of Marketing for Breastmilk Substitutes. Cow & Gate Plus products used pictures of babies on labelling in Sierra Leone in 1990, and carried no health warnings or reference to advice from health workers. Also Nutricia breastmilk substitutes were on display in a child clinic in the Netherlands Antilles in 1991.[2]

FF: Unigate owns Turners Turkeys Ltd.[21]

OAR: Unigate's interests include the manufacture of meat products and animal feedstuffs.[21]

PD: Unigate donated £50,000 to the Conservative Party between 1988 and 1990.[576]

BC: Nutricia appears on the Mid-Somerset Earth First! boycott list of companies which make health foods and which are involved in unethical practices.[9]

Unilever

Unilever House, Blackfriars, London EC4 4BQ

This Anglo-Dutch company...

SA: ...has subsidiaries in South Africa[21]...

OR: ...and in Brazil, Colombia, Egypt, El Salvador, Guatemala, Honduras, India, Indonesia, Kenya, Mexico, Morocco, Peru, the Philippines, Senegal, Sri Lanka, Turkey and Uganda.[21]

TU: In June 1989, workers occupied the Gessy Lever plant in Sau Paulo, Brazil, seeking better pay and conditions. Although the company did eventually agree to a pay rise, 87 workers were sacked for taking action, and company management failed to recognise an elected factory committee.[4] According to the company, it was "unable to recognise the trade union which those workers wished to set up, since it was illegal under Brazilian trade union law."[1849]

ENV: According to the Registers of the NRA and/or the RPBS, in the year to 31/3/91, the company exceeded its discharge consent three or more times. Also, between 1/9/89 and 31/8/91 the company was convicted for water pollution offences.[20]

In 1990, Crosfield Chemicals, was fined £5,000 after leaking fifty tonnes of concentrated sulphuric acid into a sewage system in Warrington.[372]

In 1991, a sulphuric acid plant in Nairobi which supplies Unilever was closed down for three months because sulphur dioxide emissions were above WHO limits.[799]

Lever Brothers also features on Greenpeace's 'Murder on the Mersey' list of companies polluting the Mersey.[650]
(See also refs: 3, 29, 1096, 1804)

IM: Unipath has been criticised for a free offer of multivitamins (including Vitamin A) with its pregnancy testing kits. Both the Maternal Alliance and Centre for Pregnancy and Nutrition pointed out that, in 1990, the Department of Health advised pregnant women to avoid taking dietary supplements containing vitamin A because of the risk of birth defects.[1319]

AT: The company is on the PETA list of companies that test on animals.[10] Products tested include cosmetics, toiletries, household cleaners, foods, food additives and chemicals.[139] In April 1992, Unilever was also listed as a subscriber to BIBRA.[1]

See also BC below.

OAR: In 1991 the Chairman of Birds Eye Wall's revealed that the company annually imported 30,000 tonnes of beef from Brazil for burgers and other meat products.[47] Unilever owns Birds Eye Walls, John West and other companies manufacturing meat products.[21]

BC: Unilever appears on the Mid-Somerset Earth First! boycott list of companies which make health foods and which are involved in unethical practices.[1168]

United Biscuits (Holdings) PLC

Church Road, West Drayton, Middlesex UB7 7PR

OR: United Biscuits owns companies in Brazil, China and the Philippines.[21]

ENV: UB (Ross Young's) Ltd was prosecuted in February 1991 by the NRA for a water pollution offence in the South West in August 1990. The company was fined £250 with £770 costs.[11]

OAR: Ross Young's products include frozen fish and seafood.[21]

PD: In 1991, United Biscuits was the largest contributor to the Conservative Party giving £130,000.[834] United Biscuits is the top corporate donor to the Conservative Party, having given £874,500 since 1979.[1807]

Valio Meijerien Keskusosuusliike

Meijeritie 6, SF-00370, Helsinki 37, Finland

IM: The company's UK subsidiary, Young Nutrition has been criticised for violating the WHO baby milk marketing code. The packaging of First infant milk shows pictures of babies, as do advertisements for the product which have appeared in baby journals and health trade journals.[88]

Verenigde Bedrijven Nutricia

NL-2700 MA Zoetermeer, Rokkeveenseweg 49, the Netherlands

OR: Nutricia owns a company in Indonesia.[21]

IM: Nutricia has violated the WHO baby milk marketing code by promoting baby milk in healthcare facilities and to health workers, and giving out free samples or supplies.[14] Cow & Gate Plus products used baby pictures on labelling in Sierra Leone (1990) and carried no health warnings or reference to advice from health workers. Also Nutricia breastmilk substitutes were on display in a child clinic in the Netherlands Antilles in 1991.[2]

OAR: Some of the company's baby foods contain meat.[1790]

BC: Nutricia appears on the Mid-Somerset Earth First! boycott list of companies which make health foods and which are involved in unethical practices.[1168]

Waissel's Ltd

58/60 Berners Street, London W1P 4JS

OAR: Waissel's products include snails and seafood.[1790]

Warburtons Ltd

Back o' the Bank House, Blackburn Road, Bolton, Lancashire BL1 8HJ

OAR: The company manufactures sausages and other prepared meat products.[21]

Wardell Roberts plc

79 Broomhill Road, Tallaght, Dublin 24, Ireland

OAR: The company has a subsidiary called Country Style Meat Products.[21]

Warner-Lambert Co

201 Tabor Road, Morris Plains, NJ 07950, USA

SA: Warner-Lambert owns companies in South Africa.[21]
(See also refs: 19, 1750)

OR: It also operates in Brazil, Chile, Egypt, Guatemala, Kenya, Mexico, Morocco and the Philippines.[21]

IM: In 1989, Warner-Lambert was criticised for marketing high-dose hormonal drugs in Peru. The drugs were indicated as appropriate for pregnancy tests despite the discovery in the 1970s that they could damage the foetus. These drugs were not marketed in the USA.[1149]
(See also refs: 1637, 1638)

AT: Warner-Lambert tests its drugs and other products on animals.[10]
(See also refs: 1, 1750)

OAR: It manufactures pet food[1726] and gelatine capsules.[1131]

Wasserstein Perella

Yardley, 33 Old Bond Street, London W1X 4AP

OR: Yardley owns a company in Colombia[1725]...

AT: ...and Maybelline cosmetics are listed as being tested on animals.[10]

Companies

The Watermill, Little Salkeld

The Watermill, Little Salkeld, Penrith, Cumbria CA10 1NN

OAR: The Watermill manufactures animal feeds.[1849]

Weetabix Ltd

Weetabix Mills, Burton Latimer, Kettering, Northants NN15 5JR

ENV: Weetabix was listed on 31/12/91 as a member of the BRF.[1743]

Wella AG

D-6100 Darmstadt, Berliner Allee 65, Postfach 40 28, Germany

SA: Wella owns two companies in South Africa.[21]

OR: It also owns companies in Brazil, China, Mexico and Turkey.[21]

Charles Wells Ltd

The Brewery, Havelock Street, Bedford

AT: In April 1992, Charles Wells was listed as subscribing to BIBRA through its membership of the Brewers' Society.[1]

PD: In January 1991, Charles Wells Ltd made a donation to the Conservative Party.[1076]

Whitbread plc

The Brewery, Chiswell Street, London EC1Y 4SD

ENV: Between September 1989 and February 1992, Whitbread was prosecuted and fined four times for water pollution offences in the UK.[11, 12]

AT: In April 1992, Whitbread was listed as a subscriber to BIBRA, through the Brewers' Society.[1]

PD: Whitbread gave £30,000 to the Conservative Party in the financial year to March 1991.[1076]

Whitman Corp

One Illinois Center, 111 East Wacker Drive, Chicago, Il 60601, USA

OAR: The company makes Shippam meat pastes, and through Van de Kamps it supplies frozen sea-foods.

Whitworths Holdings Ltd

Victoria Mills, Wellingborough, Northants NN8 2DT

OAR: Whitworths Holdings manufactures animal feeds.[21]

George Williamson & Co Ltd

Sir John Lyon House, 5 High Timber Street, London EC4V 3LD

OR: George Williamson owns companies in India, Kenya and Uganda.[21]

PD: Williamson Tea Holdings gave £4,000 to the Conservative Party in the financial year to 31/3/91.[1076]

Wittington Investments

Weston Centre, Bowater House, Knightsbridge, London SW1X 7LR

SA: Wittington owns Talisman Holdings which operates in South Africa.[3, 21]

ENV: According to NRA/RPB records, Associated British Foods exceeded its discharge consent at least three times in the twelve months to March 1991.[20]

IM: The health lobby, Action and Information on Sugars (AIS), formally complained to the IBA in June 1990 about a TV advertising campaign jointly funded by Wittington and Tate & Lyle which implied that sugar was natural and safe. AIS claims that sugar is highly refined and chemically treated. In December 1989, a government study by the Committee on the Medical Aspects of Food Policy condemned sugar as "the most important factor in the cause of dental caries" and recommended a reduction in its consumption.[674, 662]

The Food Commission has also criticised The Sugar Bureau (jointly funded by Wittington and Tate & Lyle) for sending biased promotional material about sugar to schools.[580]

AT: In April 1992, Associated British Foods Ltd and British Sugar plc were listed as subscribing to BIBRA.[1]

OAR: Wittington owns Power Meats Ltd, a meat processing and packing concern.[21]

PD: In the financial year to March 1990, George Weston Holdings gave £100,000 to the Conservative Party and £7,500 to the CPS.[1075]

BC: Wittington appears on the Mid-Somerset Earth First! boycott list of companies which make health foods and which are involved in unethical practices.[9]

Companies

200

> **We have not discovered any criticisms of the following companies:**

Ahmad Tea Ltd
Bridge House, 181 Queen Victoria Street,
London EC4V 4DD

AM Paper Converters Ltd
Pimbo Road, West Pimbo, Skelmersdale,
Lancashire WN8 9PD

An Bord Bainne Co-operative Ltd
Grattan House, Lower Mount Street, Dublin
2, Eire

Ark Consumer Products
PO Box 18, Melbourn Royston, Herts SG8
6JQ

Aspall Cider
Aspall Hall, Debenham, Stowmarket, Suffolk
IP14 6PD

Astley Dye and Chemical Co
Mallinson St, Bolton, Lancs BL1 8PP

Australian Canned Fruit (IMO) Pty Ltd
c/o 222-224 Northfield Avenue, West
Ealing, London W13 9SG

Austrian Moor Products Ltd
Whiteladies, Maresfield, East Sussex TN22
2HH

H Bahlsens Keksfabrik KG
D-3000 Hannover, Podbielskistr. 289,
Germany

A G Barr plc
1306 Gallowgate, Glasgow G31 4DS

Barry M Cosmetics
Unit 1, Bittacy Business Centre, Bittacy Hill,
Mill Hill East, London NW7 1BA

Beauty Without Cruelty plc
37 Avebury Avenue, Tonbridge, Kent TN9
1TL

Benson's Crisps
Marquis St, Kirkham, Lancs PR4 2HY

Berrydales
5 Lawn Road, London NW3 2XS

Bio-D
Unit 6, Applegarth Rd, Spyvee St, Hull HU8
7JJ

Blackmores Ltd
PO Box 258, Balgowlah, New South Wales
2093, Australia

The Body Shop International plc
Hawthorn Road, Littlehampton, West Sussex
BN17 7LR

Brash Brothers Ltd
Greenwood House, 6 Church Street,
Waltham Abbey, Essex, EN9 1DX

Brauerei Beck & Co
D-2800 Bremen 1, Am Deich 18-19,
Germany

Breger Gibson
Greenfield Industrial Park, Holywell, Clwyd
CH8 7HJ

Briess Holdings
Phoenix Works, Davis Road, Chessington,
Surrey KT9 1TH

Bumkins
PO Box 3008, Barnet, Herts EN2 2AZ (071
487 5665)

Busses Farm Ltd
Harwoods Lane, East Grinstead, West
Sussex RH19 4NL

Camilla Hepper Sales Ltd
51 St Mary's Street, Wallingford, Oxon
OX10 0EY

Captiva Brands International
21 Church Road, Poole, Dorset BH14 8UF

Caradoc Ltd
Goethean House, Woodman Lane, Clent,
West Midlands DY9 9PX

Cawston Group Ltd
The Winery, Chapel Street, Cawston,
Norwich

Celestial Seasonings
4600 Sleepytime Drive, Boulder, Co 80301-
3292, USA

Colorsport
Vale Road, Windsor, Berks SL4 5NY

Community Foods
London NW2 1LT

Consorzio Cooperativo Conserve Italia
40068 San Lazarro di Savena (BO), Via
Poggi 11, Italy

Constantine & Weir
29 High Street, Poole, Dorset BH15 1AB

Coochies Baby Business
12 Park Hall Rd, London N2 9PU (081 442
0491)

Cooke Bros (Tattenhall) Ltd
The Creamery, Tattenhall, Chester, Cheshire
CH3 9PX

Cottontails
JR Productions, 60 Swan St, Sileby, Leics
LE12 (0509 816787)

Creightons Naturally plc
Water Lane, Storrington, Pulborough RH20
3DP

Cristina of London
Dale Mill, Roch Street, Rochdale, Lancs
OL16 2UQ

Cygnus Venture Partners Ltd
Wellington House, 4/10 Cowley Road,
Uxbridge, Middlesex UB8 2XW

D & S (Food Products) Ltd
Union Road, Bolton, Lancashire BL2 2HQ

Dambi AB (Sweden)/Dambi UK
c/o Bodywise Ltd, 14 Lower Court Road,
Lower Almondsbury, Bristol BS12 4DX

S Daniels plc
South Quay Plaza, 183 Marsh Wall, Isle of
Dogs, London E14 9SH

Dayville Holdings Ltd
78-92 Stamford Road, London N15 4PQ

DDD Ltd
94 Rickmansworth Road, Watford, Herts
WD1 7JJ

Desilu Dresses Ltd
66-68 Margaret Street, London W1N 7SR

Dhamecha Foods Ltd
Wembley Stadium Industrial Estate, First
Way, Wembley, London

J & E Dickinson
Longley Farm, Holmfirth, West Yorkshire

Disposable Soft Goods
Boythorpe Works, Goyt Side Rd,
Chesterfield, Derbyshire S40 1YG
Although we have not discovered any
criticisms of this company, it is registered in
the Virgin Isles and we have a policy of not
recommending companies from tax havens.

Doves Farm Foods Ltd
Salisbury Road, Hungerford, Berkshire
RG17 0RF

Ducky Diapers
23 London Rd, Loughton, Milton Keynes
MK5 8AB (0908 666968)

F Duerr & Sons Ltd
15 Prestage St, Old Trafford, Manchester
M16 0HL

Earthwise
114 St Augustine's Ave, Thorpe Bay, Essex
(0702 589055)

East of Eden
Old Kingsmoor School, Railway Street,
Hadfield, Cheshire SK14 8AA

Edrington Holdings
106 West Nile Street, Glasgow G1 2QX

The End Product (Kooshies)
Northants (0280 701019)

Equal Exchange Trading
29 Nicholson Square, Edinburgh EH8 9BX

FAGE SA
35 Ermou, Athinon-Lamial National Road
(13a KM), GR-14452, Metamorfossi, Greece

Faith Products
Unit 5, Kay St, Bury, Lancs BL9 6BU

Fauser Vitaquellwerk KG GmbH & Co
D-200 Hamburg 54, Pinneberger Chaussee
60, (Einfahrt Baumacker), Postfach 540629,
Germany

P Ferrero & C. SpA
12051 Alba, Piazza P, Ferrero 1, Italy

Finaf SpA
Roma (00181) vie Amelia 70, Italy

Firstborn
32 Bloomfield Ave, Bear Flat, Bath, Avon
BA2 3AB (0225 422586)

C B Fleet Co Inc
4615 Murray Place, Lynchburg, VA 24502,
USA

Frenchie Cosmetics
Riverbank House, Putney Bridge Approach,
London SW6 3JD

Ganmill (part of Vernon-Carus)
38/40 Market St, Bridgewater, Somerset TA6
3EP (0278 423037)

Gaymer Group Ltd
Whitchurch Lane, Bristol BS14 OJZ

Charles Gordon Associates
Hoe House, Franksfield, Peaslake, Guildford
GU5 9SR

Peter Grant Papers Ltd
Stafford Park 12, Telford, Shropshire TF6
6PG

Companies

Green & Black's
222 Kensal Road, London W10 5BN

Green Baby Products
Minard, Lispole, Co Kerry, Ireland (066 57345) or Essex (0702 471378)

Green Catalogue
Freepost (BS 7348), Axbridge, Somerset BS26 2BR (0934 732469)

Greenbank Drinks Co
Church Row, Stranton, Cleveland TS24 7QS

Grolsch NV
NL-7523 EA Enschede, Fazantstraat 2, Netherlands

Gusto
269 Portobello Road, London W11 1LR

Happidog Petfoods
Bridge End, Brownhill Lane, Longton, Preston PR4 4SJ

Harlequin Fluffies
PO Box 534, Seaford, E Sussex (0323 895730)

Martha Hill Ltd
The Old Vicarage, Laxton, Nr Corby, Northants NN17 3AT

Holsten Brauerei AG
D-2000 Hamburg-Altona, Holstenstrasse 224, Postfach 50 07 49, Germany

Honesty Cosmetics Ltd
33 Markham Road, Chesterfield, Derbyshire S40 1TA

Hygieia Healthcare Holdings Ltd
Unit 2, Sunrise Enterprise Park, Ferryboat Lane, Castledown, Sunderland SR5 3RX

Inch's Cider Ltd
Hatherleigh Road, Winkleigh, Devon EX19 8AP

Indisposables
Henlie House, Hallsannery Farm, Littleham, Bideford, N Devon EX39 5HE (0237 477014) and Brighton (0273 772222)

Interbrew SA
Vaartstraat 94, B-3000 Leuven, Belgium

W Jordan (Cereals) Ltd
Holme Mills, Biggleswade, Beds

Kallo Foods Ltd
Premier House, Madeira Road, West Byfleet, Surrey KT14 6NF

Kays (Ramsbottom) Ltd
Britannia Works, Kenyon Street, Ramsbottom, Bury, Lancashire BL0 0AE

Kent Paper Products Ltd
9 Tribune Drive, Trinity Trading Estate, Sittingbourne, Kent

Kingfisher Natural Toothpaste
21 White Lodge Estate, Hall Road, Norwich NR4 6DG

Kooshies
PHP, 12 Thornton Place, London W1H 1FL (071 935 7727)

Kord Beteiligungsgesellschaft GmbH
Am Sandtorkai 2, 2000 Hamburg 11, Germany

John Labatt Ltd
451 Ridout Street North, PO Box 5870, London, Ontario N6A 5L3, Canada

G R Lane Holdings Ltd
Sisson Road, Gloucester GL1 3QB

Lindt & Sprungli AG
CH-8802, Kilchberg 2H, Switzerland

Lornamead Ltd
Lornamead House, Kings Place, 1-5 Newington Causeway, London SE1 6ED

LPC Group
Waterside Rd, Hamilton Industrial Park, Leicester LE5 1TZ

Gebr. Marz AG
D-8200 Rosenheim, Am Salztadel 2, Germany

Mavala
PO Box 1211, Geneve 11, Switzerland

Maxim Pharmaceutical
4 Allison Road, London W3 6JE

Meadow Magic
Lower Rubhay, Tedburn St Mary, nr Exeter, Devon EX6 6BS

Meridian Foods Ltd
Unit 13, WDA Advance Factories, Corwen, Clwyd, LL21 9RT

Merrydown Wine
Horam Manor, Horam, Heathfield, E Sussex TN21 0JA

Mevgal Macedonian Milk Industry SA
571-00 Koufalid, Thessaloniki, Greece

Mikey Diapers
18 Winsbury Way, Bradley Stoke, Bristol
BS12 9BE (0454 616762)

Miss Mary of Sweden Cosmetics
7 Tudor Road, Hanover Business Park,
Altrincham, Cheshire WA14 5RZ

Montagne Jeunesse
London Production Centre, Broomhill Road,
London SW18 4JQ

Morning Foods
North Western Mills, Crewe, Cheshire CW2
6HP

Morningside
274 Dalston Lane, London E8 1JG (081 986
3955)

Nairobi Coffee & Tea Co Ltd
Shakespeare Street, Watford, Herts WD2
5HF

Natural Beauty Products Ltd
Western Avenue, Bridgend Industrial Estate,
Bridgend, Mid Glamorgan CF31 3RT

Nazirs Ltd
328-344 Stockport Road, Manchester M13
0LE

Neutrogena Corp
5760 West 96th Street, Los Angeles, Ca
90045, USA

Newcel Paper Converters Ltd
Carnbane Industrial Estate, Newry, Co.
Down BT35 6QT

J N Nichols (Vimto) plc
Ledson Road, Manchester M23 9NL

Franz Niehoff GmbH
Kaffeerosterei, Sunderhooker Weg 6, 4432
Gronau-Epe, Germany

Northumbrian Fine Foods
Dukesway, Gatehead, Tyne & Wear NE11
0QP

Onken & Co
Mullerstrasse 42-54, D-4330 Mulheim/Ruhr,
Germany

Organisations Switzerland Third World
PO Box 69, Byfangstrasse 19, CH-2552
Orpund, Switzerland

**OTG (Ostfriessische Tee-Gesellschaft
Laurens Spethman)**
D-2105 Seevetal 1, AM Bauhof 13-15,
Germany

Oxfam
274 Banbury Road, Oxford OX2 7DZ

Laura Page Cosmetics
The Barracks, Barwell, Leicester LE9 8EF

Pataks (Spices) Ltd
Park Lane, Abram, Wigan WN2 5XJ

Paulig Ltd
Iiluodonkuja 2, PL15, SF00981 Helsinki,
Finland

Pecksniffs Ltd
Unit 1, Gerston Farm, Greyfriars Lane,
Storrington, West Sussex RH20 4HE

Personalized Products Ltd
Butts Road, Alton, Hampshire, GU34 3E2

Petty & Wood Co
PO Box 66, Central Way, Andover, Hants
SP10 5LA

Plamil Foods Ltd
Plamil House, Bowles Well Gardens, Dover
Road, Folkestone, Kent CT19 6PQ

Prospect Foods
1 Parliament Street, Harrogate, Yorkshire
HG1 2QU

Pure Plant Products
Europa Trading Estate, Stonelough Road,
Radcliffe, Manchester M26 9HE

Alfred Ritter GmbH
Schokolade Fabrik, 7035 Waldenbuch,
Germany

Riviana Foods Inc
2777 Allen Parkway, Houston, Texas 77019,
USA

The Robinson Group of Companies Ltd
Crown Cider Works, Tenbury Wells,
Worcestershire WR15 8HB

Rock's
Twyford, Berkshire

Rolith International
8 St George's Place, Brighton, Sussex BN1
4GB

Rubicon Products Ltd
Rubicon House, Ironbridge, London NW10
0UF

Ryecroft Foods Ltd
Smith Street, Ashton-under-Lyne OL7 0DB

Sanpoint AB (Sweden)
c/o Bodywise Ltd, 14 Lower Court Road,
Lower Almondsbury, Bristol BS12 4DX

Companies

Schwalbchen-Molkerei Jakob Berz AG
Bahnhofstrasse 38, D-6208 Bad Schwalbach,
Germany

R & W Scott Holdings/Schwartauer
52 Clyde St, Carluke, Lanarkshire

Seabrook Investments Ltd
c/o Seabrook Potato Crisps Ltd, Seabrook
House, Allerton, Bradford, W.Yorkshire
BD15 7QU

Benjamin Shaw & Sons Ltd
Willow Lane, Huddersfield HD1 5ED

Shipton Mill
Long Newton, Tetbury, Gloucestershire GL8
8RP

J M Smucker Co
Strawberry Lane, Orville, OH 44667, USA

Soya Health Foods Ltd
Unit 4, Guinness Road, Trafford Park,
Manchester M17 1AU

Speciality Foods
Rakusen House, Clayton Wood Rise, Ring
Road, West Park, Leeds LS16 6QN

Stargazer Products Ltd
Unit 5B, 9 Brighton Terrace, London SW9
8DJ

Stute Nahrungsmittelwerke GmbH
D-4790 Paderborn, Abtstrede 129,
Nordrhein-Westfalen, Germany

Suma Wholefoods
Dean Clough, Halifax, W Yorks HX3 5AN

Taunton Cider Co Ltd
Norton Fitzwarren, Taunton, Somerset TA2
6RD

Teekanne GmbH
D-4000 Dusseldorf 11, Kevelaerer Str. 21-
23, Germany

Thayers Real Dairy Ice Cream
Dairy Ice Creamery, Wentloog Road,
Rumney, Cardiff, South Glamorgan CF3
8ED

Thorncroft Vineyard
Leatherhead, Surrey KT22

Thursday Cottage Ltd
Carswell Farm, Uplyme, Devon DT7 3XQ

Tom's of Maine
Railroad Avenue, PO Box 710, Kennebunk,
ME 04043, USA

Trads
25 Gloucester St, Stroud, Glos GL5 1QG
(0453 756757)

Traidcraft
Kingsway, Gateshead, Tyne & Wear, NE11
0NE

Treats Ice Cream
Manston Lane, Crossgate, Leeds LS15 8SX

Triangle Foods
Dean Clough, Halifax, West Yorkshire HX3
5AN

Tuesdays Girl Ltd
54 Higher Ardwick, Manchester M12 6BU

Twin Trading Ltd
Fourth Floor, 5-11 Worship St, London
EC2A 2BH

Ultra Glow Cosmetics
12 St Peter's Court, Colchester, Essex CO1
1WD

Unichem
Unichem House, Cox Lane, Chessington,
Surrey KT9 1SN

Unichips SpA
Via Turati, Milan, Italy

Unimix
Aurora General Trading, 51 Shakespeare Rd,
London

Vandemoortele International NV
Kennedypark 8, B-8500 Kortrijk, Belgium

Vernon-Carus Ltd
Penwortham Mills, Preston, Lancashire PR1
9SN

Waterford Co-operative Society Ltd
Main Street, Dungarvan, Co Waterford,
Ireland

Weepee
Parm Unit 1, Marlborough Rd, Old
Courtaulds, Nuneaton CV11 5PG (0203
347773)

Weleda (UK) Ltd
Heanor Road, Ilkeston, Derbyshire DE7 8DR

H Weston & Sons Ltd
Much Marcle, Herefordshire

Whole Earth Foods Ltd
269 Portobello Road, London W11 1LR

Wilkin & Sons
Tiptree, Colchester, Essex CO5 0RF

Appendix 1

References

1 BIBRA Annual Report 1992

2 Breaking the Rules (IBFAN 1991)

3 Changing Corporate Values - New Consumer (Kogan Paul 1991)

4 Fighting Back - The Brazil Network (1989)

5 Infocheck July 1992

6 Investment in Apartheid (ICFTU May 1988)

7 Key British Enterprises 1992

8 Major Arms Traders - Campaign Against the Arms Trade (CAAT 1987)

9 Mid-Somerset Earth First! Boycott Sheet December 1991

10 PETA List May 1991 (USA) (People for the Ethical Treatment of Animals)

11 Pollution Prosecution Statistics September 1989 - August 1991 - National Rivers Authority

12 Pollution Prosecution Statistics September 1991 - February 1992 - National Rivers Authority

13 South Africa, How British Business Profits from Apartheid (Labour Research Department 1989)

14 State of the Code by Company (IOCU 1991)

15 The Better World Investment Guide - CEP (Prentice Hall Press 1991)

16 The Economic League - M Hollingsworth & C Tremayne (Liberty 1989)

17 The South African Disconnection - Anti-Apartheid Movement (AAM 1988)

18 Trade Union Rights (ICFTU 1991)

19 Unified List of US Companies in South Africa and Namibia (Africa Fund 1990)

20 Water Pollution - EIRIS (February 1992)

21 Who Owns Whom 1992 (Dun & Bradstreet)

22 World Nuclear Industry Handbook 1990 - Nuclear Engineering International

23 1001 Ways to save the Planet - Bernadette Vallely - (Penguin 1990)

27 A Review of Procter & Gamble's Environmental Balances for Disposable and Renewable Nappies (The Landbank Consultancy for WEN July 1991)

28 A Tissue of Lies? Disposable Paper and the Environment (WEN 1990)

33 Additives - Your Complete Survival Guide - Felicity Lawrence (ed) (Century Hutchinson 1986)

42 Agscene 95 May/June 1989

43 Agscene 96 August 1989

44 Agscene 97 November 1989

45 Agscene 98 Spring 1990

46 Agscene 101 November 1990

47 Agscene 103 Summer 1991

48 Agscene 104 Autumn 1991

49 Agscene 105 Winter 1991

51 Albright & Wilson Annual Report 1988

65 Animal-Free Shopper (Vegan Society 1991)

66 Animals in Medical Research: An investigation (NAVS)

75 Anti-Apartheid press release 19/3/92

82 Assault and Battery - Mark Gold (Pluto Press 1983)

86 Baby Milk Action Newsletter Summer 1989 (BMAC)

87 Baby Milk Action Update July 1992

88 Baby Milk Action Update November 1991

References

89   Baby Milk Action Update
      September 1991
97   Better World Investment
      Guide (CEP 1991)
102   Biodegradability of
      Surfactants - Ecover
      factsheet 1992
106   Blueprint for a Green
      Planet - J Seymour & H
      Girardet (Dorling
      Kindersley 1987)
110   Body Shop Ingredient
      Reference Book
113   Boycott Action News Fall
      1992
114   Boycott Action News
      Winter 1989
115   BP Half year review 1/1/91
119   Breaking the Pesticide
      Habit - Terry Gips (IOCU
      1990)
120   Breastmilk: A World
      Resource (BMAC 1992)
134   British Medical Journal 23/
      2/91
135   British National Formulary
      October 1992
136   BUAV (British Union for
      the Abolition of
      Vivisection) Approved
      Product Guide 1992-93
137   BUAV Campaign Report 1/
      12/91
138   BUAV correspondence
      with Paterson Zochonis
      1986
139   BUAV Press Release 10/7/
      91
141   BUAV Press Release 13/6/
      91
142   BUAV Press Release 14/
      10/91
143   BUAV Press Release 6/2/
      92
144   Building Economic
      Alternatives (Co-Op
      America) Fall 1989
146   Building Economic
      Alternatives Winter 1989
170   C for Chemicals - M Birkin
      & B Price (Green Print
      1989)
183   Child Slaves - BBC
      Television (BBC 2, 23-6-
      89)
186   Cities are Good for Us -
      Harley Sherlock (Paladin
      1991)
190   Co-op America Quarterly
      Winter 1991

191   Co-op America Quarterly
      Spring 1992
196   Communication with CRS
      October 1992
197   Company Statement on
      Animal Testing 29/1/91
199   Compassion in World
      Farming material
220   Consumer Currents
      (International Organisation
      of Consumers' Unions)
      April 1992
230   Consumer Currents June
      1991
235   Consumer Currents March
      1991
238   Consumer Currents
      October/November 1990
242   Consumer Reports (USA)
      October 1990
243   Consumers' Guide to the
      Protection of the
      Environment - Jonathan
      Holliman (Pan, Ballantine
      1974)
253   CWS Animal Welfare
      Sheet
257   CWS South East Retail
      Group Information
275   Daily Telegraph 9/9/91
279   Dipyrone - a drug no one
      needs (Health Action
      International-Europe/
      BUKO-Pharma-Kampagne
      1989)
284   Dirty Water - Judith Cook
      (Unwin Hyman 1989)
287   Down to Earth 11/90
288   Down to Earth 11/90
289   Down to Earth 3/90
290   Down to Earth 3/90
291   Down to Earth 3/90
296   E For Additives - Maurice
      Hanssen
298   Earth Matters 5, Autumn
      1989 (Friends of the Earth)
305   Earth Matters 13, Winter
      1991
306   Ecologist January/February
      1991
308   Ecologist July/August 1989
309   Ecologist March/April 1992
312   Ecologist November/
      December 1989
319   Ecover Information
      Handbook - R Bines & P
      Marchand 1989
320   ECRA Survey October
      1992
321   EIRIS Information Pack

360   ENDS Report 172 May
      1989
362   ENDS Report 174 July
      1989
368   ENDS Report 181 February
      1990
371   ENDS Report 189 October
      1990
372   ENDS Report 190
      November 1990
373   ENDS Report 191
      December 1990
377   ENDS Report 195 April
      1991
378   ENDS Report 196 May 91
380   ENDS Report 198 July
      1991
381   ENDS Report 199 August
      1991
382   ENDS Report 200
      September 1991
383   ENDS Report 201 October
      1991
384   ENDS Report 202
      November 1991
385   ENDS Report 203
      December 1990
386   Enjoy Healthy Eating
      (Health Education
      Authority 1991)
387   Environment Digest 2 July
      1987
396   Environment Digest 21
      February 1989
398   Environment Digest 26 July
      1989
402   Environment Digest 33
      February 1990
404   Environment Digest 41/42
      October 1990
408   Environment Digest 56
      February 1992
409   Environment Now April
      1990
418   Environmental News
      Digest vol 8 no 3 February
      1990 (Friends of the Earth
      Malaysia)
425   Ethical Consumer 7 April/
      May 1990
431   Ethical Consumer 19 May/
      June 1992
451   Factsheet 1990 - PETA
452   Failsafe April 1990
455   Farmers Guardian 8/7/88
      (cited in Chickens Lib
      newsletter Sept 1988)
457   File on Tea - Tea Council
472   Financial Times 11/12/90
478   Financial Times 13/8/91

497 Financial Times 16/5/90

498 Financial Times 16/7/91

513 Financial Times 2/12/91

521 Financial Times 23/10/91

544 Financial Times 30/4/91

549 Financial Times 4/9/91

554 Financial Times 6/9/90

558 Financial Times 8/11/91

570 First Tuesday - Granada Television 5/6/90

572 Fixed Cut-Off Date Information

573 Food First - F Moore Lappe & Joseph Collins (Abacus 1982)

575 Food Magazine April/June 1990

576 Food Magazine April/June 1991

577 Food Magazine April/May 1991

578 Food Magazine February 1992

580 Food Magazine January/ March 1991

582 Food Magazine July/ September 1990

583 Food Magazine July/ September 1991

585 Food Magazine October/ December 1989

586 Food Magazine October/ December 1989

587 Food Magazine October/ December 1991

589 Food Magazine Summer 1988

608 German and Swiss drug supplies to the Third World - R Hartog & H Schulte-Sasse (HAI-Europe/BUKO-Pharma-Kampagne)

614 Global Pesticide Campaigner - PAN October 1990

615 Global Reach; the power of the multinational corporation - R J Barnett & R E Muller (Johnathon Cape 1975)

617 Good Health on a Polluted Planet - Nigel Dudley (Thorsons 1991)

620 Green Consumer Guide - J Elkington & J Hailes (Gollancz 1988)

621 Green Consumer Supermarket Shopping Guide - J Elkington & J Hailes (Gollancz 1989)

627 Green Line August 1989

628 Green Line February 1992

629 Green Line July 1990

632 Green Line March 1991

633 Green Line November 1992

634 Green Line September 1991

639 Green Magazine Guide to Food & Drink August 1990

645 Green Magazine October 1990

650 Greenpeace Campaign Report, Murder on the Mersey, 8/10/90

651 Greenpeace Campaign Report May 1990

656 Grocer 11/11/89

660 Grocer 14/4/90

661 Grocer 16/12/89

662 Grocer 16/6/90

668 Grocer 2/5/92

669 Grocer 20/3/90

672 Grocer 23/11/90

673 Grocer 23/6/89

674 Grocer 23/6/90

678 Grocer 24/6/89: "Daylay Eggs Fined"

685 Grocer 4/3/89

691 Grocer 8/7/89

694 Grocer Price List 2/5/92

701 Guardian 1/7/91

711 Guardian 3/7/89

712 Guardian 4/3/92

714 Guardian 5/2/90

716 Guardian 5/9/91

717 Guardian 6/12/88

724 Guardian 7/10/91

726 Guardian 8/1/91

728 Guardian 8/2/91

735 Guardian 9/7/90

744 Guardian 10/2/91

749 Guardian 10/9/91

752 Guardian 11/5/90: "Gold's urgent need to slip racist leash"

761 Guardian 13/10/89

763 Guardian 13/11/90: "Ban on 'green' toilet paper ad"

768 Guardian 14/2/92

770 Guardian 14/3/91

786 Guardian 16/3/90

799 Guardian 17/9/91

802 Guardian 18/12/92

814 Guardian 19/3/91

815 Guardian 19/4/91

822 Guardian 20/11/91

823 Guardian 20/3/90

825 Guardian 20/4/90

828 Guardian 20/8/90

829 Guardian 21/1/90: "Firms who are up in arms"

834 Guardian 21/4/92

856 Guardian 23/8/91

863 Guardian 24/6/89

879 Guardian 27/9/89: "Tea strike adds to Sri Lankan despair"

885 Guardian 28/9/89: "Bank boost in England"

886 Guardian 29/1/90

900 Guardian 30/1/91

931 Guardian 9/2/89: "It's time to peal off green veneer and seek out some earthier ethics"

946 Herbal Cosmetics - Camilla Hepper (Thorsons 1987)

947 Hillsdown Holdings Annual Report 1991

949 Home Ecology - Karen Christensen (Arlington Books 1989)

952 How to be Green - John Button (Greenprint 1989)

962 Independent Food & Drink 1989/90

967 Independent on Sunday 22/ 3/92

981 International Defence Directory 1991 (Jane's Information Group 1991)

998 International Labour Reports 21 May/June 1987

1001 International Labour Reports 25 Jan/Feb 1988

1004 International Labour Reports 29 Sept/Oct 1988

1009 International Labour Reports 34/35 July-Oct 1989

1022 Jeyes Product Brochure 1/1/ 91

1053 Keynote 1991: Biscuits & Cakes

1055 Keynote 1991: Canned Foods

1057 Keynote 1991: Cosmetics

1058 Keynote 1991: Sauces & Spreads

1067 Kwik Save Annual Report 1992

1070 Labour Research April 1988

1072 Labour Research August 1989

1074 Labour Research December 1988

1075 Labour Research December 1990

References

1076 Labour Research December 1991

1078 Labour Research July 1989

1080 Labour Research June 1991

1082 Labour Research May 1988

1084 Labour Research May 1991

1087 Labour Research October 1989

1088 Labour Research September 1990

1090 LCA Studies for Chemical Substances: Major Detergent Surfactants and their Raw Materials (Procter & Gamble 1992)

1094 Letter from Company

1096 Letter from Port Sunlight Village Society August 1992

1097 Letter on BUAV files 1/11/90

1098 Letter on BUAV files 13/2/89

1099 Letter to Anti-Apartheid 30/3/89

1105 Liberator June 1990

1107 Liberator March 1990

1109 Liberator September 1988

1112 Liberator Summer 1990

1113 Liberator Summer 1991

1115 Liberator Winter 1991

1123 Lloyds List 18/4/91

1128 Lloyds List 28/8/91

1130 Lloyds List 8/1/91

1131 MacMillan Directory of Multinationals (MacMillan 1989)

1132 Magpie Summer 1992 (Manchester Wildlife Trust)

1136 Making Recycled Paper - Friends of the Earth Briefing Sheet

1137 Making your own home proteins - Evelyn Findlater (Century 1985)

1139 Margarine - J H Stuyvenberg (ed) (Liverpool University Press 1969)

1140 Market Barriers to Recycling (Friends of the Earth Feb 1990)

1144 Market Research Great Britain Oct 1990: Organic Bread Products

1149 Marketing Fertility - WEMOS 5/89

1157 Marks & Spencer Annual Report 1992

1164 Merchants of Drink - F Clairmonte & J Cavanagh (Third World Network 1988)

1168 Mid-Somerset Earth First! Boycott Sheet July 1992

1171 Military Production and Sale January 1990 - EIRIS (Ethical Investment Research Service)

1182 MINTEL May 1990

1192 Moody's Industrial Manual 1988

1195 Moody's Industrial Manual 1991

1200 Multinational Monitor April 1990

1202 Multinational Monitor April 1992

1203 Multinational Monitor December 1988

1204 Multinational Monitor December 1989

1205 Multinational Monitor December 1990

1206 Multinational Monitor December 1991

1207 Multinational Monitor February 1988

1209 Multinational Monitor January 1990

1210 Multinational Monitor January 1992

1215 Multinational Monitor July/Aug 1990

1226 Multinational Monitor May 1990

1228 Multinational Monitor May 1992

1235 Multinational Monitor October 1990

1236 Multinational Monitor October 1992

1237 Multinational Monitor Sept 1988

1240 Multinational Monitor Sept 1991

1247 National Boycott News vol II no 4 Spring/Summer 1989 (USA)

1254 Natural Food Trader Nov 1990

1258 New Consumer February 1990

1261 New Consumer Summer 1990

1288 New Internationalist 167 Jan 1987

1304 New Internationalist 205 March 1990

1306 New Internationalist 215 Jan 1991

1308 New Internationalist 219 May 1991

1315 North West Tonight ITV 13/6/89 6.30pm

1319 Observer 10/5/92

1320 Observer 11/11/90

1335 Organic Consumer Guide (Thorsons 1990)

1339 Outrage April/May 1990

1342 Overcoming Addictions - Janet Pleshette (Thorsons 1989)

1345 Packet information

1358 Peace News 23/6/92

1376 Politics of Breastfeeding - Gabrielle Palmer (Pandora 1988)

1377 Pollution by Detergents (Ecover 1990)

1378 Poultry World August 1989

1391 Pure, White and Deadly - John Yudkin (Penguin 1986)

1394 Rating America's Corporate Conscience - Council on Economic Priorities (Addison and Wesley USA 1986)

1418 Safe Food Handbook - Parents for Safe Food (Ebury Press 1990)

1419 Sainsbury Annual Report 1990

1420 Scotsman 22/1/91

1446 Shopping For A Better World (Council on Economic Priorities 1991)

1447 Shopping for a Better World (New Consumer 1991)

1454 Snack Food International Summer 1989

1460 South African Labour Bulletin March 92

1472 SPUR (World Development Movement) August/September 1990

1474 Standard & Poors Directory 1990

1498 Sunday Times 2/8/92

1502 Sunday Times 3/6/90

1504 Surfactants in Consumer Products - ed. J Falbe (Springer-Verlag 1987)

1506 Swedish Society for the Conservation of Nature material 1989

1507 Tea and Justice - D Jones (Bangladesh International Action Group 1986)

1537 The Ethical Investor July 1992 - EIRIS

1544 The Global Chocolate Factory (TIE March 1990)

1545 The Global Consumer - Phil Wells & Mandy Jetter (New Consumer/Gollancz 1991)

1546 The Globe Feb/March 1990

1551 The Greenpeace Story - Michael Brown & John May (Dorling Kindersley 1989)

1564 The Residue Report - Stephanie Lashford (Thorsons 1988)

1566 The Sanitary Protection Scandal - A Costello, B Vallely & J Young (WEN 1989)

1620 Toxics and Community 1988

1628 Traidcraft press release 14/7/89: "Fair trade begins with a cup of tea"

1636 Turning Point 8 Autumn 1987

1637 Turning Point 9 January/March 1988

1638 Turning Point 10 April/June 1988

1642 Turning Point 16 Jan/March 1990

1643 Turning Point 17 April/June 1990

1645 Turning Point 19 Oct/Dec 1990

1646 Turning Point 23 Oct/Dec 1991

1661 Unilever Monitor December 1987/February 1988 - Transnationals Information Centre London (TICL)

1666 Vegan Society publicity material

1669 Vegetarian January/February 1990

1677 Vivisection in Britain: NAVS January 1991

1687 WEN (Women's Environmental Network) press release 28/2/90: "Wrapping is a rip off"

1688 WEN Information

1689 WEN Newsletter 4

1691 WEN Newsletter 12 Autumn 1991

1698 Which? April 1989

1708 Which? July 1991

1709 Which? June 1989

1710 Which? June 1990

1723 Whiter Shade of Pale - Bandung File, Channel Four TV (21/6/88 transcript)

1725 Who Owns Whom (1988)

1726 Who Owns Whom (1989)

1728 Who Owns Whom (1991)

1729 Will My Work Make Me Sick? (June 1985)

1737 World Nuclear Industry Handbook 1991

1742 Green Line March 1992

1743 British Road Federation Membership List 31/12/91

1744 Turning Point April 1992

1745 ENDS Report 215 December 1992

1746 Corporate Examiner January 1992

1747 Survival Top Ten List of companies in the Americas 17/9/92

1748 Filthy 50 (Greenpeace 1992)

1749 Guardian 20/3/92

1750 Shopping for a Better World (CEP 1992)

1751 Dirty Dozen Campaigner (PAN June 1990)

1752 ENDS Report 213 October 1992

1753 New Consumer 10, January 1992

1754 Down to Earth 16/3/92

1755 ELTSA October 1992

1756 Guardian 25/5/90

1757 New Internationalist 234 August 1992

1758 National Boycott News 8, November 1992

1759 Multinational Monitor September 1992

1760 Turning Point October 1992

1761 Boycott Action News Winter 1992

1762 Utusan Konsumer 1/8/92

1763 Ranks Hovis McDougall Annual Report 1991

1764 Baby Milk Action - Action Pack March 1993

1765 Co-op America Quarterly Winter 1992

1766 Indians of the Americas (Survival International 17/9/92)

1767 Earth Matters December 1992

1768 Multinational Monitor December 1992

1769 Boycott Action News Winter 1992

1770 Secret Polluters Top 100 (Friends of the Earth July 1992)

1771 ENDS Report 210 July 1992

1772 Grocer 21/7/90

1773 Outrage 83 February 1993

1774 Kinder Lydenberg Domini Press Release 17/3/93

1775 Corporate Examiner - ICCR January 1992

1776 Child Slaves - Peter Lee-Wright (Earthscan Publications 1/1/90)

1777 Food Magazine August 1992

1778 Traidcraft Catalogue 1991/2

1779 Yorkshire Post 15/5/92

1780 Yorkshire Post 27/1/93

1781 BUAV Campaign Report July 1992

1782 Guardian 17/1/91

1783 Co-op America Quarterly Summer 1992

1784 Turning Point July 1992

1785 Times 23/1/91

1786 Guardian 13/9/89

1787 HMIP Annual Report 1989/90

1788 HMIP Annual Report 1990/91

1789 Environment News Digest January 1990

1790 Grocer Price List 6/3/93

1791 CEP Research Report May 1991

1792 Nuclear Free America Top 50 January 1990

1793 Independent 10/10/91

1794 ENDS Report 206 March 1992

1795 Utusan Konsumer 267 15/11/92

1796 Earth Matters September 1992

1797 Multinational Monitor November 1992

1798 Adelaide Advertiser 14/2/89

1799 Adelaide Advertiser 7/2/89

1800 Adelaide News 23/1/90

References

1801 Guardian 9/2/90

1802 The Cruel Deception - Dr Robert Sharpe (Thorsons Publishers 1988)

1803 Market Research Great Britain: Washing Powders March 1992

1804 Sunday Express 23/6/91

1805 Grocer 15/12/90

1806 Grocer 5/6/90

1807 Labour Research April 1992

1808 Observed on product

1809 Fresh Produce Journal 9/2/90

1810 Financial Times 26/1/93

1811 Letter from Allied Lyons

1812 Guardian 18/5/90

1813 Guardian 17/5/90

1814 MINTEL 1/5/90

1815 Ecologist September/October 1989

1816 Fresh Produce Journal 9/2/90

1817 The Gulliver File (Minewatch 1992)

1818 Ecologist March/April 1993

1819 The Arms Traders (CAAT September 1992)

1820 Letter to Health and Diet Food Company 16/2/90

1821 Grocer 24/11/90

1822 Britain's Best Employers - Sean Hamil/New Consumer (Kogan Page 1993)

1823 Independent 7/11/92

1824 EIRIS News Release 8/2/93

1825 Ethical Investment & The Third World - EIRIS October 1992

1826 WDM Debt Special September 1991

1827 'In Whose Interest' Press Release 15/2/90

1828 WDM Press Release 11/9/91

1829 Natural Food Trader 1/1/91

1830 Utusan Konsumer 268 1/12/92

1831 National Boycott News Update Spring 93

1832 Consumer Currents January 1992

1833 Food Magazine October/December 1990

1834 CEP Research Report February 1990

1835 Utusan Konsumer 264 1/10/92

1836 Utusan Konsumer 258 1/7/92

1837 Consumer Currents 150 November 1992

1838 Environment Digest 24 July 1989

1839 Environment News Digest 9/2-3 June 1992

1840 The Globe 4 June/July 1990

1841 Grocer 31/3/90

1842 GreenLine 88 July 1991

1843 ENDS Report 214 November 1992

1844 Guardian 2/9/92

1845 Letter from Johnson & Johnson 13/6/90

1846 Environment Digest 62 August 1992

1847 Consumer Currents 141 December 1991

1848 Boycott Action News Fall 1992

1849 Communication with company

1850 Snack Foods International 2/10 1991

1851 Marketing 15/6/89

1852 Financial Times 26/11/92

1853 Financial Times 27/1/93

1854 Letter from Booker plc 5/11/91

1855 Sanitary Protection: Women's Health & The Environment - WEN Information Pack April 1993

1856 Financial Times 27/4/93

1857 Market Research Great Britain October 1992: Canned Food

1858 Ecologist 22/6 November/December 1992

1859 Retail Business May 1992: Tinned Vegetables

1860 Retail Business February 1992: Tinned Fruit

1861 PETA News June 1992

1862 Guide to British Food Manufacturing Industry - P R Sheard (Nova Press)

1863 Green Party Press Release 16/4/93

1864 Keynote 92: Disposable Paper Products

1865 Which? May 1993

1866 Whale and Dolphin Conservation Society Newsletter February 1992

1867 Utusan Konsumer 252 April 1992

1868 Labour Research 82/4 April 1993

1869 Guardian 24/10/92

1870 ENDS Report 212 September 1992

1871 ENDS Report 215 December 1992

1872 Greenpeace Campaign Report March 1993

1873 Guardian 15/12/92

1874 Daily Express 16/12/92

1875 Consumer Currents January 1991

1876 Information from BUAV 6/4/93

1877 Multinational Monitor October 1992

1878 Environmental Digest 30 November 1989

1879 Guardian 6/6/92

1880 Turning Point 15 October 1989

1881 Britain's Worst Polluters - the South East (Greenpeace 1992)

1882 Guardian 15/5/91

1883 Business Times 13/5/91

1884 Nappies and the Environment - WEN February 1993

1885 Sunday Telegraph 6/12/92

1886 Sunday Telegraph 29/3/92

1887 Harrisons & Crosfield annual report 1992

1888 Independent 1/4/93

1889 Guardian 18/5/93

1890 Economist 29/8/92

1891 Mid Somerset Earth First! boycott list 4/93

1892 Morality and the Market: N Craig Smith (Routledge 1991)

1893 Ethical Consumer 11 Dec 1990/Jan 1991

1894 The Green Consumer 1991 - Mintel Special Report

1895 Consumerism Reconsidered: Mica Nava (Cultural Studies 5/2/91 Routledge)

1896 Ethical Consumer 12 Feb/Mar 1991

Appendix 2

Technical Information about Ratings

ECRA monitors radical and mainstream publications for criticisms of company behaviour. Research currently embraces the fourteen different categories defined in Chapter One. Each category falls into one of two groups:

Company Research

Company policy
Nine of the categories are of company policy, i.e. where companies will not usually deny the fact of involvement, and where the merits of involvement are the subject of open debate. The categories are South Africa, Oppressive Regimes, Nuclear Power, Armaments, the three Animals categories, Political Donations and Boycott Call. Particular companies may not in the past have been named by independent critics. Criticism might be levelled at 'all companies with policies of involvement in a specific field' (e.g. South Africa, Animal Testing) and ordinary business information has subsequently revealed activity in that field.

Technical Information about Ratings

Contentious issues

The five other categories are usually where all companies will want to be seen to have good records. This will occur in the sections on Environment, Trade Union Relations, Wages and Conditions, Irresponsible Marketing and Land Rights. Official statistics and worldwide surveys in these fields do not really exist. Information like this is very much more open to the writer's own interpretation of the criticisms available. Judgements in these columns will only therefore be <u>relative</u> to the other companies appearing in this book. If for example Unilever were to receive a mark under Environment, it would not mean that 'Unilever has a bad environmental record', it would mean that compared with other companies in this book, Unilever has attracted more criticism.

Company Groups

A company record is taken to be the record of the parent company and all its subsidiaries and associates (subsidiaries are usually where a parent company owns more than 50% of the shares and associates where they own 10% to 40%). It is difficult to use rules accurately, but where it seems that a company has sufficient financial power to force a board of directors to change course, it will be held responsible for not having done so if practices continue. The larger and more complex European and Japanese company groupings (such as Zaibatsus) are currently treated as single company groups. When one company buys another, the new company is deemed to have bought the history (questionable or not) of the other, unless there is evidence that practices ceased or policies changed when the purchase occurred.

Own Brands

Supermarket and other retailers' own-brands are rated by combining the following:
(i) the retailing company's own rating in the usual way
(ii) evidence of direct involvement in the following categories through both own-brand and branded product availability in their stores: South Africa, Oppressive Regimes, Factory Farming, Animal Testing, Other Animal Rights. Evidence of a lesser degree of involvement will take account of the progressiveness of company policy.

A company will receive a half square if it scores up to five points, and a whole square if it scores six or more under the following system:

Oppressive Regimes

Operations in any of the following regimes score two points: Afghanistan, Burma, Colombia, India, Indonesia, Iran, Iraq, Lebanon, Liberia, Mauritania, Morocco, Peru, the Philippines, Somalia, Syria, and Turkey. These sixteen regimes have been criticised in the Amnesty International Report 1991 for, (i) torture, (ii) extrajudicial executions or disappearances, and (iii) prisoners of conscience AND in World Military and Social Expenditures 1991 for "frequent official violence against the public".

Operations in any of the following score one point: Algeria, Angola, Bahrain, Brazil, China, Egypt, El Salvador, Guatemala, Haiti, Honduras, Jordan, Kenya, Kuwait, Mali, Mexico, Nepal, Niger, Papua New Guinea, Senegal, Sri Lanka, Sudan and Uganda. These 23 regimes have been criticised under any three of the four categories listed above.

The words CON, LAB (or other) will indicate that a donation has been made to that political party in the UK. The amount and date of the donation will be given in the Companies Section. BUI (British United Industrialists) are commonly recognised as a money laundering agency for the Conservative Party. CPS is the Conservative Party's Centre for Policy Studies.

Political Donations

A half square indicates marketing of products in a way that has been criticised as being detrimental to health generally. A square indicates marketing of products in a way that has been criticised for causing severe physical harm.

Irresponsible Marketing

Appendix 3

Abbreviations

APPEN Asia-Pacific Peoples' Environment Network.

BIBRA The British Industrial Biological Research Association. BIBRA is a large animal research laboratory which carries out contract testing for companies which may not have their own testing licence.

BRF The British Road Federation. BRF is a lobbying group which campaigns for more motorways and roads.

BUAV The British Union for the Abolition of Vivisection. BUAV is a campaigning group whose aim is an end to animal testing.

BUI British United Industrialists. BUI is commonly recognised as a money laundering agency for the Conservative Party.

CAAT Campaign Against Arms Trade.

CEP Council on Economic Priorities (US). Founded in 1969, CEP analyses and rates US companies on corporate responsibility issues.

CIWF Compassion in World Farming. CIWF campaigns for a non-violent and educated approach to our relationship with farm animals and the environment in general. It produces the magazine, Agscene.

CPS Centre for Policy Studies. The Conservative Party think tank.

ECRA The Ethical Consumer Research Association.

EIRIS Ethical Investment Research Service. Set up in 1983, EIRIS provides a consultancy service for those wishing to invest in major UK companies which meet their ethical and social criteria.

EPA Environmental Protection Agency (US).

Abbreviations

FDA Food & Drug Administration (US).

FoE Friends of the Earth.

HAI Health Action International. HAI is an informal network of about 100 consumer, health and development action groups in 60 countries. It actively promotes a more rational use of drugs.

HMIP Her Majesty's Inspectorate of Pollution.

IBFAN International Baby Food Action Network.

ICOM Industrial Common Ownership Movement. An organisation promoting the interests of worker co-operatives.

INFACT Infant Formula Action Coalition. Originated the Nestlé boycott, now campaigns on a range of corporate responsibility issues.

IOCU International Organisation of Consumer Unions. IOCU is a federation of consumer organisations dedicated to the protection and promotion of consumer rights worldwide through information, research and educational activities.

MaLAM Medical Lobby for Appropriate Marketing. MaLAM is a campaign group whose aim is to encourage companies to provide sufficient, consistent and accurate information to enable appropriate prescribing, dispensing and consumption of drugs.

NAVS National Anti-Vivisection Society. NAVS campaigns for an end to all animal testing including medical experiments and dissection for educational purposes.

NRA National Rivers Authority.

OECD Organisation for Economic Co-operation & Development

OSHA Occupational Safety & Health Administration (US).

PETA People for the Ethical Treatment of Animals (US). A US non-profit animal protection organisation dedicated to establishing the rights of all animals.

RPBS River Purification Boards of Scotland.

RSPCA Royal Society for the Prevention of Cruelty to Animals.

SIPRI Swedish International Peace Research Institute

TUC Trades Union Congress.

UNICEF United Nations Children's Fund.

WDM World Development Movement. WDM is the UK's main pressure group for changes that will benefit the world's poor on issues like aid, trade, debt, environment and development.

WEN Women's Environmental Network. A non-profit organisation staffed entirely by women, WEN aims to provide a forum for women to link environment, health, ecology and aid.

WHO World Health Organisation.

Appendix 4

Contact Addresses

Act-Up
BM Box 2995, London WC1N 3XX 071
738 4300

Amnesty International
99-119 Roseberry Ave, London EC1R
4RE 071 278 6000

Animal Aid
7 Castle St, Tonbridge, Kent TN9 1BH
0732 364 546

Anti-Apartheid
13 Mandela St, London NW1 0DW 071
387 7966

Baby Milk Action
23 St Andrews St, Cambridge. CB2 3AX
0223 464420

**BUAV - British Union for the Abolition
of Vivisection**
16a Crane Grove, Islington, London N7
8LB 071 700 4888

CAAT - Campaign Against Arms Trade
11 Goodwin St, Finsbury Park, London
N4 3HQ 071 281 0297

**CANE - Consumers Against Nuclear
Energy**
PO Box 697, London NW1 8YQ

Centre for Alternative Technology
Llwynywern Quarry, Machynlleth, Powys,
Wales SY20 9AZ 0654 702400

CEP - Council on Economic Priorities
30 Irving Place, New York NY 10003

Christian Aid
PO Box 100, London SE1 7RT 071 620 4444

CIIR - Catholic Institute for International Relations
22 Coleman Fields, London N1 7AF 071 354 0883

CIWF - Compassion in World Farming
Charles House, 5a Charles St, Petersfield, Hants GU32 3EH

CND - Campaign for Nuclear Disarmament
162 Holloway Rd, London N7 8DU 071 700 2393

Consumers' Association
2 Marylebone Rd, London NW1 4DF 071 486 5544

Co-op America
2100 M St NW, Suite 403 Washington, DC 20037, USa

ECRA - Ethical Consumer Research Association
16 Nicholas St, Manchester M1 4EJ

EIRIS - Ethical Investment Research Service
504 Bondway Business Centre, 71 Bondway, London SW8 1SQ 071 735 1351

ELTSA - End Loans to South Africa
c/o Methodist Church, 56 Camberwell Rd, London SE5 0EN 071 708 4702

ENDS - Environmental Data Services
Unit 24, Finsbury Business Centre, 40 Bowling Green Lane, London EC1R 0NE 071 278 4745

FAWN - Farm Animal Welfare Network (including Chickens' Lib)
PO Box 40, Holmforth, Huddersfield HD7 1QY

Food Commission
3rd Floor, 5-11 Worship Street, London EC2A 2BH 071 628 7774

Friends of the Earth
26-28 Underwood Street, London N1 7TQ 071 490 1555

GreenLine
PO Box 297, Oxford OX2 0BF 0865 243202

Green Party
10 Station Parade, Balham High Rd, London SW12 9AZ 071 673 0045

Greenpeace
Canonbury Villas, London N1 2PN 071 354 5100

HAI - Health Action International
Jacob van Lennepkade 334-T, 1053 NJ Amsterdam, Netherlands

IBFAN - International Baby Food Action Network
PO Box 1045, 10830 Penang, Malaysia

ICFTU - International Confederation of Free Trade Unions
Rue Montagne aux Herbes Potageres 37-41, B-1000 Bruxelles, Belgium

ICOM - Industrial Common Ownership Movement
Vassalli House, 20 Central Road, Leeds LS1 6DE 0532 461738/7

INFACT - Infant Formula Coalition
256 Hanover Street, Boston, MA 02113, USA

IOCU - International Organisation of Consumer Unions
2595 EG The Hague, Netherlands

MaLAM - Medical Lobby for Appropriate Marketing
12 Hugill Street, Bradford BD13 3JW 0274 834512

MedAct (formerly MCANW)- Medical Action for Global Security
601 Holloway Rd, London N19 4DJ 071 272 2020

Multinational Monitor
PO Box 19405, Washington DC 20036 USA

National Boycott News
6506 - 28th Ave NE Seattle, WA 98115

NAVS - National Anti-Vivisection Society
261 Goldhawk Rd, London W12 9PE 081 846 9777

New Consumer
52 Elswick Rd, Newcastle NE4 6JH 091 272 1148

New Economics Foundation
Universal House, Second floor, 88-94 Wentworth St, London E1 7SE 071 377 5696

New Internationalist
55 Rectory Road, Oxford OX4 1BW 0865 728181

Oxfam
274 Banbury Rd, Oxford OX2 7DZ 0865 311311

Oxfam in Scotland
36 Palmerstone Place, Edinburgh EH12 5BJ 031 225 9330

Parents for Safe Food
5-11 Worship St, London EC2A 2BH 071 628 2442

Partizans - People Against RTZ and its Subsidiaries
218 Liverpool Rd, London N1 1LE 071 609 1852

Peace Pledge Union
6 Endsleigh St, London WC1H 0DX 071 387 5501

Pesticides Trust
23 Beehive Place, London SW9 7QR 071 274 9086

PETA - People for the Ethical Treatment of Animals
PO Box 42516 Washington, DC 20015

Quaker Social Responsibility & Education
Friends House, Euston Rd, London NW1 2BJ 071 387 3601

Respect for Animals (formerly Lynx)
PO Box 59, Dunmow, Essex CM6 1UH

RSPCA - Royal Society for Prevention of Cruelty to Animals
Causeway, Horsham, Sussex RH12 1HG 0403 64181

SCRAM - Scottish Campaign to Resist the Atomic Menace
11 Forth St, Edinburgh EH1 3LE 031 557 4283/4

Soil Association
86 Colston St, Bristol BS1 5BB 0272 290661

Survival International
310 Edgware Rd, London W2 1DY 071 723 5535

Sustainability
The People's Hall, 91-97 Freston Rd, London W11 4BD 071 243 1277

Tapol (Indonesian human rights)
111 Northwood Rd, Thornton Heath, Surrey CR7 8HW 081 771 2904

Vegan Society
7 Battle Road, St Leonards-on-Sea, East Sussex TN37 7AA 0424 427393

Vegetarian Society
Parkdale, Dunham Rd, Altrincham, Cheshire WA14 4QG 061 928 0793

WDM - World Development Movement
25 Beehive Place, London SW9 7QR 071 737 6215

WEN - Women's Environmental Network
Aberdeen Studios, 22 Highbury Grove, London N5 2EA 071 354 8823

WWF - WorldWide Fund for Nature
Panda House, Weyside Park, Catteshall Lane, Godalming, Surrey GU7 1XR 0483 426444

Boycott Contacts

American Home Products boycott
Dr Idrian Resnick, Action for Corporate Accountability, 129 Church Street, New Haven CT 06511, USA

Anheuser Busch boycott
Whale & Dolphin Conservation Society, 19A James Street West, Bath, Avon BA1 2BT, *or*

The Dolphin Project, Po Box 224, Coconut Grove, Florida 33233, USA

Boots boycott
Animal Liberation Investigation Unit, PO Box 38, Manchester M60, *or*

London Boots Action Group, c/o Alara, 58 Seven Sisters Road, London N7 6AA

Coca-Cola boycott
US Coke Disinvestment Campaign, 92 Piedmont Avenue, NE, Atlanta, GA 30303, USA, *or*

Irish National Caucus, 413 East Capitol Street, SE Washington, DC 20003, USA

Credit Cards from the Big Four banks boycott (Lloyds, Midland, Barclays and NatWest)
World Development Movement, 25 Beehive Place, London SW9 7QR

DIY Superstores timber boycott (B&Q, Do-It-All, Great Mills, Sainsbury's Homebase, Texas Homecare, Wickes)
Friends of the Earth, 26-28 Underwood Street, London N1 7TQ

Dole pineapple and banana boycott
Fresh Fruit and Vegetable Workers' Union, UFCW Local 78B, 600 South Main Street Ste. 5, Salinas, California 93901,USA or

Colombia Solidarity Committee, PO Box 2337, London NW6 4TV

Gillette boycott
People for the Ethical Treatment of Animals (PETA), Po Box 42516, Washington, DC 20015, USA

Grand Metropolitan boycott
Committee of Displaced Workers, 434 Main Street, #222, Watsonville, California 95076, USA

Health food companies boycott
Mid-Somerset Earth First!, PO Box 23, 5 High Street, Glastonbury BA6 9DP

Kellogg boycott
Educators Against Apartheid, Paula Bower, 164-04 Goethals Avenue, Jamaica, New York 11432, USA

L'Oréal boycott
Animal Aid, 7 Castle Street, Tonbridge, Kent TN9 1BH

Mitsubishi boycott
Rainforest Action Network, 301 Broadway, San Francisco, California 94133, USA

Nestlé boycott
Baby Milk Action, 23 St Andrews Street, Cambridge CB2 3AX

Pepsico boycott
OPIRG-Carlton, 1125 Colonel By Drive, 326 UniCentre, Carlton University, Ottawa ON Canada K1S 5BG

Philip Morris boycott
Stop Teenage Addiction to Tobacco, 121 Lyman Street, Ste. 210, Springfield, MA 01103, USA

Procter and Gamble boycott
In Defense of Animals, 816 W Francisco Boulevard, San Raphael, California 94901, USA

Sainsbury's boycott
Manchester Earth First!, Department 29, 1 Newton Street, Manchester M1

Scott Paper boycott
Scott Boycott Committee, Judy Davis, RR/4 Tatamagouche, Nova Scotia, Canada BOK 1VO

Tesco boycott
Golden Hill Campaign, Golden Hill Protestors Office, Kellaway Avenue, Golden Hill, Bristol BS6

Appendix 5

More About ECRA

The Ethical Consumer Research Association, the producer of this book, is a co-operatively run voluntary campaigning group based in Manchester. It exists to publish information on the companies behind the brand names and to promote the ethical use of consumer power.

Promoting ethical purchasing involves more than just screening companies. It involves studying the phenomenon of ethical purchasing and persuading society generally of the benefits of its practice. ECRA also functions as a campaign group arguing for changes in the law which would help promote ethical purchasing. There are two main areas of potential benefit from legal changes:

(i) Screening by Public Authorities

Our position on this is covered in more detail in Chapter 2 under the heading 'Collective Purchasing'.

(ii) Freedom of Information

Our position on this is outlined at the end of Chapter 1.

If you are interested in helping to support ECRA in its broader campaigns for these kind of goals, one of the easiest ways is to take out a subscription to the Ethical Consumer magazine which provides details of our various projects as they develop. An order form appears overleaf.

We are also always interested to receive any letters, help, information or ideas on the subject of ethical purchasing at the address below. Finally we should mention that ECRA can provide a commercial screening service for individuals and institutions wishing to access our database of company information.

Our office is at 16 Nicholas St, Manchester M1 4EJ.

Ethical Consumer Magazine

... comes out six times per year, each issue usually containing three or four products reports.

Regular features also include spotlights on specific aspects of company behaviour, articles on campaigning groups and news of UK boycotts. News and Updates sections also allow readers to keep up with campaigns and details of company changes.

The Ethical Consumer *costs only £15 per year.*

(Overseas subscriptions: Surface mail £18 per year; Air mail Europe & Eire £20, Rest of World £26.)

I would like to subscribe to the Ethical Consumer magazine - please send me the next six issues

I enclose a cheque/P.O. made payable to ECRA Publishing Ltd for: £

Name _____

Address _____

_____

_____

Post Code _____

GES

Return this form with your cheque/PO to **ECRA Publishing Ltd (GES), 16 Nicholas St, Manchester M1 4EJ.**

Ethical Consumer Postcards

If ethical issues are influencing what you buy, why not tell the companies about it?

Boycotts and positive buying work most effectively if consumers can communicate the reasons for their decisions to the companies involved. The Ethical Consumer is now producing two full-colour postcards designed to be used in conjunction with the addresses at the back of the books and magazines.

The **NO** card allows readers to explain to companies why they have stopped buying their products, and the **YES** card is for sending to companies to encourage them in the pursuit of positive ethical policies.

Cards are for sale only in multiples of ten and the prices (including postage) are listed below. Readers can choose whether they want just **NO** cards, just **YES** cards or a mixed pack.

Prices

10 *Cards*	**£3.00**	**40** *Cards*	**£10.80**
20 *Cards*	**£5.80**	**50** *Cards*	**£12.50**
30 *Cards*	**£8.40**	**100** *Cards*	**£20.00**

Return this form with your cheque/PO to **ECRA Publishing Ltd, 16 Nicholas St, Manchester M1 4EJ.**

Please send a pack of Ethical Consumer postcards made up as follows   Amounts

YES cards	
NO cards	
Total Number of Cards	

I enclose a cheque/P.O. made payable to ECRA Publishing Ltd for: £

Name _____

Address _____

_____

_____

Post Code _____

GES

Two New Shoppers' Guides from the Ethical Consumer

Following on from the *Guide to Everyday Shopping*, the Ethical Consumer will be publishing two further guides:

The Ethical Consumer Guide to Major Purchases (September 1993, price £7.99) covering electrical goods, sport and leisure products, transport etc.

The Ethical Consumer Guide to Money (November 1993, price £7.99) covering banks and building societies, insurance, ethical investment, pensions etc.

Together, these three books should provide ethical consumers with the most comprehensive information available on UK products and services.

I would like to receive the following books:

Quantity		Totals
	copy/ies of The Ethical Consumer Guide to Everyday Shopping @ £7.99 each	

and as soon as they are published...

	copy/ies of The Ethical Consumer Guide to Major Purchases @ £7.99 each	
	copy/ies of The Ethical Consumer Guide to Money @ £7.99 each	

I enclose a cheque/P.O. made payable to ECRA Publishing Ltd for: £ _____

Name _____

Address _____

_____

_____

Post Code _____

Please return this form to:
ECRA Publishing Ltd,
Fifth Floor, 16 Nicholas
Street, Manchester M1 4EJ

(Bookshops or other retailers interested in stocking any of these publications should contact Central Books, 99 Wallis Rd, London E9 5LN. Tel: 081 986 4854, Fax 081 533 5821)

GES